Reaching the Standard
Series editor: Mark O'Hara

Teaching Geography 3–11

THE ESSENTIAL GUIDE

David Owen and Alison Ryan

continuum
LONDON · NEW YORK

Related titles

Graham Butt: *The Continuum Guide to Geography Education*
Mark O'Hara: *Teaching 3–8*
Lucy O'Hara and Mark O'Hara: *Teaching History 3–11*

Continuum

The Tower Building
11 York Road
London SE1 7NX

15 East 26th Street
New York
NY 10010

www.continuumbooks.com

© 2001 David Owen and Alison Ryan

First published 2001
Reprinted 2003

British Library Cataloguing-in-Publication Data
A catalogue record for this book is available from the British Library.

ISBN: 0-8264-5111-X

Designed and typeset by Ben Cracknell Studios
Printed and bound in Great Britain by CPI, Bath.

Contents

Preface

This book introduces the teaching and learning of geography in 3–11 settings. Geography features as a foundation subject in the National Curriculum for pupils in Key Stages 1 and 2, whereas the under-5s curriculum is organized into areas of learning where geography is not identified explicitly as a subject. However, in early years settings, children have many experiences and undertake a range of activities that develop their understanding of people and places.

As many early years settings are not within the mainstream education system, the contents of the Early Learning Goals are not compulsory in the same way that National Curriculum Programmes of Study are in schools. However, the Early Learning Goals set out the desired learning outcomes for children upon completion of their reception year, and those nurseries which are part of mainstream education, as well as reception classes, are expected to use these goals to structure their work with pupils aged 3–5. Therefore, although the Early Learning Goals have a slightly different status, the term *curriculum* is used throughout the book to describe the educational provision for all pupils aged between 3 and 11.

Second, the book addresses teaching and learning across the Foundation Stage and Key Stages 1 and 2. In order to avoid the text becoming indigestible, terms such as *school* are used for those settings where the whole 3–11 age range is represented. In those instances where 3–5 settings are being discussed separately, the terms *Foundation Stage*, *nursery* or *reception* are used.

Standards Information

This book is aimed at newly qualified and teacher training students working in the 3–11 age range. It is intended to be of use to those students and teachers who require non-specialist geography knowledge and those who have a subject specialism in this area of the curriculum. Students and teachers with geography as a subject specialism are required to demonstrate that they:

- have a secure knowledge of the subject to at least a standard approximating to GCE Advanced level in those aspects of the subject taught at Key Stages 1 and 2;
- have a detailed knowledge and understanding of the geography National Curriculum Programmes of Study and level descriptions across the primary age range;
- can cope securely with geographical questions which pupils raise;
- understand the progression from Early Learning Goals to Key Stage 1, the progression from Key Stage 1 to Key Stage 2, and from Key Stage 2 to Key Stage 3;
- are aware of, and know how to access, recent inspection evidence and classroom-relevant research evidence on teaching primary pupils in geography, and know how to use this to inform and improve their teaching;
- know pupils' most common misconceptions and mistakes in the subject;
- have a secure knowledge and understanding of ways in which information and communications technology (ICT) can be used effectively in the teaching of geography; and
- are familiar with geography-specific health and safety requirements and plan lessons to avoid potential hazards.

As well as demonstrating knowledge and understanding of the subject, students and teachers also have to demonstrate the ability to:

- plan, teach and manage geography;
- monitor, assess, record and report on pupils' progress in geography; and
- fulfil any other professional requirements in relation to geography, such as ensuring equality of opportunity and taking responsibility for their own professional development.

(DfEE, 1998)

The grid below provides the reader with a quick guide to where particular information about the Standards can be located.

Standards	Chapters
• Knowledge and understanding of geography and the geography curriculum	1, 2
• Planning, teaching and managing geography	3, 4, 5, 6
• Assessing, recording and reporting on geography	7
• Fulfilling other professional requirements in relation to geography	8, 9

REFERENCE

DfEE (1998) *Circular 4/98 Teaching: High Status, High Standards*. London: DfEE

Introduction

This book is intended as an introduction to geography for newly qualified teachers and teacher training students on 3–11 courses. It seeks to provide the reader with insights into the nature of the subject and effective ways of planning, teaching and assessing geography in primary and foundation settings. It also considers cross-curricular issues, such as equal opportunities and special educational needs (SEN), that affect teaching and learning in all subjects. The book concludes with an exploration of the role of a geography specialist in co-ordinating geography across a school.

Chapter 1 deals with the nature of geography as a subject as perceived by children, adults and the academic geography community. It details the key concepts that underpin current geographical thinking and concludes with a rationale for including geography in the education of children aged 3 to 11.

Chapter 2 examines the nature of geography in the Foundation Stage and in the National Curriculum at Key Stages 1 and 2 and offers suggestions on how aspects of the Early Learning Goals can be used to extend children's awareness of concepts such as place, location and environmental quality. The chapter explores the four aspects of geography as set out in the knowledge, skills and understanding component of the Programmes of Study and outlines the breadth of study at Key Stages 1 and 2. It concludes with an overview of the links between geography and the wider curriculum, focusing on numeracy, literacy, citizenship and sustainability.

Chapter 3 focuses on planning geography. It considers good practice at three levels of planning – long, medium and short term – and how teachers can provide for continuity and progression. It looks at how geography can feature in a school's curriculum and the merits of subject- or topic-based approaches to teaching the subject.

Chapter 4 deals with organizing and managing geography. It looks at how teachers can organize children, adults, their classrooms and resources in order to promote effective learning in geography. It also explores how teachers can match learning opportunities with pupils' learning needs through differentiation. The chapter concludes with guidance on self-evaluation as a means of improving practice and the quality of one's geography teaching.

Chapter 5 outlines appropriate teaching and learning approaches in early years and primary geography. It examines imaginative and evidence-based approaches and outlines some of the strategies practitioners and teachers can use to develop children's natural geographical competence successfully.

Chapter 6 reviews some of the resources for teaching and learning in geography. It focuses on the learning environment within the classroom and the use of out-of-classroom resources for fieldwork, and concludes with a review of ICT resources that can be used to improve geographical learning.

Chapter 7 deals with three further elements of good practice: assessment, recording and reporting. It describes ways in which pupils' achievements in geography can be assessed. It then suggests ways in which teachers can record their assessments and how they might report on pupils' progress to parents.

Chapter 8 explores how teaching and learning in geography can make a positive contribution to the provision of equality of opportunity in the classroom. Not only can the content of the geography curriculum be used to challenge stereotypical attitudes and beliefs, but the process of geographical enquiry can be used to ensure all children have access to a stimulating curriculum. The chapter examines strategies that teachers can employ in their geography teaching to foster fairness, equity and social justice in their classrooms.

Chapter 9 considers those pupils for whom special provision has to be made because they have special educational needs (SEN). Such pupils include those with physical disabilities or learning difficulties, and children who might be identified as gifted or talented. The chapter outlines some of the special needs that teachers may encounter and suggests how the curriculum can be adapted and delivered to promote the geographical learning of children with SEN.

Chapter 10 deals with the role of curriculum co-ordinator, one that most teachers now have to take on early in their careers. The chapter outlines the roles and responsibilities of geography co-ordinators. It considers how co-ordinators can address some of the problems and challenges they may face when trying to initiate and manage change in order to develop good practice in geography in a school.

The Subject of Geography

The standards for teachers (DfEE/TTA, 1998) insist that all primary teachers must have a specialist subject and at least A-level knowledge of that subject at Key Stage 1 and Key Stage 2. It is important for primary teachers to have good subject knowledge, a point that is reinforced by the Office for Standards in Education (OFSTED) (Smith, 1997) and by many geography co-ordinators. The subject-based curriculum has changed the nature of the primary teacher's role, and the increased emphasis on single-subject planning (DfEE/QCA, 1999) and the growing importance of the subject co-ordinator reflect this.

Knight (1993) identifies three types of subject knowledge:

- knowledge of the subject;
- content knowledge; and
- pedagogical subject knowledge.

Knowledge of the subject

Students and teachers need to know what sort of a subject geography is. This is the focus of Chapter 1. Is it a 'pub quiz' subject in which success is measured by the ability to name capital cities, mountain ranges or different types of agriculture? Is it a knowledge that is mainly a vehicle for enquiry and developing generic educational skills? Is striving for social justice the primary goal of study?

Content knowledge

Teachers need to have knowledge of the 'subject matter' of geography: locations of towns and cities in the UK, how a river system works and what has influenced the development of a distant locality that they study with their class. This content is the knowledge, skills, attitudes and values present in the geography National Curriculum at Key Stages 1 and 2. Student teachers can audit their current knowledge against this (see Table 1.1, pp. 16–17) and set targets to develop through peer support, computer-assisted learning and focused reading. Chapter 2 also explains and analyses the present content knowledge in the National Curriculum and Early Learning Goals.

Pedagogical subject knowledge

The third type of subject knowledge, pedagogical subject knowledge, is crucial for the student or teacher. This is the knowledge of how teachers can share their understanding of geography with their pupils, and how they recognize their children's abilities as geographers. Teachers use this knowledge when they plan strategies for children to use aerial photographs effectively, or build on children's local knowledge to develop their understanding of settlement concepts. This knowledge is explored in subsequent chapters.

This chapter is concerned with the different definitions of geography as a subject so that students and teachers can make informed judgements about what sort of geographical work they plan with their classes; so they can look critically at resources such as the Qualifications and Curriculum Authority (QCA) Geography Schemes of Work (DfEE/QCA, 1998); and so they are able to contribute to the development of geography in the twenty-first century. It investigates how children and adults view geography, and how academic geographers define their subject, and it discusses why geography has a claim to be taught and learned in early years and primary settings.

Children's Views of Geography

Students and teachers are often exhorted to start 'where the children are at' when beginning a unit of work or lesson. This might mean beginning a lesson by reviewing the children's existing understanding of sinking and floating in science, or asking 'What do we already know about St Lucia?' and then categorizing the children's answers. When asked the question 'What is geography?', children often provide illuminating and sometimes amusing answers. In 1989 Catling posed that question to Year 4 children when making an inservice training film (BBC, 1991). These are two highlights from the children's replies: 'It's about countries' [long pause] . . . 'It's . . . kind of art. . . like modern art.'

Ten years later, after a decade of National Curriculum geography, Catling and Brown asked the same question to another group of Year 6 children. Their answers make for surprising reading when matched against National Curriculum content. Children thought that geography was concerned with learning about countries, locating places around the world and naming some geographical features such as mountains, towns and rivers. None of them focused on the local environment or small-scale features such as the local street or school grounds. Considering that these places have been the focus for much National Curriculum geography work, they raise more questions than they answer.

> Geography is where you learn about countrys and continents like Europe Asia, Oceiance, capitals like paris, Mexico city, it is a really good subject, seas, countrys, towns, villages, rivers, lakes, islands, flags, places, the world basicly and maps, roads.
>
> (Year 6 pupil in Catling and Brown, 2000, p. 1)

Many writers such as Blyth and Krause (1995), Wiegand (1993), Palmer (1994) and Matthews (1992) have highlighted the distinction between geography as a subject and the child as a natural geographer. In The Whole World in Our Hands (Catling, 1993), Catling suggests that geographical exploration is a natural part of a child's development and that geographical education in the early years and primary school should start from that premise rather than seeking to impose a set academic curriculum on the children. Spencer *et al.* (1998) have produced evidence that mapping is a 'cultural universal' – they found that children as young as 3 from a variety of cities around the world could read maps and use aerial photographs. Their tentative conclusions were that spatial way-finding was part of natural human behaviour. Other researchers (Altman and Low, 1992) have considered the concept of 'place attachment' and suggest that having a good understanding of your local environment is essential for psychological well-being. Clearly, knowing where you are, being able to navigate to another location, and being able to make some sense of the environments you find yourself in are skills that have developed separately from any school-based curriculum.

The child as natural geographer

Paul, aged 3, enjoyed the drive from his parents' house to Millhouses Park. He was able to recognize landmarks on the route such as the shops and the building site. On the way back from the park his mother stopped to visit a friend and her baby for coffee and cakes. During the visit Paul played with baby Susan. Each time Paul passes the road where Susan lives he now exclaims, 'There's baby Susan's house!'

'A baby learning to crawl is already developing an understanding of physical geography' (Tina Bruce, 2000).

Adults' Views of Geography

Adults' views of geography or their geographical abilities are occasionally featured in the media. 'History is about chaps and geography is about maps', a phrase adapted from E. C. Bentley, was the title of a *Guardian* editorial discussing the virtues of each subject, and maps and the ability to locate places on them are recurring themes in the popular view of the nature of the subject. Indeed, geography graduates and teachers nationwide are wary of revealing their background when asked to join a quiz team. Often three years spent studying the sense of place in Thomas Hardy's novels has ill-prepared them for taxing questions such as 'Which is the biggest lake in the world?' or 'What's the capital of the former Yugoslav Republic of Macedonia?'.

Many adults' views of geography are inevitably coloured by their school experiences. Some people may remember their primary school experiences of 'people in other lands' – learning about the exotic costumes of former colonial citizens. Others recount secondary school tests about the meaning of unusual vocabulary: the oxbow lake, the drumlin and the nunatak. For others, locational knowledge looms large in the ability to use an atlas or an Ordnance Survey map or name places on a world map. What is interesting about many adults' views is that they often see geography as a subject studied in an educational institution. Ask people what a scientist is and the answer will be someone who does science. Ask people what a geographer is and the answer may be more confused. Johnston (1997) makes the point that most geographers are employed as higher education teachers rather than as social scientists in their own right. The next section will explore what geography is like in higher education and how this relates to school and early years geography.

What Is Academic Geography?

In 1998 the Quality Assurance Agency (which has a role similar to that of OFSTED, but with a focus on higher education) required the academic geography community to undertake a benchmarking exercise. It created a document that could be said to be a geography 'National Curriculum' for undergraduate university study. The document stated:

> Geography occupies a distinctive place in the world of learning, offering an integrated study of the complex reciprocal relationships between human societies and the physical components of the Earth. The geographer's canvas is coloured by *place, space and time:* recognising the great differences and dynamics in cultures, political systems, economies, landscapes and environments across the world, and the links between them.

> The discipline is characterised by a breadth of subject matter in which the traditional division has been between human and physical Geography. In recent years, however, the third category of 'environmental geography' has sometimes been recognised, encompassing the many courses that deal explicitly with human–environment relations and sustainable development, *and building upon the role of Geography in schools as the main discussion platform for environmental concerns.*

Geography in higher education would seem to have a wide range of approaches to investigate a vast subject matter. If something is different in particular places, or has changed over time, or has an unusual spatial pattern, then today's geographers can study it. Trainees who have completed a first degree in geography before taking a postgraduate certificate of education (PGCE) may have written essays about the geography of exclusion in the books of Enid Blyton, considered how the media shape the concept of place in tourism television programmes, and possibly attended a more traditional field course where they interpreted changing sediment discharges from a glacial lake. The subject's breadth and diversity may be a considerable strength, but it also makes defining it very difficult. Some writers now discuss 'geographies' rather than geography in an attempt to highlight the difference in interpretation. Saying 'Geography is what geographers do' (Johnston, 1997) is a convenient way of illustrating the way academic geographers have defined the subject, but it does not help the new geography co-ordinator or the well-established primary geography specialist communicate the nature of their subject. In order to help them do this, the following key concepts common to geography at all levels and age phases are defined.

What geographers study

Environments and landscapes

Geographers study how physical processes create particular environments. They study how people have modified environments and landscapes. A more recent development is the study of how our experience of the world is socially constructed.

Scarborough, North Yorkshire

Specific geological and coastal processes have created the physical landscape of Scarborough. Geological processes have led to the development of a prominent headland and impressive cliffs and wave-cut platforms over millions of years. Coastal processes of erosion, transport and deposition have constantly been altering the coastline, creating beaches, cliffs and wave-cut platforms and modifying these features through mass movement processes such as slumping and mudflows.

People have modified the coastal and headland environments for the past thousand years. Once the headland was settled, successive settlers modified the environment to create a landscape used for farming, fishing, residential use and tourism. In the nineteenth and twentieth centuries people have modified the coastline in an attempt to control the geological and coastal processes by building breakwaters and sea defences. This type of intervention is at present being reviewed as stakeholders, such as the local council and environmental groups, consider the long-term costs of sea defence engineering.

Scarborough is many things to many different people. It has an image that is socially constructed through people's direct experience, exposure to the media and exposure to

5

'place marketing' by tourism and commerce departments. Is it a bracing traditional seaside resort, a twenty-first-century university town, or a place to be left as soon as possible to live in Manchester, Leeds or London? The film *Scarborough Ahoy* (Channel 4 Films, 1996) depicts the town as having a vibrant nightlife and a reputation as a popular place for heterosexual and homosexual romantic liaisons – an image very different from that of a seaside resort popular with senior citizens. During the past decade human geographers have also been interested in investigating alternative conceptions of particular environments, and have broadened their studies to take in some of the concerns of sociology such as sexuality and everyday life.

The concept of spatial variation

Geographers can demonstrate knowledge and understanding of spatial distributions in physical and human features. They can explain the patterns and changing nature of the physical world of earth surface processes, water landforms, climate vegetation and soils.

The El Niño Southern Oscillation (ENSO)

'El Niño' has been blamed for periods of heavy rainfall and droughts in many areas of the world. It is caused by the interactions between ocean currents and atmospheric circulation in the Pacific Ocean. Sea surface temperature increases over the equatorial Pacific Ocean and heavy rainfall events occur in the central Pacific, western South America and California, with corresponding droughts in Australia and Pacific regions. Geographers have sought to explain the El Niño event, forecast its frequency and predict its impact on global weather.

Geographers can recognize and explain how spatial relations are important features of economic, social and political activity. Spatial relations show the connections and relationships between places. The patterns that are created by how people use the physical landscape for work, recreation and everyday life are a major focus for human geographers.

The changing structure of urban settlements in the USA and Europe

Joel Garreau's (1991) concept of 'Edge City' has been becoming reality in many cities across Europe and the USA over the past decade. Across nations city centres are declining unless they have heritage value, and the new growth is on the outskirts. Malls, hypermarkets, tourist attractions, housing, call centres, e-commerce industries are all developing on the periphery of the city. Spatial advantages on the edge are increasing and the task of attracting investment into the central city is becoming more difficult.

The distinctiveness of place

Places are distinctive and physical, economic and cultural processes create this

6

distinctiveness. Geographers investigate this alongside the place-specific characteristics such as the site of a settlement and the particular advantages and disadvantages of its location at any point in time. Everyone can have a different view of what a particular place is like, the phrase 'a place is an environment touched by feeling' (Clay, 1973) gives a clear message about how geographers view place as a concept that is experienced by the individual rather than only defined by social and scientific processes.

Park Hill School catchment area, Sheffield

The area around Park Hill Primary School in Sheffield is indeed distinctive. Its site on the valley side of the River Don above the centre of the city demonstrates the importance of physical processes in its creation. Changing economic processes led to cramped inner-city housing being replaced by 1960s concrete high-rise flats known as 'Streets in the Sky'. They have recently been designated as Grade 2 listed buildings and dominate the landscape of the city centre. Such areas are good examples of how local, national and sometimes global processes combine to create distinctive places. Places can also demonstrate the links between different people, environments and processes that act on a local and global scale (see Massey, 1997). Park Hill's distinctive characteristics link Sheffield to the Balkans in the movements of refugees (many refugees from Kosovo were housed in the flats in 1999 and many still live on the estate), and reflect the changing economic history of the steel and cutlery industry in Sheffield in the former jobs of the senior citizens that dwell there. Different people experience the distinctiveness of Park Hill as a place in very different ways. To some it is an inexpensive place to live which still retains a sense of community, but to others it is an eyesore and a symbol for the failings of post-war modernist architecture and local government social policy.

Bangalore, India

Global economic processes and local factors have combined to make the city of Bangalore a centre for India's huge information technology (IT) industry. The city has become a focus for inward investment in IT, with IBM, Cisco Systems and other multinationals locating in the area. This process highlights the interdependence between places based on the global economy and illustrates the impact of globalization on places around the world.

Systems

Geographers recognize the linkages between events in the physical and human environments. The links between inputs, processes and outputs in systems is a focus for geographical enquiry from primary school (Wiegand, 1993, pp. 125–32) to post-doctoral research.

Global warming and the human impact on the atmospheric system

Geographers are able to explain the workings of atmospheric processes as a system with specific inputs (solar radiation), processes (such as flows of heat and circulation of water vapour) and outputs (long-wave radiation). The increase of carbon dioxide, methane and chlorofluorocarbons (CFCs) in the atmosphere causes the greenhouse effect, in which the long-wave radiation is either absorbed by greenhouse gases or re-radiated back to the earth's surface. The impact of this atmospheric warming is analysed and projected; a 3-metre sea-level rise at the coast in Bangladesh could flood 29 per cent of the land and affect 21 per cent of the population. Such a systems approach can be valuable in modelling people–environment relationships such as changing sea defences, flood prevention systems in river basins and the impact of people in fragile ecosystems such as those of the Arctic or the Sahel.

The significance of scale

Geographers study human and physical features and processes at a variety of temporal and spatial scales. Social geographers will study the movement of people around a single street and create space–time diagrams showing how different members of a single family interact with the environment. Economic geographers study the flows of capital around the globe within multinational companies, and chart the movement of people at local, national and global level in response to changing economic patterns.

The water cycle in the school grounds

One can study the water cycle in a small section of the school grounds as well as at the global scale. Start by recording where the inputs to the system arrive. Where does the precipitation enter the school? How is it transported from the buildings to the ground? What happens when it reaches different ground surfaces? What throughputs are there; how does water enter your area of the school and leave – maybe via pipes, culverts or drains? What areas of water change state and evaporate or melt or freeze? What is driving this process? Aspects of the water cycle can be observed at this small scale as well as at a larger scale, for example when investigating the contrasting weather found on the east and west coasts of the UK, or the northern and southern extremes of Egypt.

An appreciation of change

Change is a central concept in geography and other humanities subjects such as history. So when is learning about changing places geography and when is it history? There is no simple answer to this question, as learning about changes in the geography of Greece or Egypt in past times could be seen as both geography and history. This highlights the advantages of skilful subject integration rather than potential problems of definition. Foley and Janikoun (1992) advised primary teachers that geography focuses on 'recent change' and 'changes that may happen in the

8

future'; however, the new geography National Curriculum requires children to learn about the history behind present-day settlement patterns, and historical geography is a strong specialism within academic geography. Whoever 'owns' the concept of change, it is in the end irrelevant, as the study of how places, spaces and environments change is crucial to understanding the world of today and tomorrow.

The development of UK settlement patterns

The majority of UK settlements were already established by AD 1066. Successive groups – Roman, Saxon, Celtic and Viking settlers – have influenced the development of this pattern, as have the agricultural, industrial and information technology revolutions. Knowledge of these changes allows future developments to be put in context. Awareness of the past geopolitical history of the Balkans or the Euroland countries can lead to a more perceptive analysis of the human and economic geographies of such regions.

The nature of difference and inequality

Difference can be defined simply as the variation found in particular geographical phenomena across physical space or time. It is used in human geography to express the variation in quality of life or human experience from one place to another.

The North–South divide

There are more telephones in the state of New York than in the whole of Africa. Approximately the same numbers of people suffer from obesity in the Northern parts of the globe as suffer from malnutrition in the South. Greater Manchester has the highest number of millionaires in one district and some of the poorest people in another when statistics are compared against other UK localities. Difference in human circumstances and difference in perception and construction of those circumstances are key concerns of twenty-first-century geography. The educational work of development education centres and charities such as Oxfam, Save the Children and CAFOD has been critical in raising the general public's and teachers' awareness of such difference.

The concept of globalization

Globalization is a term that rapidly entered the public domain during the 1990s. It can be defined as 'the conditions and consequences of financial, technological, cultural and political global interactions that are being put in place by and for national governments and transnational businesses' (Smart, 1993).

A common stereotype of globalization is that everything is becoming more standardized, similar and Americanized. Jargon words such as McDonaldization, Coca-Colaization and Disneyfication have been created to illustrate this alleged global convergence. However, detailed investigation (Potter *et al.*, 1999) reveals that inequality is being perpetuated through economic and cultural globalization. Only the affluent urban dwellers, who have access to relatively abundant cultural and economic resources, are living a more 'global' and standardized lifestyle. Many people in economically developed and less economically developed countries are the victims of unequal development which sees the fortunes of the few prosper at the expense of the many. Such *uneven development* is the focus for much development and social geography.

Doing Geography: Using Geographical Skills in the Process of Enquiry

The concepts discussed in the past few pages were not handed down from teacher to teacher and geographer to geographer. They have been developed through research, through the questioning of existing data and ideas, and the sharing of new developments in understanding people, places and environments. Geographers at all levels have used geographical skills to *enquire* about the world and its people. This concept of enquiry will feature widely in this book.

Geographical enquiry can be interpreted in different ways: using a series of questions to provide a structure for a unit of work in school (for example, learning about a distant locality such as Antarctica); the identification of particular enquiry skills such as using a map; or planning for specific investigations. It may be focused on primary data, acquired through fieldwork, or on secondary data. The main focus of enquiry is on the participants taking an active role both individually and with others to make sense of the world around them. There is a range of specific skills such as fieldwork and using maps and photographs that allow geographers (of whatever age) to create and obtain evidence in order to gain answers to their enquiries.

Enquiry is part of the 'subject knowledge' of geography as defined by the QAA and QCA. The geographical skills needed to construct an understanding of place or of local or global patterns, or to learn about people in local or distant places are acknowledged at all levels of geography. These are:

- Posing and answering appropriate questions about geographical environments or phenomena.
- Gathering a variety of data to answer these questions.
- Using skills such as fieldwork, secondary data analysis, map and photograph analysis to gather these data.
- Presenting the results of these enquiries in poster, oral, written, visual or hypertext forms for a variety of audiences. Academic geographers may communicate the results of their enquiries (or research) to the wider geographical community through journals, books or conference presentations. Primary children may communicate the results of their enquiries to their teachers, parents and members of the wider school community, as well as perhaps to local planners or environmental organizations.
- Evaluating the results of these enquiries. Academic geographers' work is reviewed by their peers before it is published and is commented on after it appears in print; this is one of the

main ways in which the subject develops. Likewise, nursery and primary children can evaluate the success of their own enquiries and gain feedback from practitioners and teachers as well as other adults.

Enquiry as a day-to-day learning approach is less linked to subject knowledge acquisition. However, geography in the early years and primary school is not based on transmission of knowledge but is instead based on questioning and evidence-based approaches. Most academic geographers would now assert that the subject matter of geography is not fixed and is open to many interpretations; so questioning existing views of the subject would be seen as part of today's study of geography at all levels.

Enquiry example: developing subject knowledge

Primary geography specialist students used the enquiry approach to develop their subject knowledge through fieldwork and ICT-based enquiries. Figure 1.1 shows the outline of one of these enquiries.

The students wished to develop their knowledge about place; specifically, how people constructed their own sense of place in the Derbyshire village of Monyash. Their key question was 'What senses of place are associated with Monyash?' One group focused on the objects or experiences that epitomized Monyash as a place for local people and themselves as visitors. They decided to gather data by interviewing local people, by visiting Monyash and investigating what sense of place they themselves formed, and by using a geographic information system (GIS)

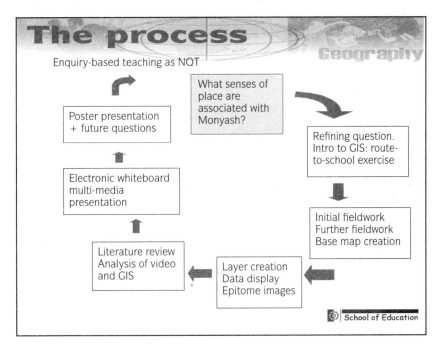

Figure 1.1 Enquiry-based teaching

mapping package to display and present the data they recorded. They learned the requisite GIS skills by practising using the package to draw a simulated route-to-school map, and then collected the data in the field. They made video recordings of their interviews with the local people, took digital images of their own epitomes of Monyash and combined this information into a presentation using a variety of presentation software and a poster. They read widely in the literature concerning place and rurality and used their findings to inform their conclusions. The students' evaluations suggested that they had both gained confidence in using an enquiry approach and developed their subject knowledge in place and rural geography.

As this above example shows, enquiry-based learning is an excellent way of acquiring subject knowledge at any level of geographical study. From nursery children investigating the route to the shops, to a PhD student enquiring into recent developments in green tourism, enquiry could be seen to be the key feature that links twenty-first-century geography at all age phases.

Summary

This section has sought to introduce some of the different ways in which geography is defined at the start of the twenty-first century. Geography exists as a way of grouping human experiences of places and environments and as a school and academic discipline. A number of points have been highlighted.

Geography and people's perceptions of it

- Children do have an understanding of what geography is. They favour explanations based on knowledge about countries and global location above local studies and enquiry-based work. Their definitions of what geography is may be very different from the statutory geography curriculum.
- Adults perceive geography as a school subject with a strong focus on location. The media often highlight the failings of children and adults in relation to their locational knowledge.
- Academic geography is a wide-ranging subject with many tools for analysis, ranging from cultural and social theory to geographic information systems (GIS).
- The wide range of geographies available makes defining the subject and communicating it to non-specialists a difficult task.
- Enquiry or research-based learning plays a major part in the construction of geographical knowledge.

Why Learn Geography?

What is our knowledge worth if we know nothing about the world that sustains us, nothing about natural systems and climate, nothing about other countries and cultures?

(Porritt, in DfEE/QCA, 1999, p. 108)

What other subject tells us so much about the great issues of the age – global change, natural and human?

(Goudie, *ibid.*)

These impassioned quotations in the introduction to the geography section of the National Curriculum (2000) would seem to render this section of the chapter irrelevant. Surely everyone involved in education in the twenty-first century would endorse Andrew Goudie's and Sir Jonathon Porritt's words? Surely geography in early years settings, schools and universities must be thriving? However, anyone with any experience of nursery and primary education will know that in many institutions this is not the case and that geography can still, in the words of Patrick Wiegand, be viewed as a 'cinderella subject' (Wiegand, 1993, p. 2). Literacy, numeracy and ICT are the priorities for today's child, and geography, along with other foundation subjects and science, must compete for that child's attention in the afternoon, after the important business of basic skills has been addressed. Even though geography has been a compulsory subject for 5- to 14-year-old pupils since the advent of the National Curriculum (apart from the 'relaxation' of the primary curriculum from 1999 to 2000 to focus on literacy and numeracy), many specialist primary geography students still report that their school 'is not doing geography' during their school experience, or that 'no one wants to be the geography co-ordinator'. So perhaps a rousing defence of geography is needed, and a case should be made for the inclusion of this statutory subject in the curriculum that children actually experience. The final section of this chapter makes this case, outlining five arguments in support of young children being allowed to learn what they are entitled to learn: geography as part of a broad and balanced curriculum.

1 Geography offers children the means to develop from 'natural geographers' who have made sense of the environments around them, to become 'global citizens' who can make sense of what they experience of the world though first-hand and mediatized experience. The world is shrinking: learning geography can help to make sense of the interdependent yet constantly changing global scene.

2 Geography's focus on *people* as well as places can contribute to education that seeks to promote a fair and just society (see Chapter 8).

3 Geography provides opportunities to learn about the big issues that will affect life in the twenty-first century. Questions of access to drinking water, globalization, and rising levels of resource consumption and inequality can all be addressed through geography, alongside the opportunity to act to create positive change.

4 Geography can help children to 'learn how to learn'. The subject matter is intrinsically interesting and has the potential to motivate, stimulate and fire children's curiosity and sense of awe and wonder, whilst the process of geographical enquiry fits well with research on how children (and adults) learn.

5 Geography provides opportunities for the development of key skills that are used across the curriculum and in later life. Yes, geography can contribute to learning in literacy and numeracy, but equally it can contribute to the development of critical thinking and decision-making, and can use ICT to investigate real-world issues. Geography is uniquely placed to deal with the exponential growth of spatially referenced information (postcodes, digital map data and photograph data) and continues to develop children's graphicacy skills.

Geography is a broad and wide-ranging subject. This is both its strength and its weakness at all age phases. On the one hand, the subject integrates a wide range of academic disciplines, learning strategies and global locations, and on the other hand it can be seen as difficult to define, fragmented or a mere compendium of useful and not-so-useful facts to be learned before going a few rounds with Chris Tarrant on *Who Wants to be a Millionaire?*. However, geography deserves its place in the early years and primary curriculum for the five reasons stated in the previous paragraph. The next chapter examines how these merits of geography as a discipline have been translated into a curriculum for children in the Foundation Stage and those at Key Stages 1 and 2 of the National Curriculum.

Box 1.1　The geography journey

From natural geographers to global citizens
Personal development and citizenship

Education for a fair and just society
Social and emotional development

Learning about twenty-first-century issues
Intellectual development: futures

Learning how to learn
Academic development

Developing key skills
Vocational development

Professional Development Tasks: Specialist Subject Knowledge

Create a portfolio with evidence of your specialist subject knowledge ability using the following evidence:

- audit data: complete the audit that follows and review it, setting targets for development;
- work from school experience files. Keep copies of work that shows evidence of your subject knowledge;
- materials from schools, unit handouts, photocopies of key articles concerning subject knowledge or teaching and learning (e.g. from *Primary Geographer*, academic journals and texts);
- your own notes;
- use of GEOCAL computer-based learning modules;
- use of Acacia Geography Revision CD-ROM or other similar products.

Geography subject knowledge audit

Complete the audit (Table 1.1 on pp. 16–17) and set targets to meet the contents of column 2. Share the results of the audit with fellow students and form learning groups to gain this knowledge.

Reflective Questions

- What do you remember as geography from your own primary education?
- How do you see the subject of geography developing in the twenty-first century?
- Is enquiry a learning approach, or part of the subject matter of geography?
- Are children natural mappers? What evidence have you seen or read that bears on this question?
- How would you justify geography's place on the 3–11 curriculum?

FURTHER READING

Kent, A., Lambert, D., Naish, M. and Slater, F. (eds) (1996) *Geography in Education: Viewpoints on Teaching and Learning*. Sheffield: Geographical Association.

Kneale, P. E. (1999) *Study Skills for Geography Students: A Practical Guide*. London: Arnold.

Skinner, M., Redfern, D. and Farmer, G. (1996) *The Complete A–Z Geography Handbook*. London: Hodder & Stoughton.

Tilbury, D. and Williams, M. (eds) (1997) *Teaching and Learning Geography*. London: Routledge.

Table 1.1 **An audit of one's subject knowledge**

Elements of NC geography	Good personal understanding to back up teaching at KS1 and KS2	Need more subject knowledge	Have observed in school
Physical geography			
Major landforms – hills, valleys, cliffs			
Simple geology			
River systems			
Coastal features and processes			
Weather – measuring			
Seasonal weather patterns			
Weather conditions around the world			
Human geography			
Characteristics of urban settlements			
Characteristics of rural settlements			
Land use in the above			
Concept of settlement hierarchy			
Reasons for settlement location			
Functions of settlements			
Issues arising from land use			
Environmental geography			
Impact of people on the built environment			
Impact of people on the landscape			
Sustainable development			
How people manage their environment			
Environmental quality			
Children's perception of the environment			
Geographical skills			
Use of			
1:1250/1:2500 maps			
1:10,000 maps			

Elements of NC geography	Good personal understanding to back up teaching at KS1 and KS2	Need more subject knowledge	Have observed in school
1:25,000 maps			
1:50,000 maps			
Other maps and plans			
Electronic mapping/using GIS			
Using 3D models to develop mapwork			
Aerial photographs			
Satellite images			
Confidence in using enquiry approach			
Using an atlas			
Using a compass			
Fieldwork			
Organizing a visit			
Using the school catchment area			
Using the school grounds			
Investigating a river/coast			
Planning a land use survey			
Use of ICT in geography			
Word processing			
Desktop publishing			
Spreadsheets			
Databases			
Drawing/painting			
Mapping packages			
Roamer			
CD-ROMs			
Email			
Internet			
Contrasting localities			
A locality in Europe			
A locality in an economically developing country			

REFERENCES

Altman, I. and Low, S. M. (eds) (1992) 'Place attachment', *Human Behaviour and Environment: Advances in Theory and Research*, Volume 12. New York: Plenum.

BBC (1991) *Teaching Today: Primary Geography*. London: BBC School TV.

Blyth, A. and Krause, J. (1995) *Primary Geography: A Developmental Approach*. London: Hodder & Stoughton.

Bruce, T. (2000), quoted in K. Grimwade, 'Geography's back in business', *Primary Geographer*, 41,1.

Catling, S. (1993) 'The whole world in our hands', *Geography* 78 (4), 340–58.

Catling, S. and Brown, M. (2000) 'Primary children's definitions of 'geography', unpublished paper presented at Charney Manor Primary Geography Research Conference, March.

Clay, G. (1973) *Close up: How to Read the American City*. New York: Praeger.

DfEE/QCA (1998) *Geography: A Scheme of Work for Key Stages 1 and 2*. Sudbury: Qualifications and Curriculum Authority.

DfEE/QCA (1999) *The National Curriculum: Handbook for Primary Teachers in England, Key Stages 1 & 2*. London: QCA.

DfEE/TTA (1998) *Circular 4/98: High Status, High Standards*. London: HMSO.

Foley, M. and Janikoun, J. (1992) *The Really Practical Guide to Primary Geography*. Cheltenham: Stanley Thornes.

Garreau, J. (1991) *Edge City: Life on the New Frontier*. New York: Doubleday.

Johnson, R. J. (1997) *Geography and Geographers*. London: Arnold.

Knight, P. (1993) *Primary Geography, Primary History*. London: David Fulton.

Massey, D. (1997) 'Questions of locality', *Geography* 178 (2), 142–9.

Matthews, M. H. (1992) *Making Sense of Place: Children's Understanding of Large-scale Environments*. Hemel Hempstead: Harvester Wheatsheaf.

Palmer, J. (1994) *Geography in the Early Years*. London: Routledge.

Potter, R. B., Binns, J. A., Elliott, J. A. and Smith, D. (1999) *Geographies of Development*. Hemel Hempstead: Addison Wesley Longman.

Smart, B. (1993) *Postmodernity*. London: Routledge.

Smith, P. R. (1997) 'Standards achieved: a review of geography in primary schools in England 1995/96/97, *Primary Geographer* 31, 4–5.

Spencer, C., Blades, M., Blaut, J., Darvizeh, Z., Elguea, S., Sowden, S., Steer, D., and Uttal, D. (1998) 'A cross-cultural study in young children's mapping ability', *Transactions of the Institute of British Geographers* 23 (2), 278–88.

QAA (2000) *Academic Standards (Geography)*. London: QAA.

Wiegand, P. (1993) *Children and Primary Geography*. London: Cassell.

Geography in the Foundation Stage and Key Stages 1 and 2

This chapter examines two particular geographies: the geography laid down by the Secretary of State as the statutory entitlement for school children in the National Curriculum; and the geography implicit in the Early Learning Goals. These two geographies are closely related, but do differ. Prior to the introduction of the National Curriculum, primary children would rarely have learned geography as a single subject. However, from 2000 onwards it is suggested that children aged from 5 to 11 will learn geography as a single subject, linked to other subjects where appropriate (DfEE/QCA, 1999). The Early Learning Goals are not subject based, but rather are focused on areas of experience.

The chapter begins by offering suggestions on how aspects of the Early Learning Goals can be used to develop children's emerging awareness of the concepts of location, place, geographical patterns and processes, and understanding of issues involving the environment and sustainability, based on their own experiences. Children in the Foundation Stage are already geographers, so it is highly appropriate that they should be experiencing activities that develop their natural geographic abilities. The chapter continues by outlining the current nature of the geography curriculum at Key Stages 1 and 2. It begins with the process of geography and introduces the four aspects of the geography curriculum that are or can be present in children's learning from Year 1 to Year 9 in the National Curriculum Programme of Study. Examples are given of how these four aspects are developed in children's classroom work and fieldwork. The chapter then outlines the breadth of study in the geography curriculum, again offering examples of how teachers have developed children's understanding of local and distant places and environments. Finally the chapter considers geography in the context of the whole curriculum, particularly in relation to literacy, numeracy, citizenship and sustainability.

Geography in the Foundation Stage

Children aged between 3 and 5 are currently working towards the Early Learning Goals in the Foundation Stage. The Early Learning Goals are structured around six broad areas of experience rather than the narrower subject boundaries to be found in the education of children aged from 5 to 14. As a result, no subject named geography exists in the Foundation curriculum. This does not mean that young children are not expected to have any geographical experiences in their early years education; rather it means that geographical learning takes place through play, first-hand experience and adult intervention in a more holistic and integrated manner, in keeping with current thinking on how young children learn.

The six areas of experience are shown below. Geography has been most keenly associated with 'Knowledge and Understanding of the World', but equally children as 'young geographers' can use their geographical skills to further their learning in any of the six areas.

The Early Learning Goals

- Personal, social and emotional development;
- Communication, language and literacy;
- Mathematical development;
- *Knowledge and Understanding of the World*;
- Physical development; and
- Creative development.

The geography in the Early Learning Goals (DfEE/QCA, 2000) is based on the 'child as young geographer' approach. Geography is seen as a way of classifying learning experiences about people and places rather than as a discrete subject area. Content and teaching and learning are closely linked and the guidance provided to early years practitioners stresses the progression in what children can already do between the ages of 3 and 5 and then what the practitioner needs to do to develop children's existing skills to meet the Goals. Opportunities exist to develop geographical learning in each of the areas of experience. The lists below show these opportunities. Study them and see if you can identify some of the key geographical concepts discussed in Chapter 1.

Personal, social and emotional development

Children should be able to:

- have a developing respect for their own culture and the cultures of other people, celebrating and acknowledging differences;
- gain knowledge and understanding of their own culture and community; talk freely about their home and community;

- respond to significant experiences, showing a range of feelings; talk about similarities and differences in their experiences and the reasons for these;
- undertake problem-solving;
- identify issues, find solutions, think about issues from the viewpoint of others; and
- select and use resources independently.

Communication, language and literacy

Children should be able to:

- imagine and recreate experiences in play;
- question why things happen and give explanations;
- build up their vocabulary; and
- use books and ICT for information.

Mathematical development

Children should be able to:

- use positional language; and
- describe a simple journey.

Knowledge and understanding of the world

Children should be able to:

- use a range of information sources (books, CD-ROMs, photographs, maps, artefacts, visits, visitors);
- ask questions;
- develop and use appropriate vocabulary;
- have real experiences (of weather, buildings that surround them);
- work on a large scale (construction, mapping, sand play);
- make models of buildings seen;
- carry out close observation;
- become familiar with their surroundings and the natural world (sensory trails, visits to shops, looking at pictures, videos);
- visit or use photographs to identify features in their local area (library, mosque, station);
- talk about observations, findings, ask questions and speculate on reasons;
- investigate, using a range of techniques and senses:
- record their findings (via drawing, writing, a model, photography)
- look closely at similarities and differences, patterns and change, e.g. seasonal patterns;
- observe and talk about the use of ICT in the environment on local walks (traffic lights, street lights, telephones);
- use ICT (for communication, finding out);
- create their own environments in play;
- develop an awareness of features of the environment through visits;
- notice differences between features;

- listen to stories about other environments;
- investigate the environment (interview local people, examine maps and photographs, make visits);
- create simple maps and plans, paintings, drawings and models of observations of the local area and imaginary landscapes;
- design practical and attractive environments;
- express opinions on built and natural environments and listen to others' points of view; and
- learn about other cultures through books, stories, artefacts, visitors, visits.

Physical development

Children should:

- develop spatial awareness and positional vocabulary.

Creative development

Children should:

- explore their environment, learning through all the senses;
- explore shape, form and space in two or three dimensions (e.g. by constructing models);
- undertake role-play, e.g. going on an imaginary journey; and
- develop an appreciation of the natural world and responsibility to care for it.

The statements above highlight the opportunities for young children to develop the following key geographical abilities through skilful planning by practitioners. The curriculum guidance and research evidence are clear: young children can develop as geographers, and the following teaching activities can help them develop.

Asking geographical questions, using geographical skills

Early years practitioners can introduce geographical vocabulary such as 'park', 'town', 'village', 'house', 'flat' and 'temple' to enable children to talk about what they observe and ask questions about their surroundings. Practitioners can provide opportunities for children to find out about the environment by interviewing local people, examining photographs and simple maps, and involving the children in fieldwork concerning the local built and natural environment.

Developing a sense of place

Practitioners can arouse interest in features of the environment around the nursery and immediate local area and use stories that help children make sense of different environments. Children can identify the places they have been to on holiday and use play maps and 'small world' equipment to create their own environments.

Exploring space: the concept of location

The early years setting has innumerable opportunities to develop children's spatial awareness. Practitioners can develop their directional language, help them create and work out routes around play equipment and in the immediate local area, and provide resources to make paintings, drawings and models of observations of the local area and imaginary landscapes.

Valuing the environment

The Early Learning Goals encourage practitioners to plan activities to enable children to find out about their environment and talk about those features they like and dislike. Practitioners are asked in the Goals to encourage children to express opinions on natural and built environments and give opportunities for children to hear different points of view on the quality of the environment. They are asked to encourage the use of words that help children to express opinions, such as 'busy', 'quiet', 'noisy', 'attractive', 'ugly', 'litter', 'pollution'. Finally, practitioners are asked to give opportunities to design practical, attractive environments, such as taking care of flowerbeds or organizing equipment outside.

(Based on QCA/DfEE, 2000a, pp. 96–7)

Thus it is clear that opportunities for geographical learning are alive and well in the guidance for the Foundation Stage. Old ideas (based on a misinterpretation of the work of Jean Piaget, and curriculum guidance written in the 1970s) of geography being somehow too hard for young children appear to have been superseded. More and more evidence from practitioners and researchers (e.g. Scoffham, 1998; Bowles, 2000) is now showing how well young children can develop as 'natural geographers' given the right support.

Geography in the National Curriculum

Geography provokes and answers questions about the natural and human worlds, using different scales of enquiry to view them from different perspectives. It develops knowledge of places and environments throughout the world, an understanding of maps, and a range of investigative and problem-solving skills both inside and outside the classroom. As such, it prepares pupils for adult life and employment.

Geography is a focus for understanding and resolving issues about the environment and sustainable development. It is also an important link between the natural and social sciences. As pupils study geography, they encounter different societies and cultures. This helps them realise how nations rely on each other. It can inspire them to think about their own place in the world, their values, and their rights and responsibilities to other people and the environment.

(DfEE/QCA, 1999, p. 108)

This statement attempts to define the geography experienced by 5- to 14-year-old pupils. This geography is again a questioning subject that acknowledges the natural and human influences in the world. It uses enquiry and geographical skills to investigate these worlds. The key concepts of place, spatial awareness and environment are again central to this vision of school geography in the twenty-first century. The present geography National Curriculum is divided into two related sections: *knowledge, skills and understanding* in geography and *breadth of study* in geography.

Knowledge, skills and understanding relates to the geographical concepts children must learn using geographical enquiry and skills. Collectively this body of knowledge, skills and understanding is known as the four *aspects* of geography (DfEE/QCA, 1998):

- geographical enquiry and skills;
- knowledge and understanding of places;
- knowledge and understanding of patterns and processes; and
- knowledge and understanding of environmental change and sustainable development;

The breadth of study specifies the localities and themes through which pupils should be taught the four aspects, and specifies at what scale and at what locations children should learn about the key ideas of geography. It also states that children should learn some of this geography at first hand by engaging in fieldwork.

The Programme of Study is a statutory document; what has been discussed above is the legal entitlement curriculum that children must learn in Years 1 to 6. At present teachers in primary schools can use this document to build a scheme of work that suits their location, catchment area, school community and teaching strengths. The curriculum planning involved in this enterprise is discussed in Chapter 3. However, schemes of work published by the Qualifications and Curriculum Authority (DfEE/QCA, 1998) and updated in 2000 on the DfEE Standards and Effectiveness Unit Web site (www.standards.dfee.gov.uk/schemes) have provided teaching units which give non-statutory exemplars of how the Programme of Study can be implemented. These have become increasingly popular with primary teachers, although the exemplars do need to be viewed with a critical eye when customizing them to any specific school situation. The following two subsections outline the four aspects of geography, and give examples of how the breadth of study can be covered at Key Stages 1 and 2, using examples from this non-statutory guidance.

Developing the four aspects of geography

Gg1a   Geographical enquiry

> In undertaking geographical enquiry, pupils should be taught to:
>
> **Key Stage 1**
> **a** ask geographical questions;
> **b** observe and record;
> **c** express their own views about people, places and environments; and
> **d** communicate in different ways.
>
> **Key Stage 2**
> **a** ask geographical questions;
> **b** collect and record evidence;
> **c** analyse evidence and draw conclusions;
> **d** identify and explain different views that people including themselves, hold about topical geographical issues; and
> **e** communicate in ways appropriate to the task and audience.
>
> (DfEE QCA, 2000, pp. 110–12)

Geographical enquiry was introduced in Chapter 1 as a key method of building on any learner's existing geographical knowledge, values and skills as well as an effective learning strategy to access the subject of geography. The Programme of Study breaks enquiry into four or five stages, which can be illustrated by the model below

> **Stage 1**
> **a** Awareness raising
> **b** Generating enabling questions – key and subsidiary questions
>
> **Stage 2**
> Collecting and recording information
>
> **Stage 3**
> Processing the gathered information
>
> **Stage 4**
> Drawing conclusions from the processed data
>
> **Stage 5**
> Sharing the learning and effective outcomes
>
> **Stage 6**
> Evaluation by all concerned
>
> (Dinkele, 1998, p. 155)

These stages should be applied to a stimulating geographical issue that the children will be interested in; they are not just a way of collecting data to turn into charts or written work for a wall display. The question(s) need to be interesting to the children (as well as the teacher) and there needs to be a recognized audience for the results of the enquiry.

Asking geographical questions

At its simplest, geographical enquiry involves asking questions and finding answers, as illustrated in Figure 2.1. Effective enquiry depends initially on the quality of the questions. Choice of questions can be guided by the following exemplar or 'key' questions (after Storm, 1989):

- What/where is it?
- What's it like?
- Why is it like it is?
- How is it connected to other places?
- How and why is it changing?
- What would it be like to be there?
- How is it similar to/different from another place?

These questions can be applied to all the places and themes prescribed for study. They can be adapted for Foundation, Key Stage 1 and Key Stage 2 study. Each question focuses on a different aspect of what is being investigated. The questions encourage different types of thinking, investigation and use of language. They are the basis for any geographical enquiry, whether it is based on questioning an artefact or picture for 20 minutes, or designing a half-term unit of work enquiring into coasts and the processes associated with them. Enquiry is taught, not just caught (see Chapter 5), and needs to be modelled carefully by the teacher.

Generating enquiry questions for use in an enquiry-based unit of work

Gunmeet Kapoor used the enquiry approach effectively with her Year 5 class at Abbey Lane Primary School, Sheffield. She decided to adapt the QCA 'Water' unit of work to her school situation. In the first lesson of the unit of work, after recapping their existing knowledge of the water cycle gained from science lessons, she asked the class to think of questions that they would like to answer based on the movement of water around the school grounds. She gave the class some exemplar questions, then collected the class's questions on the Post-it Notes they had written them on. With the help of some members of the class she grouped the questions into categories and displayed them on the wall. These questions then formed the basis for the first part of the 'Water' unit of work.

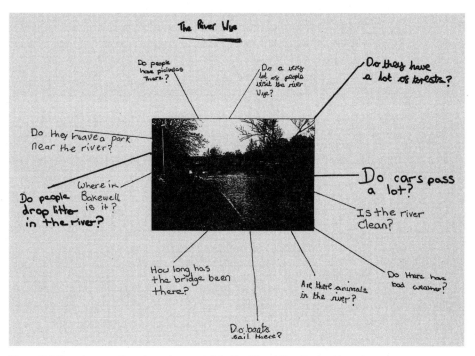

The River Wye

Do people have picnics there?

Do a very lot of people visit the river Wye?

Do they have a lot of forests?

Do they have a park near the river?

Where in Bakewell is it?

Do people drop litter in the river?

Do cars pass a lot?

Is the river Clean?

How long has the bridge been there?

Are there animals in the river?

Do there have bad weather?

Do boats sail there?

Figure 2.1 Enquiry questions based on a visit to the River Wye, Derbyshire

Gg1b Geographical skills

Key Stage 1
In developing geographical skills, pupils should be taught to:
a use geographical vocabulary;
b use fieldwork skills;
c use globes, maps and plans at a variety of scales;
d use secondary sources of information; and
e make maps and plans.

Key Stage 2
a use appropriate geographical vocabulary;
b use appropriate fieldwork techniques and instruments;
c use atlases and globes, and maps and plans at a range of scales;
d use secondary sources of information, including aerial photographs;
e draw plans and maps at a range of scales;
f use ICT to help in geographical enquiries; and
g develop decision-making skills.

Geographical skills are the tools employed in the enquiry process to gain the best understanding of the subject of the enquiry and communicate that understanding in the best possible way. For many non-geographers, geographical skills simply equate to mapwork! If the children are asked to draw their route to school or make a map of the classroom, then geography can be ticked off for another year. (This is only a slight exaggeration.)

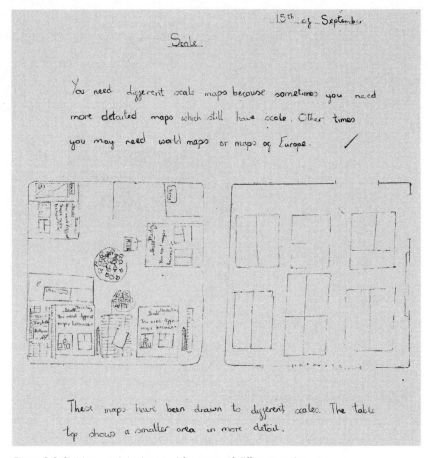

Figure 2.2 Children explain the need for maps of different scales

Teachers and students have to convince their colleagues that children need to widen their geographical vocabulary and that they should be confident in drawing a field sketch or be able, with instruction, to use a digital thermometer. They have to convince their colleagues that the children need focused teacher intervention to succeed in drawing maps and interpreting photographs and that they should use ICT.

Vocabulary

Geography is a well-established subject with its own specialist vocabulary. Many geographical terms are also used in everyday speech and could be considered part of everyday language used to describe location (near, far) or name familiar features in the landscape (town, river, motorway). Many other words in the vocabulary of any geographer have more than one meaning (transport is a verb as well as a noun) or sound the same as another word (sauce and source). Research by Platten (1995) suggests that much of the geographical vocabulary used by children at Key Stage 1 can be and is misunderstood. Box 2.1 shows suggested vocabulary developing from everyday language about the local area to more specialized vocabulary such as 'settlement', 'scale (see also Figure 2.2)' and 'land use'.

Box 2.1   Geographical vocabulary used by children at Key Stage 1 and upper Key Stage 2

KS1 vocabulary – local area

Traffic, survey, busy, quiet, street, parking, yellow lines, pedestrian crossing, council offices, address, near, far, travel, journey, routes, attractive, buildings, offices, church, shop, houses, flats, garage, playground, park

Upper KS2 vocabulary – local area

Environment, volume, pedestrian precinct, diversion, benefits, shopkeepers, deliveries, senior citizens, survey, points of view, planning, issues, decisions, hamlet, village, town, city, settlement, north, south, east, west, route, scale, distance, direction, key, symbol, services, factory, transport, land use, repair, damage, pollution, slopes, valleys, streams, soil

(Based on DfEE/QCA, 1999, Vocabulary for Geography units)

Maps, plans, globes and aerial photographs

Geography develops graphicacy. Graphicacy is part of visual literacy and allows children to express their spatial awareness and environmental cognition. Crucial in interpreting this section of the Programme of Study is the realization that these forms of spatial communication should be *used* to answer geographical questions and interpret geographical themes. Being able to draw a map or find a place on the globe, and locate your house on an aerial photograph of the school locality,

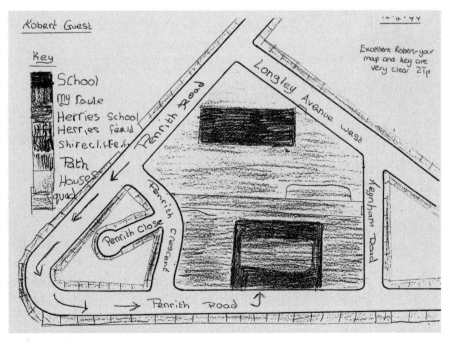

Figure 2.3 Designing a key for a local area map

are skills that should be learned as part of a unit of work that develops children's understanding of place, patterns and processes, and environmental change and sustainable development. Key Stage 1 children can be introduced to the concept of plan views and representing a 3D world in two dimensions by modelling sections of the classroom. Key Stage 2 children can map the land use of the local area, as in Figure 2.3, or locate particular types of feature (forest, buildings) on an aerial photograph of the distant locality they are studying. The development of children's map skills and their use of ICT is discussed in more detail in Chapter 5.

Decision-making skills

Children at Key Stages 1 and 2 make critical decisions all the time. Who should I stand next to in the dinner queue? Who should I sit next to on the bus? The current programme of study emphasizes that children's decision-making skills should be developed at Key Stage 2.

Gg2 Knowledge and understanding of places

Key Stage 1

Pupils should be taught to:

a identify and describe what places are like;

b identify and describe where places are;

c recognize how places have become the way they are and how they are changing;

d recognize how places compare with other places; and

e recognize how places are linked to other places in the world.

Key Stage 2

Pupils should be taught:

a to identify and describe what places are like;

b the location of places and environments they study and other significant places and environments;

c to describe where places are;

d to explain why places are as they are;

e to identify how and why places change and how they may change in the future;

f to describe and explain how and why places are similar to and different from other places in the same country and elsewhere in the world; and

g to recognize how places fit within a wider geographical context and are interdependent.

Place is a key geographical concept. Each place is distinctive and is experienced by different people in different ways. Likewise, places are interconnected, whether by telecommunications, movement of people or historical factors. Pupils are asked to identify, recognize, describe and explain the nature of places, how they are changing and how they are connected. The Programme of Study explores the holistic concept of place based on the geographical questions. It asks:

- What is this place like?
- Where is this place?
- Why is it like that?
- How is it changing? How might it change in the future?
- Why is it similar to or different from place x?
- How is it linked to place y?
- What factors make it interdependent with place z?

Study of chosen localities (the local area (see Figure 2.4), a contrasting location in the UK or overseas) is the focus for learning how geographers interpret places and the focus for learning about the localities themselves using these place questions. This section of the current geography curriculum develops children's understanding of location and their ability to observe and describe physical and human features in a locality (the school is built on a hillside, the river flows through farmland then into the town) and their ability to recognize change. Children learn the skills of comparison, of identifying similarities and differences between places (most people in our locality work in the city, most people in Grasmere work in tourism or farming). There is a progression from Key Stage 1 children identifying links between places (such as the movement of people between them) and Key Stage 2 children beginning to understand the concept of interdependence between places.

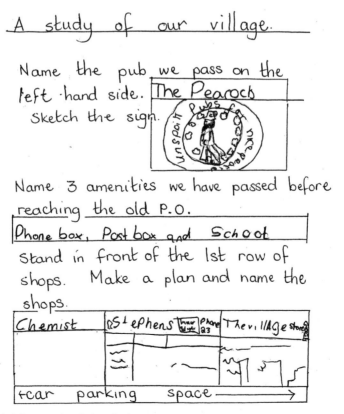

Figure 2.4 A focus on local place features

Gg3 Patterns and processes

Key Stage 1

Pupils should be taught to:

a make observations about where things are located and about other features in the environment; and

b recognize changes in physical and human features.

Key Stage 2

a recognize and explain patterns made by individual physical and human features in the environment; and

b recognize some physical processes and explain how these cause changes in places and environments.

Places are distinctive. But not every place is different in a different way. The geography of people and environments is not completely random. Patterns of physical and human features are visible: mountain ranges, coastal cities, roads, rail and canals in a valley. Children need to be able to analyse what they see and what others have seen in as near to an objective way as possible. This is the aspect of geography that is closest to science. But what do they need to do? Use of their observation skills is the first step; the second is first to recognize changes in any patterns, then to try to explain these changes (see Figure 2.5).

Teachers need to give children experiences that allow them to observe patterns then attempt to explain them. Children need to know that being a 'geographical detective' is a key part of geography. When they look at the surrounding area of their school, or study a photo of children playing next to the River Amazon, or see a video of how the coast is changing near Whitby, they need to be able to analyse the scene. What things are similar to their experience? What is different? Why might this be? What other information do they need to explain what they see? The Programme of Study specifically focuses on explaining physical processes at Key Stage 2. Children must be given opportunities to observe physical processes such as erosion and deposition, evaporation and condensation, mass movement and the impact of rainfall on different surfaces. Not all of this can be observed as it happens, but much of it can be modelled in the sand tray or school grounds.

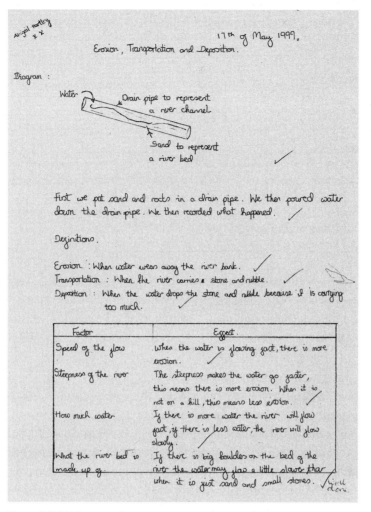

Figure 2.5 Writing up a river processes enquiry experiment

Box 2.2   *What are patterns and processes?*

What is a pattern?

In geography the way that physical and human features are arranged in a landscape or environment is referred to as a pattern. Examples include the way that streets are arranged in a town; the layout of fields and hedgerows in a rural landscape; the arrangement of a river and its tributaries; the way in which temperatures and rainfall totals vary across the UK. These all form patterns.

What is a process?

A process is a series of human or physical events which cause a change in a place or environment. Examples include deposition of material by rivers; deforestation; suburbanization of villages.

(SCAA, 1997)

Gg4 Environmental change and sustainable development

Key Stage 1
Pupils should be taught to:
a recognize changes in the environment; and
b recognize how the environment may be improved and sustained.

Key Stage 2
a recognize how people can improve the environment or damage it, and how decisions about places and environments affect the future quality of people's lives; and
b recognize how and why people may seek to manage environments sustainably, and identify opportunities for their own involvement.

Environmental change in the geography Programme of Study is change caused by people. The Programme of Study asks teachers to teach children how they can recognize these human changes. The changes may be positive (reclaiming of derelict land) or destructive (e.g. vandalism; see Figure 2.6, or pollution of a river; see Figure 2.7).

Geographical issues almost invariably arise through the interaction of the environment, development and society. The development of human society has depended on the exploitation of natural resources with its consequent impact on the environment (although most resources are not freely available to everyone). Thus environmental and development issues are often inextricably linked. Examples range from the local – which often reflect what is happening on a global scale – to the global. An example of the former would be plans for a bypass through green belt land. Tourism is an example of the latter. The past few years have seen the development of so-called 'ecotourism' in an attempt to benefit the tourist, the tour operators and the local community without damaging the environment.

Sustainable development was implicit in the 1995 National Curriculum but has been emphasized explicitly in the 2000 version. In 1992 at the Earth Summit in Rio de Janeiro, 180 of the world's leaders signed up to Agenda 21, a blueprint for sustainable development. Local Agenda 21 is the process of developing local strategies for sustainable development. It is often defined as 'development which meets the needs of the present without compromising the ability of future generations to meet their own needs' (Brundtland Commission, 1987).

QCA suggests that sustainable development is about:

- the interaction and interdependence of society, economy and environment;
- the needs of both present and future generations; and
- the local and global implications of lifestyle choices.

Education for sustainable development involves learning about issues and acquiring the knowledge, understanding, values and skills to enable participation in working

NEIGHBOURHOOD VANDALISM SURVEY

We conducted a survey of the local area around Hardings School

ACT OF VANDALISM	WHERE WE FOUND IT	HOW SERIOUS IT WAS	
School broken fencing. graffiti	infant and junior yard/boundary of yard and superfram	dangerous wood sticking out could harm child. an eyesore	Replace with stronger fencing. Reminders from teachers to respect boundary try to secure yard.
Shops graffiti on everything	walls, bins, security shutters, boarded up windows and on notice boards.	makes shops look unattractive and run down	extra police patrols or camera surveillance.
Park graffiti. holed wire fencing illegal dumping of mattress.	probable toilet wall and benches tennis courts under a tree.	make park unattractive dangerous—could cut children with spiked wire unsightly and unhygienic.	some graffiti artists increase Park Patrols to prevent damage fine dumpers Leighton Road stop
Bus stop glass broken/signal broken machines broken superfram windows scratched bus shelter damaged.	Leighton Road stop	no shelter from the weather, driver at risk without signals unattractive eyesore	Security cameras better, stronger glazing.

Figure 2.6 Assessing the environment around the school

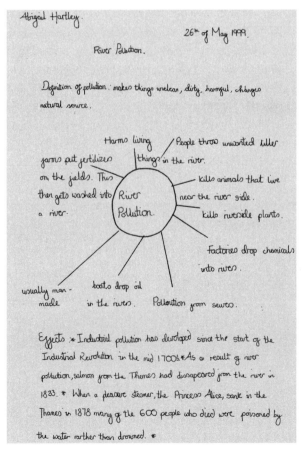

Figure 2.7 Researching river pollution

towards global equity and justice and solutions to local, national and global issues. It is seen as cross-curricular although it features most prominently in the geography curriculum. An energy policy in a primary school and the use of traditional methods of irrigation in Egypt (appropriate technology) are examples of sustainable development.

Learning about sustainable development at Key Stage 2

Sara Graham accompanied a Year 5 class to the Earth Centre at Conisbrough. The Earth Centre education staff had planned activities so that the children would learn about sustainable development through the 'Water and the Landscape' theme. The children learned about the water cycle through hands-on activities: how water is used, how it can be recycled and how it can be conserved.

Breadth of study

The previous subsection outlined the *process* of geography, and what children must learn through enquiry when doing geography in school in Key Stages 1 and 2. The children will progress in their understanding of the four aspects of geography from the ages of 5 to 11. This section explains the *content* of geography – specifically, the topics that the children must learn, with information about the scale and context in which these topics should be investigated. It begins by outlining the current requirements at Key Stages 1 and 2, highlighting the breadth of study requirements.

Geography at Key Stage 1

During KS1 pupils investigate their *local area* and a *contrasting area in the UK or abroad*, finding out about the *environment in both areas and the people* who live there. They also *begin to learn about the wider world*. They carry out geographical enquiry *inside and outside the classroom*. In doing this they ask geographical questions about people, places and environments, and use geographical skills and resources such as maps and photographs.

(DfEE/QCA, 1999, p. 111)

Key Stage 1 breadth of study

During the Key Stage, pupils should be taught the KSU (knowledge, skills and understanding) through the study of two localities:

a the locality of the school;

b a locality either in the United Kingdom or overseas that has physical and/or human features that contrast with those in the locality of the school.

In the study of their localities, pupils should:

a study at a local scale; and

b carry out fieldwork investigations outside the classroom.

The breadth of the Key Stage 1 geography curriculum entitles children to learn geography through the study of two localities. This is in keeping with the understanding that primary geography is about real people in real places and that young children learn geography best through focusing on real places at an appropriate scale. But what scale is this? What is a locality at Key Stage 1?

The locality of the school is its immediate vicinity, including the school buildings and grounds and the surrounding area within easy access (DfEE/QCA, 1999, p. 111). This is an appropriate scale at which children can enquire, ask geographical questions and do some of this enquiry learning through fieldwork outside the classroom.

The second locality can be either a contrasting locality in the UK or a locality overseas. Its size should ideally be similar to the area defined as the locality of the school. So what is a contrasting locality? The teacher must select a locality that has a physical or human geography that is different from that of the school locality. If the teacher is working in an urban school, he or she may choose a village locality in the UK or overseas.

Choosing the second locality

Many urban Sheffield schools have chosen a rural village in the Peak District as their Key Stage 1 contrasting locality. Teachers at Park Hill School have chosen the village of Edale, a small village which sits at the foot of Kinder Scout and has a population of around 250. The human and physical features at each location are certainly contrasting, and the Year 2 children go to Edale on a day field visit to investigate what is similar in the two localities and what is different.

Both localities should be studied at a local scale – that is, focusing on what children and their parents do within a small area. This can be seen as fitting in with how young children learn, and building on their pre-existing experiences of places. However, it has been criticized as encouraging children to think that all settlements in India are like Chembakoli, or all rural villages have the same characteristics as Godstone or Stanton-on-the-Peak, or even that all towns are like Croydon (although some might agree . . .), depending on what locality pack was chosen to support the unit of work. To begin to counteract this problem, teachers can also develop children's location knowledge of other places through using continuous study units such as 'Where in the world is Barnaby Bear?'

Geography at Key Stage 2

During Key Stage 2 pupils investigate a *variety of people, places and environments at different scales in the United Kingdom and abroad,* and start to *make links between different places in the world.* They find out how *people affect the environment and how they are affected by it.* They carry out geographical enquiry *inside and outside the classroom.* In doing this they ask geographical questions, and use geographical skills and resources such as maps, atlases, aerial photographs and ICT.

(DfEE/QCA, 1999, p. 112, my emphasis)

Geography in Years 3–6 also involves the study of two localities. One of these must be in the UK (as at Key Stage 1, it can be the school's locality, but at this more advanced stage it should instead match the size of the pupil catchment area). The other should be in a country that is less economically developed (a country of 'the South' or what used to be called 'the Third World' – most countries in Africa, Asia and South and Central America, including the Caribbean). Again pupils should use enquiry and their developing geographical skills to learn about the other three aspects of geography through the study of these localities.

However, in addition to the two localities, junior school pupils should also be taught three geographical themes. Geographical themes have been present in the 1990 and 1995 geography curricula and were an introduction to thematic study of physical, human and environmental geography. The geographical themes in the present curriculum are as follows.

Water and its effects on landscapes and people

An introduction to physical geography. Children will learn about the crucial issues of water supply and demand and will focus on either rivers or coasts to explore the patterns and processes (such as erosion and deposition) involved.

How settlements differ and change

An introduction to human geography. Children will learn how and why villages, towns and cities are different and are constantly changing, as well as focusing on an issue arising from changes in land use (such as the impact of building a new leisure centre).

An environmental issue

An introduction to people–environment issues, environmental change and sustainable environmental management. Children will learn about an environmental issue caused by a change in an environment and learn about attempts to manage this issue in a sustainable manner (for example, learning about drought and attempts to manage drought, such as by reducing water consumption and use).

Study of these themes *can* be carried out as part of the study of the two localities, but, as the Orders require junior school pupils to study at regional and national scales as well as local, a curriculum must be designed to reflect this. Junior school pupils must also learn geography by studying a range of places and environments in the European Union and the wider world, as well as in the UK. This demands careful curriculum planning (see Chapter 3), and the QCA non-statutory units of work give examples of how this may be done, as well as, more importantly, fleshing out the bare bones of the current 'slimmed-down' Programme of Study for Key Stage 2. A selection from the Key Stage 2 units of work is given below.

Unit 14   Investigating rivers

In this unit the children are asked to select a river and produce a project folder about it using ICT. This allows the teacher to guide the children towards rivers in Europe (the Rhine, the Rhône) and rivers in other locations of the UK (the Severn, the Trent, the Thames) or anywhere in the world (the Nile, the Mississippi, the Amazon) and so provides experience of the 'water and the landscape' theme at a national scale from many global locations, including the European Union.

Unit 15   The mountain environment

In this unit the class is divided into groups and each group investigates a mountain environment using the geographical questions. This allows groups to cover locations in the Lake District, Himalayas or the Alps at a regional scale, and focus on similarities and differences in upland settlement as well as an environmental issue such as tourism.

Key Stage 2 breadth of study

During the Key Stage, pupils should be taught the KSU (knowledge, skills and understanding) through the study of two localities and three themes.

Localities:
a a locality in the UK; and
b a locality in a country that is less economically developed.

Themes:
c water and its effects on landscapes and people, including the physical features of rivers or coasts and the processes of erosion, and deposition that affect them;
d how settlements differ and change, including why they differ in size and character, and an issue arising from changes in land use; and
e an environmental issue, caused by change in an environment, and attempts to manage the environment sustainably.

In the study of their localities, pupils should:
a study at a range of scales – local, regional and national;
b study at a range of places and environments in different parts of the world, including the UK and the EU; and
c carry out fieldwork investigations outside the classroom.

Locational knowledge: examples of significant places and environments

Locational knowledge has been an area of controversy in the new curriculum. Should children know where places are in geography or should they know how to find out? Is it important to be able to locate cities and rivers in the UK or is this an outdated view of geography? Is the curriculum about learning how to learn or knowing what to learn? Geography as a school subject gained some perhaps much-needed publicity over the summer of 1999 as these questions were debated on radio and television.

Revenge of the progressives

As David Blunkett relaxed in his flat in Sheffield on a sunny bank holiday morning, he was startled to hear an official from Britain's most powerful educational quango declare on national radio that schoolchildren need not know exactly where Paris was. Here was Tony Millns, the public face of the Qualifications and Curriculum Authority, the body responsible for deciding what the nation's children are taught, apparently down-grading a basic geographical principle: the knowledge of maps and the location of capital cities.

(*Sunday Times*, 16 May 1999, cited by Rawling, 2000, p. 214)

The outcome of this debate was that 'the maps' available at http://www.nc.uk.net, are indeed part of the new National Curriculum. By the end of Key Stage 2, children need to know the location of the key features and environments shown in Table 2.1 p. 42). The inclusion of 'the maps' indicates that National Curriculum geography still has a strong element of place knowledge in it, and that the National Curriculum is still content focused, although the processes of enquiry needed to learn this content have been made more explicit.

Geography and Its Contribution to the Whole Curriculum

The new National Curriculum now has a distinct rationale. It claims to be flexible and responsive to the needs of individual children, to their special educational needs, and to local school strengths. Literacy, numeracy and ICT are emphasized as important, and the document stresses the importance of developing these areas through each subject.

The introduction to the current National Curriculum (DfEE/QCA, 1999, pp. 10–13) suggests that key skills should be embedded in each subject. The following section suggests how geography contributes to the wider aims of primary education by showing examples of how geography contributes to literacy, numeracy (see Figure 2.8, citizenship and education for sustainability. Geography's contribution

Drawing River Profiles

Use the results below to draw your river profiles. You need to use a new sheet of graph paper for each profile.

When you finish, answer the questions on the question sheet.

Profile 1 Distance from start	Depth (in cm)
0	0
25	15
50	27
75	34
100	24
125	29
150	28
175	34
200	35
225	40
250	41
275	50
300	39
325	39
350	61
375	54
400	34
425	25
450	10
475	5
490	2

Profile 2 Distance from start	Depth (in cm)
0	0
25	5
5	10
75	12
100	14
125	15
150	20
175	32
200	48
225	44
250	42
275	43
300	44
325	28
350	25
375	20
400	20
425	18
450	16
475	14
500	0
525	12
550	12
575	5
600	0

Label the axes:
Depth of water.
Distance across the river channel.

Add these titles to your profiles:
A River Profile of the River Porter at a location with steep banks.

A River Profile of the River Porter at a location with gentle banks.

Figure 2.8 Using numeracy skills in presenting fieldwork data

to the developing of children's thinking skills and ICT use will be discussed in Chapter 5 when we discuss teaching and learning approaches.

Geography supporting literacy and numeracy

Geography lessons should aim to develop children's geographical knowledge, understanding and skills. Geography, however, can also provide a real-world context, particularly for the development and practice of literacy and numeracy skills. It should be noted that although the literacy hour can provide a context for geography, it has little potential for developing children's geographical skills. Table 2.2 (see p. 43) shows some links between geography and literacy and Table 2.3 some links between geography and numeracy.

Table 2.1   Places and environments children should be able to locate by the end of Key Stage 2

British Isles	Significant places and environments
The two largest islands of the British Isles	Great Britain, Ireland
The two countries of the British Isles	The United Kingdom, the Republic of Ireland
Parts of the United Kingdom	England, Scotland, Wales, Northern Ireland
Capital cities	London, Dublin, Edinburgh, Cardiff, Belfast
The largest mountain areas in Wales, Scotland and England	The Cambrian Mountains, the Grampian Mountains, the Lake District, the Pennines
The three longest rivers in the United Kingdom	River Severn, River Thames, River Trent
The seas around the United Kingdom	The English Channel, the Irish Sea, the North Sea

Europe	Significant places and environments
The two countries of the British Isles and their capital cities	The United Kingdom, the Republic of Ireland; London, Dublin
The three countries in the EU with the highest populations and their capital cities	France, Germany, Italy; Paris, Berlin, Rome
The three countries in the European Union with the largest areas and their capital cities	France, Spain, Sweden; Paris, Madrid, Stockholm
The largest mountain range in Europe	The Alps
The longest river in the European countries identified above	River Rhine
The two largest seas around Europe	The Mediterranean Sea, the North Sea

The world	Significant places and environments
The continents	Africa, Asia, Europe, North America, Oceania, South America, Antarctica
The largest city in each continent	Lagos, Tokyo, Paris, New York, Sydney, São Paulo
The six countries with the highest populations	Brazil, China, India, Indonesia, Russia, the USA
The six countries with the largest areas	Australia, Brazil, Canada, China, Russia, the USA
Areas of family origin of the main minority ethnic groups in the United Kingdom	Bangladesh, the Caribbean, India, Pakistan, the Republic of Ireland
The three largest mountain ranges in the world (on the basis of height and geographical extent)	The Andes, the Himalayas, the Rocky Mountains
The three longest rivers in the world	River Amazon, River Mississippi, River Nile
The largest desert in the world	The Sahara
The oceans	The Arctic, Atlantic, Indian and Pacific Oceans
Two canals linking seas and/or oceans	The Panama Canal, the Suez Canal
Main lines of latitude and meridian of longitude	The poles, the equator, the tropics, the prime meridian

Task: cover the right-hand column of the above table and try to name the places and environments described on the left-hand side. How did you do?

Table 2.2 **Some geography–literacy links**

Literacy	Examples of geographical activities
Speaking and listening	Debate about the use of a derelict piece of land Assembly presentation on fieldwork Interviewing for a shopping survey Role play in a travel agent's Describing the weather
Reading	Fiction or poems to develop a sense of place Newspaper article on a local issue Information on the World Wide Web or CD-ROMs Using reference books to find information on a locality Research skills: evaluating the usefulness of different resources, e.g. holiday brochures
Writing	Poster campaigning on walking to school Captions or speech bubbles for photographs Diary of a child's life in another locality Description of a human or physical feature Letter to the local council suggesting improvements to a local park List of what to take on holiday Poem following coastal fieldwork Questionnaire on shopping habits Geographical enquiry will also extend children's vocabulary (nouns – physical and human features; verbs and adverbs – e.g. when describing processes; prepositions – location)

Table 2.3 **Some geography–numeracy links**

Collect and record data	Present data	Interpret data
Traffic survey – tally chart	Pictogram of different types of vehicles	Why are there so many lorries on the road?
Measuring temperature – chart	Graph to show temperature over two weeks	How is the temperature related to the wind direction?
Measuring river channel width and depth at several sites – table	Cross-section linked to map	What affects the shape of a river channel?
Preferred holiday destination – questionnaire	Tally chart	Why do we prefer certain places?
Land use survey – map	Graph to show different land uses	What is the main land use?

Children can also interpret data obtained from a variety of other sources such as

- travel brochures/World Wide Web – data on weather/climate, costs of holidays and flights
- timetables
- road atlas matrices

Children can investigate numbers and shape in the local environment. Mathematical skills can also be developed in the context of map-making and map-reading, for example through work on coordinates, grid references, distance, direction and scale.

Geography and the 'new agenda': citizenship and sustainability

One of the new features of the current geography curriculum is the explicit focus on citizenship, education for sustainability and the recognition that attitudes and values about people, places and institutions are an important component of a child's education. Those teachers who have been involved in development education (TIDEC, 2000) and environmental education (see Palmer, 1994) have always seen a strong values dimension in their work, but the introduction of this 'new agenda' has not been without controversy. When the draft new curriculum was released and viewed by the media, some commentators derided the changes as substantially altering the nature of geography – 'maps out and politics in' would summarize this viewpoint. Whilst any discussion of values could lead to controversial issues being debated, this is no bad thing for children or for the continued health of geography as a subject. Children *are* interested in child labour (who sewed the footballs for the World Cup?), global warming and animal rights. They deserve the chance to become informed contributors to debates that will affect their futures.

Box 2.3   Some geography–citizenship links

Education for citizenship is seen as having three distinct but interconnected strands that will prepare young people for adult life: social and moral responsibility, community involvement and political literacy. Geography provides opportunities for children to acquire skills, understanding and attitudes that will contribute to their development as global citizens.

- using an enquiry-based, participatory approach which involves critical thinking;
- developing ideas about fairness and the nature of responsibilities;
- recognizing their own values and attitudes;
- sharing opinions, discussing and analysing relevant issues;
- recognizing other people's perspectives;
- working in groups;
- developing a sense of place and sense of community;
- carrying out fieldwork in the community (a survey on the effects of environmental change on different people; proposing changes to improve the local park);
- learning how decisions are made at a local scale (role-playing a public meeting; writing to the local council about parking issues);
- identifying how local and global events and issues are connected and interact;
- identifying similarities and differences between people and places, on a local to global scale, valuing diversity and developing positive attitudes (linking with children nationally and internationally by email);
- inviting members of the local community into school;
- investigating how people use local facilities; and
- understanding events in the news, locally and globally.

Students and teachers should not avoid addressing controversial issues in their teaching but they need to think through their approach carefully. Children need to be aware of different perspectives on an issue; teachers need to avoid indoctrination.

> **Box 2.4   Some geography–sustainability links**
>
> Geography provides opportunities for children to investigate relevant environmental and development issues. As with citizenship, this involves looking at issues at various scales from the local to the global and identifying how they are connected and interact. This again necessitates a practical approach and the use and development of skills such as enquiry and critical thinking. Geography promotes environmental awareness and responsibility whilst at the same time making children aware that solutions to environmental issues are not always easy to find and agree on. Children can address sustainability through activities such as:
>
> - learning about physical processes;
> - learning about the needs of society;
> - investigating the impact of traffic and how it can be managed more effectively;
> - investigating how a derelict piece of land might be used to be of benefit to the community; and
> - investigating the impact of tourism on a locality and how it could be managed more sustainably.

The next chapter focuses on how teachers can interpret this statutory and non-statutory guidance to plan the geography curriculum in early years and primary settings. It considers long-term planning, medium-term planning and lesson planning in geography.

Reflective Questions

- Is the geography shown in the National Curriculum different from the geography you studied in order to qualify as a teacher or start a specialist geography course?
- Should children learn about distant places in the Foundation Stage and Key Stage 1?
- What similarities does the geography curriculum have with the science curriculum at Key Stages 1 and 2?
- What similarities does the geography curriculum have with the history curriculum at Key Stages 1 and 2?

FURTHER READING

Grimwade, K., Jackson, E., Reid, A. and Smith, S. (2000) *Geography and the New Agenda: Citizenship, PSHE and Sustainable Development in the Primary Curriculum*. Sheffield: Geographical Association.

Martin, F. (1995) *Teaching Early Years Geography*. Cambridge: Chris Kington.

46

REFERENCES

Bowles, R. (2000) *Raising Achievement in Geography. Occasional Paper: No.1*. Blackheath: Register of Research in Primary Geography.

Brundtland Commission (1987) *Our Common Future/World Commission on Environment and Development*. Oxford: Oxford University Press.

DfEE/QCA (1998) *Geography: A Scheme of Work for Key Stages 1 and 2*. London: Qualifications and Curriculum Authority.

DfEE/QCA (1999) *The National Curriculum: Handbook for Primary Teachers in England, Key Stages 1 and 2*. London: Qualifications and Curriculum Authority.

DfEE/QCA (2000) *Curriculum Guidance for the Foundation Stage*. London: Qualifications and Curriculum Authority.

Dinkele, G. (1998) 'Geography questions and enquiry' in R. Carter *Handbook of Primary Geography*. Sheffield: Geographical Association.

Palmer, J. (1994) *Geography in the Early Years*. London: Routledge.

Platten, L. (1995) 'Talking geography: an investigation into young children's understanding of geographical terms, part one' *International Journal of Early Years Education* 3 (1), 74–92.

Rawling, E. (2000) 'Ideology, politics and curriculum change: reflections on school geography 2000' *Geography* 85 (3), 209–20.

SCAA (1997) *Geography at Key Stage 2: Curriculum Planning Advice for Teachers*. London: SCAA.

Scoffham, S. (ed.)(1998) *Primary Sources: Research Findings in Primary Geography*. Sheffield: Geographical Association.

Storm, M. (1989) 'The five basic questions for primary geography', *Primary Geographer* 2 (2), 4.

TIDEC (Teachers in Development Education) (2000) www.tidec.org

Planning Geography

Knowledge of what geography is as a subject and what content is included in the National Curriculum and Early Learning Goals is not sufficient to develop as a successful teacher of geography. Knight's third category of subject knowledge is still needed to translate an understanding of the nature of geography and the content of the 3–11 curriculum into effective and exciting learning experiences. This is the focus of the next three chapters.

Good teaching is characterized by sound subject knowledge, thorough preparation and clear, detailed planning. Good planning is fundamental to effective teaching and purposeful learning, and takes place on three levels: long-term across the Foundation Stage and Key Stages; medium-term planning of units of work; and short-term planning of lessons or activities. Geography has a distinctive contribution to make to children's learning, as do all the foundation subjects. Consequently, teachers' planning for the subject should be as rigorous as for the core subjects. At each level, planning needs to be structured and systematic and not only fulfil the requirements of the National Curriculum (2000) or the Early Learning Goals but also reflect an individual school's overall aims, objectives and policies. Different views exist as to how a geography curriculum should be planned and where the emphasis should be placed (Chapter 2), and teachers need to make professional judgements about how to work within the current context in order to develop a worthwhile curriculum for their pupils.

This chapter is aimed at trainee and newly qualified teachers with a specialist interest in geography as well as experienced teachers new to the role of geography co-ordinator. It describes what is generally acknowledged as good practice in the three levels of planning and different ways in which geography might feature in a school's curriculum. Examples of planning are given for the Foundation Stage and Key Stages 1 and 2. The chapter also suggests how progression and continuity can be incorporated into planning.

Long-Term Planning

Long-term planning involves all the teaching staff in the development and approval of Foundation or Key Stage plans. Long-term planning for the Foundation Stage should provide for a range of experiences which will enable children to work towards the Early Learning Goals. At Key Stages 1 and 2, planning needs to meet the statutory requirements of the National Curriculum (2000) in terms of knowledge, skills and understanding within the programme of study for geography as well as incorporating the appropriate breadth of study. The geography co-ordinator can ensure that this coverage is achieved by completing a matrix, listing the National Curriculum (2000) or Early Learning Goals requirements and then indicating where these are covered within different units of work (Table 3.1). This should identify whether the different aspects of geography are adequately catered for: for example, are skills, such as the interpretation of photographs, revisited on a regular basis to ensure continuity and progression? Is fieldwork a prominent feature? Is sufficient time allocated to developing children's knowledge and understanding of other places? Completing a matrix for Key Stage 2 units would also be useful to indicate that the breadth of study requirements are being met – in other words that children are studying at a range of scales across the Key Stage.

The breadth of study requirements for Key Stage 2

- local scale (a small area such as a village or small town);
- regional scale (a larger area such as a stretch of coast);
- national scale (a country);
- United Kingdom;
- European Union;
- elsewhere in the world;
- fieldwork.

Table 3.1 **Section from a matrix indicating coverage of the Key Stage 1 Programme of Study**

	Programme of Study requirements Key Stage 1	Y1 Local area	Y1 on the farm	Y1 improve school grounds	Y1/2 Barnaby Bear	Y2 Bangladesh
1a	Ask geographical questions	•	•	•	•	•
b	Observe and record	•	•	•		•
c	Express own views	•	•	•	•	•
d	Communicate in different ways	•	•	•	•	•
2a	Use geographical vocabulary	•	•	•	•	•
b	Fieldwork skills	•	•	•		

However, long-term planning which will result in effective teaching and learning needs to go beyond mere coverage of the geography Programme of Study or Early Learning Goals. Any guidance for curriculum planning must be adapted to reflect a school's particular circumstances: its location, the interests of the children, the expertise of the teaching staff and the resources available. Has the school built up a wealth of resources and contacts on a particular locality? Does a stream within the school grounds lend itself to enquiry work for different year groups? (This is not to suggest that schools should not acquire new resources or make new links, or that teachers should not extend their knowledge and skills!)

When developing long-term plans, schools need to consider a number of points.

Points to discover when developing long-term plans for teaching geography

- How much time is available for teaching geography or developing knowledge and understanding of the world, and when does it occur?
- What opportunities are provided by the local physical, economic, social and environmental context?
- What opportunities are offered by the school buildings and grounds?
- What links exist within the local community, and with other places in the UK as well as overseas?
- What approaches to teaching and learning can resources (human as well as physical) support?
- What is the staff's level of subject knowledge, expertise and interest?
- To what extent can geography contribute to other aspects of the curriculum, such as citizenship or the development of literacy and numeracy?
- How can planning reflect the school's aims, objectives and policies, for example on equal opportunities?
- What are the needs, abilities, interests and achievements of the children? What sorts of experiences do they have?
- How do children learn? How do they acquire knowledge and skills and develop understanding in geography?

A school may use units of work from the QCA scheme (QCA/DfEE, 1998, 2000), either in their entirety or as a source of ideas. Teachers need to view these critically to ensure that the units take the above points into consideration and that they are relevant and appropriate. Is there, for instance, a more pressing local issue than traffic on the local high street (Unit 12) but which could follow a similar structure for enquiry? Does the unit provide further opportunities for developing key skills such as the use of ICT other than those which have been identified?

Other published schemes should also be scrutinized carefully. They may be useful as a source of ideas but often fail to create a 'sense of place'. Nor do the accompanying worksheets always provide for differentiation.

A long-term plan outlines the geographical content to be covered and how that will be organized; in other words:

- when geography is taught to each year group and how often;
- in what depth it is taught;
- whether it is taught separately or linked with other subjects;
- whether it is organized and taught as a distinct and cohesive unit of work ('blocked' units of work) or as 'continuing' work (SCAA, 1995);
- the focus and broad content of each unit, which should be manageable and coherent; and
- links with other subjects or aspects of the curriculum.

From a long-term plan it should be clear that:

- Children have a worthwhile and recurring experience of geography which includes work outside the classroom.
- There is progression both within and between different stages in terms of knowledge, understanding and skills.
- There is continuity within and between different stages.
- There is a mixture of place- and theme-focused units and a balance between human, physical and environmental aspects of geography.
- Places, themes and skills are integrated in each geography unit.

Skills, themes and places have been identified as encapsulating the nature of school geography and are often referred to as the geographical 'cube' (DES, 1990). These three elements are seen as of equal importance and as interactive with each other. In particular, skills should be taught with reference to places and thematic studies. A further dimension, attitudes and values, could be added as these are increasingly a concern both of geographical education and for the reflective teacher (Halocha, 1998). Skills, places and themes will usually be present within individual units of work although the focus may be on either a theme, place(s) or an issue.

Long-term planning also needs to ensure that adequate attention is paid to the four aspects of geography:

- geographical enquiry and skills;
- knowledge and understanding of places, both local and beyond children's direct experience;
- knowledge and understanding of patterns and processes; and
- knowledge and understanding of environmental change and sustainable development.

These should be developed through the localities and themes set out in 'Breadth of study' (DfEE/QCA, 1999).

The four aspects of geography

A Year 5 unit of work on water and its effects on the landscape focuses on rivers (**theme**). The class uses and develops the following **skills** in the classroom and in the field: enquiry skills, such as asking questions about a contrasting river; collecting and analysing data about a local stream; using appropriate vocabulary for features and processes; using atlases and maps; drawing maps; and using photographs and ICT. They investigate features and processes associated with a local stream, look at the stream in its wider context and then

50

make comparisons with a European river (**place**). The investigation includes water pollution and the efforts being made to improve water quality, and so as well as integrating skills, places and a theme, the unit also incorporates the four aspects of geography.

Planning for Continuity and Progression

Continuity and progression are often talked about in the same breath but they are different features of planning and the presence of one does not necessarily indicate the presence of the other. For instance, children may undertake fieldwork on a regular basis but develop little in the way of geographical skills unless these are specifically taught and practised. On the other hand, fieldwork may appear rarely on long-term planning, providing children with little continuity of experience.

Continuity

Continuity focuses on the teacher's or school's provision and the children's experience. It should be evident in long-term planning through significant features of geographical education occurring on a regular basis:

- content, for example an emphasis on the study of real places; considering values and attitudes; a mix of both local and global material;
- types of learning activity, for example fieldwork; the integration of ICT; learning through play;
- common assumptions about the nature of the subject, for example that geography is active and enquiry based;
- geographical skills such as using secondary sources and drawing maps and plans; and
- the use of certain resources such as maps, photographs and ICT.

Progression

Progression has been defined as 'the careful and deliberate sequencing of learning so that children can build their current learning on previous experience and also prepare for future learning' (Chambers and Donert, 1996, p. 27). It focuses on how children's learning advances in terms of the acquisition of knowledge and skills and the development of understanding, values and attitudes.

Teachers need to plan for progression in two ways. First, the content and sequence of learning activities should be structured through long- and medium-term planning. The notion of a 'spiral curriculum' is useful here (Bruner, 1966): children revisit key elements of the curriculum throughout their school experience, each time at a higher level of understanding or refinement. Second, teachers need to use their assessments of individual children's learning to match new tasks to their capabilities in order to

Table 3.2   **Progression in the four aspects of geography from Early Learning Goals to Key Stage 3**

	Enquiry and skills	Knowledge and understanding of places	Knowledge and understanding of patterns and processes	Knowledge and understanding of environmental change and sustainable development	Scale
EL Goals	• Talk about observations • Record observations in different ways • Ask questions • Gain information from primary and secondary sources • Use positional language • Express opinions	• Make focused visits to local environment • Talk about where they live and their environment • Notice differences between features of local environment • Find out about other cultures	• Look closely at patterns and change • Ask questions about why things happen	• Express opinions on natural and built environments • Listen to others' views on environmental quality • Design new environments	Show knowledge, understanding and skills in studies at a local scale
Level 1	• Make observations • Express views • Use resources provided and own observations to respond to questions	• Recognize and make observations about human and physical features of localities	• Recognize and make observations about human and physical features	• Express views on features of the environment of a locality	
Level 2	• Describe features • Express views • Select information from sources provided • Use information provided to ask and respond to questions • Begin to use appropriate geographical vocabulary	• Describe physical and human features of places • Recognize features that give places their character • Show awareness of places beyond own locality	• Describe physical and human features • Begin to use appropriate vocabulary	• Express views on features of the environment of a locality and recognize how people affect the environment	
Level 3	• Describe features and make comparisons • Use skills and sources of evidence to respond to a range of geographical questions • Begin to use appropriate vocabulary to communicate findings	• Show awareness that different places may have both similar and different characteristics • Offer reasons for some of their observations and judgements about places • Describe and compare human and physical features of different localities	• Describe and compare human and physical features of different localities • Offer explanations for location of some of these features	• Compare physical and human features of different localities • Offer reasons for some of their observations and judgements about places • Recognize how people seek to improve and sustain environments	

	Enquiry and skills	Knowledge and understanding of places	Knowledge and understanding of patterns and processes	Knowledge and understanding of environmental change and sustainable development
Level 4	• Describe patterns and processes • Explain own and others' views • Suggest suitable questions • Use primary and secondary sources of evidence • Use a range of skills (from KS2/3) in investigations • Communicate findings using appropriate vocabulary	• Appreciate the importance of location in understanding places • Show understanding of how physical and human processes can change the features of a place and how changes can affect the lives and activities of people living there	• Begin to recognize and describe geographical patterns and to appreciate the importance of location • Recognize and describe physical and human processes • Show understanding of how processes can change features of places and affect people's lives	• Understand how people can both improve and damage the environment • Explain views of self and others about an environmental change • Show understanding of how processes can change features of places
Level 5	• Describe geographical patterns and processes • Explain own views • Begin to suggest relevant questions and issues • Select and use appropriate skills and ways of presenting information (from KS2/3) • Select sources of evidence and information, suggest plausible conclusions, present findings graphically and in writing	• Describe how processes can lead to similarities and differences between places and people's lives • Recognize links and relationships making places interdependent	• Describe and begin to explain geographical patterns and processes • Draw on knowledge and understanding to investigate themes and to reach plausible conclusions	• Suggest explanations for how human activities cause changes to the environment and people's different views • Recognize how people try to manage environments sustainably
KS 3	• Suggest relevant questions and issues and appropriate sequences of investigation • Select a range of skills and sources of evidence and use effectively in investigations • Present findings in a coherent way and reach conclusions consistent with evidence	• Appreciate many links and relationships making places interdependent • Recognize that processes interact to produce distinctive characteristics of places • Describe how processes operating at different scales lead to changes in places	• Describe and explain a range of processes and recognize that processes interact to produce distinctive characteristics of places • Describe how processes operating at different scales create patterns and lead to changes in places	• Recognize how conflicting demands on the environment may arise • Describe and compare different approaches to managing environments • Appreciate that different values and attitudes result in different approaches with different effects on people and places

Show knowledge, understanding and skills in studies of a wide range of places and environments at various scales, from local to global, and in different parts of the world

Show knowledge, understanding and skills in studies of a range of places and environments at more than one scale and in different parts of the world enable them to make progress. Progression in the four aspects of geography can be identified within the Early Learning Goals (ELGs) and level descriptions in the National Curriculum of 2000 (Table 3.2). Teachers can find these useful for identifying the next stage for individuals or groups of children. QCA/DfEE (2000) and SCAA (1997) provide examples of children's activities and work which demonstrate achievement across the 'stepping stones' of the Early Learning Goals and at different levels in the National Curriculum. More specifically, Foley and Janikoun (1996) suggest how children from Reception to Year 6 progress through the different elements involved in drawing and using maps (e.g. as in Table 3.3).

Progression in geography involves:

- an increasing **breadth** of geographical knowledge – for example where places are, what they are like;
- an increasing **depth** of geographical understanding – for example, describing geographical features, explaining physical processes;
- an increase in the **scale** of places investigated, starting from the school grounds and the local area;
- an increasing **complexity** in what is studied – for example, from daily weather observations to microclimate investigations;
- the use of more **abstract ideas** such as interdependence;
- an increasing understanding of social, political and environmental **issues** involving different attitudes and values, from an enquiry into litter in the playground at Key Stage 1 to an investigation into the impact of tourism in Kenya at Key Stage 2; and
- the development and use of geographical **skills,** especially in mapwork and enquiry, whether in the classroom or in the field.
- The following list, for example, summarizes how teachers can provide for progression in children's use of maps and photographs.

Providing for progression in children's use of maps and photographs

- the **scale** of the maps/photographs: from large to small scale;
- the **type** of the maps/photographs: from picture maps to Ordnance Survey maps; from postcards or ground-level photographs to oblique and vertical aerial photographs;
- the **places** represented: from plans of the school grounds and photographs of features in the local area to maps and photographs of unfamiliar places;
- the **detail** and **complexity** of the maps/photographs;
- **enquiry**: asking children geographical questions and then encouraging them to formulate their own; and
- the **type** of activities: from observing, naming and describing features to interpreting photographs and maps (for example, identifying patterns).

Table 3.3   **The development of map skills: location**

Level	Skill
ELGs/Level 1	Follow directions: e.g. up and down, left and right, behind, in front of
Level 1/2	Follow directions: north, south, east, west
Level 3	Use letter/number coordinates and four compass points
Level 4	Use four-figure coordinates to locate features on a map; use eight compass points
Level 5	Use six-figure grid references to locate features on OS maps; latitude and longitude on atlas maps

Medium-term Planning

Medium-term planning, usually for half a term, is done by class teachers, supported by subject co-ordinators and year group or Key Stage co-ordinators. In a nursery setting, all the teaching team will usually be involved at some point. As well as demonstrating continuity and progression in the context of long-term planning, a unit of work should have carefully planned coverage of a number of features.

Planning a unit of work

A unit of work should feature:

- at least two of the four aspects of geography, for example enquiry and skills and knowledge and understanding of places;
- integration of skills with places and thematic work;
- integration of geographical enquiry, encouraging children to ask and answer questions and using key questions to plan;
- a logical progression in the enquiry questions and tasks children undertake, for example acquiring knowledge about a place before investigating any issues there;
- progression in at least one of skills, knowledge or understanding;
- fieldwork wherever possible, integrated with classwork;
- clear learning objectives (knowledge/understanding/skills), derived from the geography Programme of Study or Early Learning Goals and linked to assessment criteria;
- contexts within which the Early Learning Goals will be covered, such as role-play or an outdoor area;
- lessons where children are taught particular skills, such as those involved in enquiry;
- variety in the modes of assessment, approaches to teaching and learning, organization, activities and resources;
- opportunities for supporting literacy, numeracy and ICT;
- opportunities for differentiation other than by outcome; and
- links with other subjects or cross-curricular elements.

Above all, a unit of work should be interesting, motivating and relevant to children's lives.

Blocked and continuing units of work

Ideally, children's experience of geography should be continuous, recurring throughout their nursery and primary school life. This experience can be provided in several different ways. Geography can be taught through blocked units within a specific amount of time such as half a term. These units will focus on a distinct and cohesive body of knowledge, understanding and skills. They may stand alone or link with other units of work or aspects of the curriculum. It may be more effective for certain units of work, such as an enquiry with younger children, to be concentrated into a relatively short period of time, whereas other units, such as a locality study at Key Stage 2, can be taught on a weekly basis over half a term.

However, teaching geography solely in blocked units may mean that children have little contact with the subject at certain times. Thus it is useful for schools and individual teachers to plan for geography to be taught other than through discrete units of work. Continuing work is particularly valuable where aspects of the curriculum, whether skills, knowledge or understanding, require time for their systematic and gradual acquisition, practice and consolidation (SCAA, 1995). Children in the Foundation Stage, for example, may regularly observe and record the weather over a period of time. This will develop their geographical vocabulary and their ability to recognize geographical patterns.

Various strategies for developing and reinforcing children's geographical skills and knowledge when geography is not the main focus of attention can also be used. These may not appear in planning documents but it is worth considering the potential of the following contexts and activities.

Developing and reinforcing children's geographical skills

Any or all of the following can be used:

- children's interests, such as major sporting events;
- children's holiday locations and souvenirs;
- children's family connections;
- postcards, stamps, paper money and coins;
- children's fiction, poems and non-fiction set in different places;
- geographical contexts for work in literacy and numeracy;
- jigsaw puzzles of Britain, Europe and the world;
- using compass points and directional vocabulary, for example in PE lessons; and
- events in the news, whether local or further afield, or evidence of physical processes at work such as an earthquake, a tsunami, a volcano erupting, or tales of human endeavour such as a trek to the North Pole.

Use of the last of these may need care to avoid children gaining the impression that life in less economically developed countries is dominated by disaster.

Units 5 (Barnaby Bear), 16 (What's in the news?) and 24 (Passport to the world) (QCA/DfEE, 2000) suggest similar ways in which children can develop knowledge about places, their location and how they are connected, throughout Key Stages 1 and 2. Through this work they will also practise skills such as using secondary sources.

Subject- or topic-based approaches

Students or newly qualified teachers may encounter a bewildering variety of methods of curriculum planning as schools and nurseries attempt to combine their own aims and priorities with effective coverage of the National Curriculum (2000) or Early Learning Goals and the demands of the national literacy and numeracy strategies. All lessons may focus on separate subjects with few or no links being made between subjects. At the other extreme, all subjects may be integrated in so-called 'topic work'.

The merits and limitations of both these approaches have been a source of debate for many years. Integrated topic work has been criticized as undemanding and failing to provide for progression, with subjects losing their identity and characteristics within it. Subjects are seen as 'some of the most powerful tools for making sense of the world which human beings have ever devised' (Alexander *et al.*, 1992, p. 17) and OFSTED has noted that geography rarely flourishes in integrated topics unless it is the subject receiving most attention (Smith, 1997). On the other hand, those in favour of topic work would argue that a well-planned, carefully structured, integrated approach reflects the holistic way in which children view the world and allows them to construct their own meanings (Knight, 1993). Furthermore, the National Curriculum (2000) identifies elements, such as sustainable development and citizenship, which are cross-curricular rather than fitting neatly into subject 'boxes'.

There are, however, sound reasons for linking a limited number of subjects or aspects of the curriculum, rather than adopting the all-embracing type of topic work (SCAA, 1995). The benefits of linking subjects should be seen in terms of providing relevance and curriculum coherence, but at a pragmatic level it is an effective use of time. It would be educationally valid to link geography with other subjects if:

- they contained common or complementary knowledge, understanding and/or skills – for example, work on water in science could link with physical processes (weather and climate, rivers or coasts) in geography;
- the skills acquired in one subject or aspect of the curriculum could be applied or consolidated in the context of another – for example, scale and distance, coordinates and grid references in maths and geography; or
- work in one subject could provide a useful stimulus for work in another – for example, a topic on St Lucia in geography could provide the context for investigating music from the Caribbean and vice versa.

Table 3.4 demonstrates how Early Learning Goals for 'Knowledge and Understanding of the World' have been translated into work for a reception class. The unit seeks to develop children's enquiry skills such as asking questions, observation and using different sources of information. It also has links with the English, history and geography Programmes of Study in the National Curriculum (2000).

Table 3.4   **Example unit of work for a reception class: 'Where we live now and then'**

learning objective	activity
• Find out about where they live • Use appropriate vocabulary • Use and draw maps	• Go on short, focused walks in the local area; identify features • Talk about the route; use and draw a simple map • Identify and talk about/label local features in photographs
• Distinguish between past and present • Notice similarities and differences • Identify change in the environment • Express opinions about the environment • Suggest how the environment can be improved	• Sort old/new photographs/pictures of the local area • Compare houses they have seen, paint pictures • Talk about old photographs and pictures of the local area; identify how it has changed • Ask older relatives about how it used to be • Talk about what is happening on a building site • Talk about what they like and dislike about the park • Draw pictures of what they would like the park to be like

Note: *The main areas of learning covered are 'Knowledge and Understanding of the World' and 'Language and literacy'.*

Figure 3.1 illustrates how one school plans its geography curriculum, using blocked and continuing units and making links with units of work in other subjects.

	Autumn		Spring		Summer	
Y1	Where we live (history, science)		On the farm (science)		Holidays	
Y2		Local enquiry				Tocuaro (art)
Y1/2	Where in the world is Barnaby Bear?					
Y3		Settlement (history)		Local land use issue		
Y4	Water – Mayfield (science)				Egypt (history, DT)	
Y3/4	Passport to the world					
Y4		Antarctica			Whitby – residential	
Y5	Improving the environment		Rainforests (science)			Tudors – mapwork
Y6	Rivers (history)				Our twin town	
Y5/6	What's in the news?					

Figure 3.1 A school's long-term planning for geography

The most effective geography curriculum is most probably one that is planned flexibly and combines teaching through separate subjects and teaching through topics, exploiting the advantages of both approaches. Children's learning can be kept focused by restricting the numbers of subjects or aspects of the curriculum which are linked and avoiding contrived or artificial links. Whichever approach is taken, geography's basic concepts and skills must be clearly identified and incorporated into activities. Indeed, it has been suggested that making children aware of the nature of a subject and its skills and knowledge (metacognition) can lead to higher levels of achievement (Knight, 1993). Careful planning should also ensure that children are able to progress from one level of knowledge, understanding and skill to the next.

Supporting other elements of the curriculum

It could be argued that teachers are increasingly required to adopt the role of technicians who deliver a prescribed curriculum and assess and stratify pupils by reference to standard norms (Halocha, 1998). Geography has a distinctive role to play in this curriculum but it also contributes to the wider aims of primary education, and teachers need to identify where this is possible when planning units of work.

In the first place, it provides a wealth of opportunities to contribute to children's social, moral, spiritual and cultural development, personal, social and health education (PSHE) and citizenship. It can, for example, bring a European and global dimension to their understanding of the world as well as enrich and reinforce cross-curricular elements of the curriculum such as education for sustainable development.

Second, geography provides opportunities for developing a range of skills which are common to several subjects, such as creative thinking or the enquiry skills involved in observing, recording and interpreting data required in science and history. Although lessons in geography should aim to develop children's knowledge, understanding and skills in the subject, they can also provide real-world contexts, particularly for the development and practice of skills involved in numeracy, literacy and ICT. These features of the geography curriculum have been considered in more detail in Chapter 2. As has already been indicated (p. 57), teachers may also be able to make valid links between subjects. The study of a contrasting locality, for example, might be enhanced by making links with history, art, music, design and technology, religious education or dance, where appropriate.

Incorporating variety in units of work

Children learn in different ways and have different strengths. Teachers need to motivate pupils and maintain their interest. Consequently, it is important that teachers plan to use different approaches to teaching and learning, such as fieldwork, drama, ICT, creative work and learning through play, within a unit of work. Ways in which

59

this can be done are considered in more detail in Chapter 5. For the same reasons, and to enable all children to demonstrate what they have learned, teachers also need to involve them in a range of activities within a unit of work, such as:

- following a map
- using a CD-ROM atlas
- interpreting photographs
- structured play
- making a model
- reading a reference book
- designing a poster
- undertaking a traffic survey
- assessing environmental quality
- searching the World Wide Web
- interpreting weather data

- drawing a map
- carrying out a land use survey
- orienteering
- role play
- sketching
- producing a booklet
- writing a newspaper article
- measuring temperature
- discussing a local issue
- emailing other children
- taking photographs

Furthermore, teachers need to incorporate lessons, within the context of the unit, where children are taught, develop and practise particular skills such as using four-figure grid references or enquiry skills. Otherwise, children are likely to be merely 'doing' geography, increasing their geographical knowledge but making little progress in their geographical skills and understanding.

Tables 3.5 and 3.6 illustrate features of good practice in planning units of work that have been mentioned. The first unit is an enquiry based on Unit 2 in the QCA scheme (QCA/DfEE, 1998). It would be most effective if it were taught over a fairly short period of time. The second unit of work involves children in investigating a contrasting locality outside the UK. This could extend over half a term and links with topics in art and/or music. By using a computer to create templates for planning documents such as these, teachers will find it relatively straightforward to make any adjustments to planning that may be necessary following teaching and assessment of children's learning. QCA units of work can also be adapted on screen.

Table 3.5 **Unit of work for Year 2: 'How can we make our local area safer?'**

Learning objectives	Assessment	Activity and organization	Special resources	Links
Is our school on a busy road?				
• Know how to carry out a traffic survey and analyse data (1b, d, 2b, 4a)	Can carry out a traffic survey and analyse data (mode: tally, graph with comments)	Carry out simple traffic survey on road outside school; graph and analyse results (pairs)	Clipboards, graphing software	ICT, numeracy
• Compare the features and atmosphere of their road with school road (1a, c, 2b, 3d)	Can compare features and atmosphere of their road with school road (mode: table/written/wp task)	Lower ability: complete table Higher ability: give reasons for preferring one road to another	Word processing software	Literacy, ICT
Is parking a problem?				
• Identify when and where parking is a problem (1d, 2b, e, 4a)	Can children identify when and where parking is a problem? (mode: annotated map)	Carry out survey at different times of day, map results	Base maps, local studies software	ICT
How is parking controlled?				
• Recognize how parking is controlled (1a, d, 2a, b, 5b)	Can children recognize how parking is controlled? (mode: sketch)	Visit road outside school, sketch/photograph ways to control parking on map, incorporate photos into map	Digital camera, local studies base map	ICT
How could the area be made safer?				
• Identify a variety of solutions (1a, 5b)	Children can identify a variety of solutions (mode: poster)	Use photographs, brochures, ref. books etc. to identify ways of making an area safe (group work)	Ref. material	Sustainable development
• Use evidence to present a case (1d, 5b)	Children can use evidence to present a case (mode: letter)	Using data collected, write/wp letter to transport dept of local council with suggestions for new safety feature Lower ability: use writing frame	writing frames word processing templates	Literacy, ICT, citizenship

Table 3.6   **Unit of work for Year 4: 'St Lucia'**

Learning objectives	Assessment	Activity and organization	Special resources	Links
Where is St Lucia? • Locate St Lucia (2c, d, 3b, c, g, 4a)	Can locate Caribbean, St Lucia and major features (mode: worksheet, map)	Use atlases/satellite images to complete worksheet and annotate blank map	Atlases, satellite images, blank maps	
What are St Lucia and Castries like? • Search WWW for information on St Lucia (1a, 2a, f, 3a)	Can devise and answer questions on St Lucia (mode: word processing)	Raise questions (class); learn to use Ask Jeeves; answer questions (ability pairs); contribute to St Lucia fact file	Access to Internet	ICT, music
What is it like for children to live in Castries? • Know about children's lives in Castries (1a, e, 2f, 3a, d)	Can produce diary of child from Castries (mode: written work)	Watch *Pen Pals* video; email children in Castries with questions about their life; write illustrated diary of child from Castries	Email, *Pen Pals* video	Literacy, ICT
Why is the island like it is? • Recognize impact of weather on St Lucia (1c, 3c, 4a, b)	Can identify patterns in rainfall and temp. data and relate to physical environment (mode: conclusions from graph)	Draw graphs of temperature and rainfall, identify patterns, relate to vegetation, tourism, etc.	St Lucia pack graphing software	Numeracy, ICT
How does tourism affect St Lucia? • Know why tourists come to St Lucia (2d, 3d)	Can produce poster to identify tourist attractions (mode: poster)	Use travel brochures to identify tourist attractions and produce tourist poster	Travel brochures	
• Identify benefits and drawbacks of tourism (1e, 5a)	Can identify benefits and drawbacks of tourism (mode: role play)	Discussion about impact of tourism; role play – groups take roles in debate over new development	Role cards	Sustainable development
How does Castries compare with here? • Identify similarities and differences between Castries and own locality (1e, 3f)	Can identify similarities and differences (mode: letter/table)	Write/word-process letter as a tourist comparing St Lucia with own locality Lower ability: complete table	St Lucia pack, wp software	ICT, literacy

Short-term Planning

Short-term planning for the Foundation Stage and Key Stages 1 and 2 is done by class teachers or by members of the nursery team. This level of planning, whether for a lesson or an activity, should be sufficiently detailed to indicate clearly what is being taught, how it is being taught and how the children are expected to learn. It is important that planning is adjusted in the light of teaching and assessment of children's learning. When planning lessons or activities, teachers must make a number of decisions. The learning objective will have been identified in medium-term planning: does it involve knowledge or a skill to be acquired, a concept to be grasped or an issue to be investigated? Is it more concerned with the children's ability to engage in the enquiry process? Teachers will need to decide on the most effective approach which will enable children to learn and demonstrate what they have learned, as well as using the available time and resources efficiently.

Planning a lesson or activity

A good lesson plan has the following features:

- a clear, specific, relatively small-scale learning objective, derived from the Programme of Study or Early Learning Goals, which can be assessed, stating what the children will be able to do, know or understand at the end of the session;
- what will be assessed (linked to the learning objective) and how;
- key teaching points/questions/action and how the children are expected to respond;
- the incorporation of ICT if appropriate;
- details of how the children will be organized;
- stimulating tasks and resources matched to children's experience and ability and informed by assessment;
- provision for differentiation, if appropriate;
- precise details of resources such as the name of a video or the scale of a map;
- opportunities for feedback; and
- clear progression from the introduction to the conclusion.

Introduction

This section should include:

- telling the children what they are going to learn;
- recapping or recalling previous experience;
- key teaching points or key questions, new vocabulary to be introduced;
- how the children will respond.

The first few minutes of a lesson are crucial and it is well worth the beginning teacher spending time on thinking how he or she is going to gain the children's attention and interest them in what is to follow. This will often involve something visual: a map, a picture or an artefact, or reference to a display. An alternative is a brief anecdote (true or fictitious!) to introduce the lesson's content.

At some point during the introduction, the children need to be told the purpose of the lesson in order to help them learn more effectively. This also means that they can reflect on their learning at the end of the session. It is advisable to write down key teaching points and any new vocabulary, otherwise teachers can be sidetracked or interrupted unnecessarily.

Beginning teachers have a tendency to try to pack too much into an introduction. They need to ensure that they do not talk too much or for too long; that time is left for children to ask questions; that time is left for them to clarify points and ensure that the children are clear about what they have to do.

Development

This section should include:

- the task/s on which the children are engaged;
- how the children are organized;
- differentiation if other than by outcome – for example by resources, by task, or by support;
- how the teacher and children will interact; and
- the nature of adult intervention, if any.

It is important for teachers to consider their role and the form that any adult support or intervention might take during this period of a lesson. Is it to work with a particular group or to monitor each group, deciding who needs more input or encouragement, or extending by appropriate questioning? If this is relayed to the children, it will encourage them to work more independently.

Extension

This section should only include geographical tasks which more able children, or those who finish early, will complete in order to extend their learning. These could include using different reference sources or applying a skill in a different context. The task should not involve drawing a picture or colouring in!

Conclusion

Sufficient time should be left at the end of a lesson not only for resources to be put away but also for reviewing and consolidating the children's learning. This can be achieved by, for example:

- playing a game;
- children sharing and discussing their learning;
- the work being connected to future activities; or
- a similar question being asked in a different context.

Figures 3.2 and 3.3 give examples of lesson activity plans drawn from the units of work detailed in Tables 3.5 and 3.6. In the lesson in Figure 3.2 there is a strong link with literacy; Figure 3.3 is an example of a lesson where children are being taught a particular skill.

Reflective Questions

- How do long-term plans for geography reflect the school's particular circumstances, such as its location?
- Do long-term plans provide adequate coverage of the four aspects as well as balance in integrating skills, places and themes?
- How do you adapt QCA or published schemes?
- How do you make the most of geography's potential to support other areas of the curriculum?
- How do you incorporate the development of geographical skills and knowledge in the curriculum when it is not timetabled?
- Do you plan to use a range of approaches to teaching and learning, ways of organizing pupils, resources and activities within units of work?
- How do you plan for children to make progress in some way during a unit of work?
- Is your short-term planning clear and concise while providing sufficient information on what you are teaching and how the children are learning?

Subject Geography: Making our road safer   **Class** Y2   **Date**   **Time** 1 hour

Learning objective
Children will be able to present a case to improve the environment (1d, 5b)
Other purposes: letter writing

Assessment
Criterion: Can children use evidence to present a case?
Method/mode: marking letter

Resources
Templates, writing frames (hard copy and templates on computer)

Teaching points/questions/action	Children's activities
Introduction	
• Ask children about survey results and ways of making roads safe	• Recall previous work
• Discuss what would be appropriate in our road	• Make suggestions with reasons
• Explain how decisions about local environment are made	• Suggest writing to local council
• Ask/tell children about features of a letter	
• Stress need to use evidence to support case	
• Ask more able children for appropriate persuasive language they could use	
Development	
• CCA (Child Care Assistant) to work with less able group	• Use template to produce letter
	• Less able – use writing frame
	or
	• In pairs, word-process letter using template/writing frame
	• More able include scanned photographs
Extension	• Produce map/diagram to accompany letter
Plenary/conclusion	
• Ask whether children have made sensible suggestions	• Selected children read out letters
• Ask whether letters are effective	• Respond with reasons
	• Children identify use of evidence, etc.

Figure 3.2 Lesson plan for Year 2

Subject Geography: What is St Lucia like? **Class** Y4 **Date** **Time** 20 mins (intro)

Learning objective

Children will know how to search WWW for information on St Lucia (1a, 2f, 3, 6b)

Other purposes: co-operative working

Assessment

Criterion: Can children search WWW for information on St Lucia?

Method/mode: observation of printout

Resources

OHP, OHTs, ref. sources, computer with access to Internet and factfile set up, list of children in ability pairs

Teaching points/questions/action	Children's activities
Introduction	
• Ask children to suggest what they'd like to find out about St Lucia, write questions on board	• Suggest appropriate questions
• Recap on different sources of information (ref. books, video, photographs, maps etc)	• Make suggestions
• Teach how to use Ask Jeeves – use OHTs of computer screen – keep questions simple	• Suggest appropriate questions from those on board
• Recap on how to cut and paste into another file	
Development	
• Identify one question for each pair of children (differentiate between simple questions which need one-word answer and those where children will need to read)	• Work in pairs (ability) to find answer to question
• Read through list of instructions (OHT) with children and put up by computer	• Cut and paste question and answer into St Lucia factfile
• Put up list of paired children by computer	• Tell next pair it's their turn
• Check how each pair is working	
Extension	• Edit and print out factfile
Plenary/conclusion	
• Ask children what they have learned	• Respond to questions
• Ask if there were any problems using Ask Jeeves	
• Outline next session – using factfile and other resources to find out about children's lives on St Lucia	

Figure 3.3 Lesson plan for Year 4

REFERENCES

Alexander, R., Rose, J. and Woodhead, C. (1992) *Curriculum Organisation and Classroom Practice in Primary Schools*. London: DES.

Bruner, J. S. (1966) *Towards a Theory of Instruction*. Cambridge, MA: Belknap Press.

Chambers, B. and Donert, K. (1996) *Teaching Geography at Key Stage 2*. Cambridge: Chris Kington.

DES (1990) *Geography for Ages 5 to 16*. London: DES.

DfEE (2000) *Curriculum Guidance for the Foundation Stage.* London: QCA.

DfEE/QCA (1999) *The National Curriculum: Handbook for Primary Teachers in England, Key Stage 1 and 2*. London: QCA

Foley, M. and Janikoun, J. (1996) *The Really Practical Guide to Primary Geography*. Cheltenham: Stanley Thornes.

Halocha, J. (1998) *Co-ordinating Geography across the Primary School*. Lewes: Falmer Press.

Knight, P. (1993) *Primary Geography, Primary History*. London: David Fulton.

QCA/DfEE (1998) *A Scheme of Work for Key Stages 1 and 2: Geography*. London: QCA.

QCA/DfEE (2000) *A Scheme of Work for Key Stages 1 and 2: Geography Teacher's Guide Update* London: QCA. www.standards.dfee.gov.uk/schemes

School Curriculum and Assessment Authority (SCAA) (1995) *Planning the Curriculum at Key Stages 1 and 2*. London: SCAA.

School Curriculum and Assessment Authority (SCAA) (1997) *Expectations in Geography at Key Stages 1 and 2*. London: SCAA.

Smith, P. (1997) 'Standards achieved: a review of geography in primary schools in England, 1995–96', *Primary Geographer* 31, 4–5.

68

Organizing and Managing Geography

Children in a primary class or nursery are usually taught by one teacher or a small group of adults, and thus these adults are responsible for helping children to reach their full potential. Organizing and managing children's learning effectively plays an important part in this process. The Early Learning Goals provide clear guidelines as to how young children should be taught, whereas the National Curriculum (2000) dictates the content of teaching but not the process. Children also learn in different ways and have different needs. Consequently, teachers have to decide when it is appropriate to use particular teaching and learning strategies to ensure that geography is accessible and of interest to all children.

Beginning teachers tend to focus on the content of lessons and 'getting through it' rather than on what the children are learning and how this is organized. The previous chapter focused on planning to enable children to learn and make progress. This chapter explores different ways in which children can be organized in order for them to learn. It then considers how teachers can provide for differentiation to enable all children to achieve success. Other aspects of classroom management are also covered, including organizing other adults, organizing resources and producing a classroom environment which enhances children's geographical learning. The chapter concludes by considering how practitioners can assess the effectiveness of their teaching through self-evaluation.

Organizing the Children

The way in which teachers organize children for an activity is determined by the nature of the task being undertaken and the type of learning which is anticipated. Children may work as a whole class, in groups, in pairs or on an individual basis. Although practicalities, such as the availability of resources, may need to be taken into consideration, effective teachers choose the most appropriate form of organization for the task in hand. In general terms, the benefits of these different forms are as follows:

Ways of working and their benefits

- individually: for developing children's ability to work independently and autonomously;
- in groups: for developing language and social skills; as a means by which children can support, challenge and extend their learning together;
- whole class: for direct teaching (exposition and questioning); for introducing new work, recalling and recapping on previous learning; for summarizing, reviewing and consolidating learning; for giving instructions.

Most geography lessons in primary settings will begin and end with the teacher engaging with the whole class. In between, children will work either individually or collaboratively. Effective teachers aim to achieve a balance between these different forms of organization in their teaching as each has its strengths and limitations. For instance, a focus on individual work means that similar points will have to be repeated and children may make less progress, lacking the stimulus of other children and having limited contact with the teacher. Children may have to work in groups on different tasks because of the availability of resources: this takes careful planning and again points may be repeated. On the other hand, whole-class teaching tends to be directed at the middle ability range and there may be children who will be bored with the pace or unable to follow what is happening. Beginning teachers need to develop good exposition skills, a feeling for appropriate pace and timing, and the ability to involve all members of the class through both directed questioning and body language such as constantly scanning the children or walking to different parts of the room.

Within geography lessons, it would be appropriate to use particular forms of class organization as shown in Table 4.1.

Table 4.1 **Suitability of different forms of class organization according to activity being undertaken**

Form of organization	Activity
• Individual	Drawing a map, reading a reference book, using a digital camera, writing a poem about the weather, drawing a graph
• In pairs	Searching the World Wide Web, measuring and recording the weather, carrying out a survey, using Roamer, using a map
• In groups	River fieldwork (measuring and recording), interpreting photographs, role play, producing a report on an enquiry, watching a demonstration of river processes
• Whole class	A debate, listening to a story, watching a video

Several forms of organization may also be employed within one lesson, as the following example demonstrates.

Use of different forms of classroom organization within a lesson

A Year 3 class suggested a number of questions about the lives of children who live in Lima which they would like to answer. Their teacher wrote the questions on the whiteboard. They then watched relevant parts of a video. The teacher asked the children to work in groups to answer the questions and choose one child to record the answers. He also asked them to think individually whether there was anything else which they had learned from the video. During the plenary session, each group read out their answers to see if everyone agreed and then the children shared any further observations they had made.

Group work

Teachers find it valuable to work with small groups of children as this can provide opportunities to:

• use higher-order questioning	extending an able group analysing data from a questionnaire;
• provide further input	enabling a less able group to complete a task by introducing and explaining additional resources;
• engage children in discussion	encouraging a mixed group to discuss how they intend to plan an enquiry and what each child will be responsible for.

Teachers can group children by age, ability, friendship or interest, or place them in mixed ability groups. Each method has advantages and drawbacks. Grouping by age in mixed year classes is usually not very useful as the groups will contain children with different levels of ability, interests and needs. Grouping by ability can be appropriate for specific differentiated tasks; for extending more able children; for giving closer attention to those requiring additional help; or for teaching a group which has reached a particular stage. However, the groups are often determined on the basis of the children's level of literacy and numeracy, whereas it is more important to consider the task on which the children are engaged. For example, there may well be children whose spatial awareness bears little relation to their ability to read and write. Constantly grouping by ability can lead to children being labelled or developing a sense of inferiority or superiority.

Friendship groups are popular and so can be motivating, but they can also be divisive, isolating children or reinforcing stereotypes. Teachers can plan for children to work in interest groups for certain activities and thus capitalize on their enthusiasm. For instance, children could be grouped when investigating a locality according to their interests – whether the approach is 'encyclopedic', focusing on stamps, flags and currency, or on children's school and leisure activities. Mixed ability groups can be useful where different roles can be assigned to each child, for example in order to produce a report on an enquiry. They can provide role models for less able children, although teachers should ensure that more able children work to their potential and are not exploited as surrogate teachers.

The benefits of children working as a group are well documented (Bennett and Dunne, 1992). By discussing an issue, for example, children may extend their understanding across their 'zone of proximal development' in a way which they would have been unable to do alone and thereby 'scaffold' each other's learning (Vygotsky, 1978). It is sometimes claimed that children are engaged in group work when in fact they are working in a group as individuals rather than as a group. Co-operative group work, however, does not happen automatically and children need to be taught certain social skills from an early age to enable them to work effectively with others. These skills can include listening carefully to others, taking turns, and deciding on roles for each member of the group.

Routines

Like any other lesson, geography lessons will run more smoothly if classroom routines are clear to children. What are the procedures for getting out and putting away different resources? What do they do with finished work? Can they rub out? What do they do if they 'get stuck'? It is a good idea to work out these routines and procedures with the children: ownership means they are more likely to be followed. However, in order to make routines work, teachers need to be clear, consistent and, if necessary, persistent and insistent. It is also useful if children are aware of certain expectations, for instance that they should always look and think carefully, take care with presentation, check completed work and try to work independently and autonomously. There will always be some children who ask questions for reassurance. Teachers should try to pre-empt such questions and thus help to build up a child's confidence.

A pupil with low self-esteem

For a variety of reasons, Carly's self-esteem was at a low ebb. She was constantly bringing her work to show her teacher and asking 'Is it right?' (it invariably was). In a geography lesson the class was using maps of the area to describe features of the physical and human landscape along the course of a river they were studying. Carly's teacher made sure that she knew exactly what she had to do before starting the task. He also asked her to bring her work to show him when she had written about one feature. He subsequently praised her for her efforts and said that he would come and see what she'd done in a few minutes, by which time he expected her to have written about a further two features. He returned to see what Carly was doing throughout the lesson, praising her work, making his expectations clear and extending the intervals at which he visited her table.

Differentiation

Nurseries and schools have a responsibility to provide a broad and balanced curriculum for all pupils. The National Curriculum (2000) and Early Learning Goals provide a starting point for planning a relevant and interesting geography curriculum. However, children learn in different ways, at different rates and have different levels of attainment, interest and confidence. Thus, the curriculum also needs to accommodate differences between children and match learning opportunities with individual learning needs. Differentiation involves providing all children with work at an appropriate level which enables them not only to participate but also to learn, demonstrate what they know, understand or can do, and make progress.

Teachers tend to focus on differentiation in the core subjects. However, it is an essential element in effective teaching as it provides all children with access to the curriculum and with opportunities to fulfil their potential. It is also perhaps one of the hardest aspects of teaching to 'get right', particularly for beginning teachers with little knowledge of the children in their class, and it is far easier to identify differences between children than to work out what to do about them. Also, teachers aim to use their time efficiently, yet teaching a class as a whole may be ineffective since it means that the individual needs of particular children are ignored. Nevertheless, differentiation is not about creating individual programmes for every child in a class. This is not only impractical and unworkable but also undesirable. It may isolate the children and they will not be able to reap the benefits from working in a group.

Hart (1992) suggests that teachers should focus on the difficulties that arise from the curriculum rather than those related to pupils. There are a number of steps teachers can take at the medium-term planning stage to ensure that children are able to achieve and make progress.

Steps to take at the medium-term planning stage

- Incorporate a variety of teaching and learning strategies such as organizing the children in different ways; using different approaches to teaching and learning; involving the children in different types of activity.
- Plan to use a range of different resources – for example, videos rather than textbooks may appeal to some children.
- Identify different methods for assessment to enable children to demonstrate their learning.

Enabling all children to achieve can also be helped by the following features of good practice.

Enabling children to achieve

- Give clear instructions, explanations and expectations.
- Identify clear learning objectives which are shared with children.
- Sequence questions towards the learning objective.
- Recap on previous knowledge.
- Ensure that learning is consolidated.
- Provide resources that are easily accessible.
- Use an appropriate level of language.
- Balance teacher exposition with independent and collaborative work.
- Have high expectations of attainment and involvement.
- Value the children's responses (and not just the correct answer).
- Give positive, quality feedback, written or oral, promptly and with points for improvement.
- Produce displays which encourage learning and reflect high expectations.
- Promote a supportive classroom atmosphere which focuses on positive discipline and praise.

Experienced teachers often differentiate their lessons without consciously acknowledging that they are doing so. However, actually planning for differentiation ensures that all children should be able to participate. Within individual geography lessons there are various ways in which children's needs can be catered for. Some of these will need planning; others are standard features of experienced teachers' practice. Both apply to fieldwork as well as to classroom-based work.

Outcome

Differentiation by outcome is probably the most common form of differentiation where children use the same resources and have a common task which is sufficiently open-ended for them all to achieve success at their own level. Activities need to be accessible to all children and should not be dependent upon knowledge or skills that only some of them possess. Differentiation by outcome can be overused and, to ensure it is effective, teachers need to make their expectations clear to ensure that the task is sufficiently challenging for all children.

Differentiation by outcome

A Year 4 class designs posters to entice tourists to St Lucia. They have access to a range of resources which they have used in previous activities. This particular task is useful as an assessment exercise: it identifies the information children have gleaned from the resources and their understanding of the nature of tourism.

Task

Differentiation by task can be achieved in various ways. Children may be engaged on different tasks with the same objective; alternatively, a task can be open-ended or more structured and clearly sequenced for less confident children. Teachers need to be aware that they may over- or underestimate what children may be able to achieve.

Differentiation by task

A class of Year 3 children produce plans of the classroom, working in ability pairs. The work is planned at three levels, from arranging pre-cut shapes on a piece of paper to taking and using measurements of the room and furniture.

Recording

Recording is closely linked to differentiation by task. There are many different ways in which children can record their geographical knowledge and understanding (sketches, graphs, maps and plans, tape, video, photographs, tally, chart) other than in written form, thus ensuring that they are not restricted by any lack of ability to write properly.

Recording of results and observations

A Year 6 class is undertaking an enquiry into a local environmental issue. The children are able to choose an appropriate method of recording their observations, such as annotated maps or sketches, digital photographs (to which they will later add text) or notes to be written up.

Organization

A teacher may plan for children with similar needs or abilities to work on a particular task. He or she may also pair children, a less able with a more able child, although this needs to be done with care, with the teacher's expectations of each child being made clear, to avoid the more able taking control.

Feedback and target-setting for future learning

Most teachers differentiate the feedback, whether oral or written, they give children and the targets they set. A child who has low self-esteem, for example, will be highly praised; a more able child will be set questions to extend his or her thinking.

Stepped tasks/extension

Children can be given a series of increasingly demanding tasks to enable them to work at their own pace and own level. Teachers need to ensure that children do not see this as a form of competition; or that more able, less motivated children linger unduly on the less demanding tasks. Stepped tasks could cause difficulties in that children may not have a common starting point for a subsequent geography lesson. The solution to this is to have core tasks achievable by all children, with extension activities for those who are capable of taking their learning further in the time available.

Stepped tasks

Year 1 children use a sketch of the school grounds produced by their teacher to recognize and record geographical features. A series of stepped tasks is planned as follows:

- recognize and colour in three features;
- identify three named features;
- add three extra features;
- add directions;
- add estimates of distances and size.

Questioning

Most experienced teachers automatically use questioning as a form of differentiation. Beginning teachers may need to consider more carefully what type of questions, whether oral or written, are appropriate for particular children and in particular circumstances.

Differentiated questioning

A class of Year 1 children is engaged on tasks following fieldwork in the school grounds. Their teacher asks each (mixed ability) group appropriately differentiated questions, ranging from questions involving factual recall to ones which require higher-order thinking. For example:

- What did we see on the ground around the school gates?
- What kind of litter was there?
- Where do you think it had come from?
- If you were the school caretaker, how do you think you would feel?

Support

In providing for differentiation by support, teachers plan to work with particular children, either individuals or groups, because they have identified a specific need.

A group of children, for example, may be particularly able and would benefit from extra support to enable them to extend their thinking; or an adult helper might be assigned to help a child who appears to lack motivation.

Providing support for children who need it

A Year 3 class is using atlases to answer questions. Their teacher has identified a group of children who have had difficulties in the literacy hour in using reference books. He plans to work with this group until he is satisfied that they are confident about using an atlas.

Intervention

Differentiation by intervention, unlike differentiation by support, is not planned but is part of everyday teaching. It makes an important contribution to effective teaching as it involves not only being aware of children's individual needs but also being able to make quick yet accurate decisions about their level of understanding or particular problem and responding appropriately to enable them to progress. The ability to do it develops with experience.

Appropriate intervention

Emma, a Year 1 child, is having difficulty drawing a plan view of a model she has made. The teacher puts the model on an overhead projector to make the outline clearer.

Resources and materials

Resources can be provided which, for example, make different demands on children's ability to read reference books, newspapers or maps. Worksheets may be differentiated to give more scope for initiative.

Providing appropriate resources

Year 5 children are working in pairs on the computer to access information about the weather and climate of St Lucia. Some pairs are provided with a short list of bookmarked Web sites to enable them to locate information with appropriate 'readability'.

Worksheets/Activity Sheets

OFSTED inspectors sometimes comment on the excessive use of commercial worksheets, often as a means of keeping children occupied, with little thought having been given to what might be learned through their completion. However, worksheets or activity sheets produced by class teachers can be a useful tool for teaching and learning. They can be used to promote discussion, help foster research skills and support practical activities as well as being useful for assessment purposes. Good worksheets can take time to prepare, so it is worth ensuring that they are well designed and promote children's active, enquiry-based learning in geography. Using ICT to produce worksheets means that they can be of high quality, include scanned photographs or maps if appropriate, and thus be attractive and motivating for children to use. It is also relatively straightforward to produce differentiated work.

When children are engaged on fieldwork, it is important that they are encouraged to observe closely, use their senses and talk about what they can see. However, there are times when worksheets are useful as a way both of stimulating enquiry and of providing a structure for recording. The principles underlying the devising of good worksheets are similar whether they are to be used in or out of the classroom.

Worksheets

Good worksheets should:

- be well laid out and clear;
- be motivating to use, perhaps with some graphics included;
- be easy to understand, with straightforward vocabulary;
- not be overloaded with text;
- have a clear purpose;
- be open-ended or graded to provide for differentiation;
- provide for independent and collaborative working; and
- ask questions such as *how?, why?* and *which?* that promote higher-order thinking as well as questions which require a factual response;

They should not involve colouring in unless this is related to a mapping task. In addition, worksheets for use during fieldwork should:

- include questions which involve thinking rather than simply doing;
- require different types of response, such as drawing, deciding or estimating;
- not contain too many directions; and
- encourage children to use their senses where appropriate and safe.

The following is an excerpt from a worksheet which begins with a simple cloze procedure that children can answer through the use of secondary sources. The subsequent questions are open-ended to allow for a range of responses.

St Lucia is one of the _____ islands. It is located in the _____ sea, to the east of _____

The climate is _____

Where are bananas grown on St Lucia?

Could we grow bananas in the UK?

How do bananas reach the UK from St Lucia?

Would you like to work on a banana plantation?

The next example engages children in problem-solving and involves them working collaboratively.

Imagine that you are hotel developers and you want to build a new hotel on St Lucia.

In your group, decide on a good location for the hotel and mark it on the map.

Why do you think this would be a good location?

Do you think that anyone would object to your new hotel?

Why?

How could you convince them that it would be a good idea?

Organizing Other Adults

Most teachers sometimes work with other adults in the classroom. These may include special needs teachers, language support teachers, students and ancillaries as well as parent helpers and other volunteers. Indeed, it would be unusual to find a school which did not encourage the involvement of parents and other adult helpers in the classroom. They can help make the most effective use of equipment and materials, perhaps utilizing a particular skill such as cartography; foster a sense of security by providing more support; and act as role models, for example by displaying an enthusiasm for geography. For parents, involvement in the classroom develops home–school links and can contribute to their understanding of geography in 3–11 settings.

Parental involvement

The class teacher displays a poster outside the classroom explaining what the children will be learning in next term's geography topic on a contrasting locality. Parents are asked if they would like to be involved, particularly in the field trip, and whether they have any resources which could be used. They are subsequently invited to a school assembly on the topic.

Organizing and managing possibly older and more experienced adults can be a daunting task for beginning teachers. This is particularly true for those working in the Foundation Stage. Nursery nurses often have roles and responsibilities very similar to those of qualified teachers yet do not attract the same level of pay or status.

It is important that the role of each staff member is made clear in order to establish good working relationships. In the case of voluntary helpers, most schools have policies to follow which will cover issues such as volunteers' suitability for work with children and the need to maintain confidentiality. There are also a number of steps teachers can take in order to make the most effective use of adult assistance.

Using adult assistance effectively

- Make the classroom a welcoming place.
- Find out about the role of support staff and procedures for briefing them.
- Discover the interests and abilities of potential helpers.
- Find out if they can help on a regular basis; this will provide more continuity for the children and perhaps more satisfaction for the helper.
- Avoid assigning helpers on a stereotypical basis (women helping with cooking samosas while men assist children in using a CD-ROM on India).
- Involve helpers in planning activities: they need to be clear about what the children should be learning and how they are to go about this.
- Make sure that roles, responsibilities and procedures, for example for discipline, are clear, to the children as well as to the adults involved.

Organizing the Learning Environment

An environment which is stimulating and accessible, and contains high-quality resources, is likely to support and encourage children's learning in geography. Initially teachers need to take children's safety into account when organizing the classroom. In addition, particular activities, such as making and tasting food from different places, will need to take the school's health and safety requirements into account. Children should also understand and observe nursery or school rules and conventions and be encouraged to take responsibility for their own actions. The way in which the available space and furniture are arranged should not cause major disruption or hinder teachers' observing and monitoring of the children's learning. Where possible, use should be made of the 'outdoor classroom', for example when using a model to demonstrate river processes.

Many of the points considered in this chapter apply equally to the organization of fieldwork. However, because it involves more complex planning, organization and management, particularly to ensure children's safety, fieldwork is considered at length in Chapter 5.

Organizing Resources

Selecting and using a range of up-to-date, appropriate resources which support active, investigative learning is essential to good geography and these will be considered in more depth in Chapter 6. Their organization also requires some thought and attention to detail, particularly where they are shared with colleagues. The geography co-ordinator has a responsibility for resources, but class and nursery teachers will still need to:

- identify resources which may need to be booked or borrowed, such as artefacts from other places, in medium-term planning;
- ensure that there are sufficient resources for the task in hand – for example, is there a class set of atlases?;
- check that resources they intend to use are durable – for example, that maps and photographs have been laminated;
- check that resources they intend to use have been well maintained: dog-eared photographs and crackly videos are not motivating;
- ensure that children know how the school or class library system works: can they find a book on life in a particular country, or on rivers, or on pollution? (books to support geography are usually found in more than one place); and
- check that resources in the classroom or base are clearly labelled (using pictures if appropriate) and easily accessible so that children know where to find them and where to return them.

Making resources easily accessible will enable children to make choices when selecting appropriate equipment or materials as well as encourage them to take responsibility for keeping the classroom tidy. Again, establishing routines, say for getting out and clearing away painting materials, is important.

Organizing resources effectively

A member of the nursery staff had produced 1:1 plans of equipment that children used in the sand and water. These had been laminated and stuck on a low shelf next to the sand and water trays. When the children had finished with a particular item, they were taught to replace it on the shelf, matching the object with its plan.

Organizing Information and Communications Technology

Teachers are required to integrate ICT into their teaching whenever it is appropriate and possible. Geography provides a range of contexts for incorporating ICT, but some forethought and planning is required in order to make the most effective use of what, apart from adults, is the most expensive resource in the classroom. Schools vary greatly in the hardware and software that are available, although most bases and classrooms have at least one computer and some schools have dedicated computer suites. They may also have other hardware such as digital and video cameras and programmable floor turtles, which can be used in a geographical context.

New teachers will need to ascertain what resources are available and where they are stored, the systems for booking out equipment and the procedure to be followed when there is a problem such as a faulty machine. They should also find out whether a computer is permanently accessible before planning units of work, as this will have implications for incorporating its use in geography lessons. The next stage is to decide when the use of ICT would be appropriate in terms of both more effective teaching and assisting children's learning. For example, do children gain anything from using an interactive CD-ROM atlas or could the computer be put to better use? In this case it might be that children with reading difficulties would benefit from hearing the text read out, whereas other children would develop their research skills better through the use of a conventional atlas.

Once these decisions have been made, checking the following points will help to ensure that ICT is used safely and efficiently.

Safe and efficient use of ICT

- Before school starts, check that hardware (including the printer) is functioning correctly and that software is working.
- Make sure that any batteries are fully charged, there is sufficient paper and that ink cartridges are not likely to run out.
- Avoid trailing cables.
- Keep hardware away from water, paint, food and drink.
- Position the computer so as to have an overview of the activity.
- Position the screen to avoid reflections from windows and lighting.
- Position the monitor so that the screen does not distract other children.
- Maintain the volume of any sound at an acceptable level.
- Make sure children are sitting at an appropriate height.
- Reinforce children's awareness of precautions to be taken, such as when handling software.
- Understand specialist terms in order to give precise explanations to children.
- Provide a record sheet for children to tick when they have completed the task (they should then inform the next pair).

When planning tasks involving the use of a computer, teachers need to know the level of the children's skills: for example, do they know how to search a CD-ROM for information or will this have to be taught? Can they teach their peers? They can then decide how best to introduce the activity, for example by preparing instruction cards that enable children to work independently. Whole-class teaching will need supporting with appropriate visual aids such as an overhead transparency or key instructions on the computer screen, using a large television as the computer monitor.

Planning the size and composition of working groups also needs some consideration. Ideally, children should work in twos or threes as this stimulates collaboration and discussion. Again children will work more effectively if they have been taught group work skills: they can then, for example, decide on who is going to operate the keyboard or the mouse or read the screen. Children could be in single- or mixed-sex groups, ability or mixed ability, friendship groups or paired with a child of a similar personality (which can generate lively discussion). What is important is that one child, through either personality or experience, does not dominate the activity. In certain situations, individual work may be appropriate, for example to reinforce a particular skill or for a child with special educational needs.

It is essential that teachers spend time with groups using ICT, intervening when appropriate, asking questions and stimulating discussion. Adult helpers need their role explaining carefully. It may not be possible for all children to have access to particular software or tasks during one unit of work. It is therefore important to keep records of who has done what to ensure that over the year all members of the class gain experience of, for example, using a CD-ROM in a geographical context.

Display

There is no doubt that assembling and maintaining attractive and worthwhile displays takes a considerable amount of time and effort. Some teachers seem to possess a natural flair for it, whereas it takes others some time to develop the requisite skills. However, display can be seen as an integral part of the teaching and learning process and geography provides a wealth of opportunities for creating displays.

Displays

Displays can:

- celebrate children's achievements and enhance their self-image;
- provide an attractive, lively and stimulating environment;
- exemplify and set standards;
- inform staff, parents and other visitors about children's experiences and work;
- provide opportunities for children to interact, for example by posing questions, inviting participation in a quiz or setting a problem-solving activity;
- provide a resource for teachers to refer to and for children to use during lessons;
- demonstrate an enquiry-based approach to geography, either as a stimulus or as a summary;
- consolidate and reinforce learning, such as the learning of new vocabulary; and
- act as a stimulus for future learning.

Displays should reflect the variety and breadth of the geography curriculum, including evidence of practical activities as well as written work, and material which reflects both the use of skills and acquisition of knowledge and understanding. Teachers need to ensure that the work displayed reflects the genuine efforts of all children to avoid some being overlooked whilst others receive disproportionate recognition. Involving children in some of the decision-making about which resources and work to display and how to do so can help to ensure that displays are used and referred to.

Teachers should aim to use a range of techniques: displays can be 2D and 3D, on vertical and flat surfaces, hang from the ceiling, encourage observation or be more interactive. They can be the starting point of a topic, stimulating interest and curiosity, or summarize what has been learned. Displays can also take the form of a role-play area such as a travel agent's or an environment such as a rainforest. Children's work can be mixed with commercial material such as maps and photographs, as well as artefacts. Beginning teachers will find it useful to make annotated sketches or take photographs of displays which they feel are effective, to inform their future practice.

Teachers' displays may be subject to outside influences such as the availability and quality of resources as well as their own confidence and expertise. Many schools have guidelines about display, for example about mounting and colours for backing paper and sometimes, unfortunately, about displaying work with errors. It is, however, the quality of a display which demonstrates that children's work is valued, and high quality can be achieved if teachers prepare displays carefully.

Preparing a display

- Plan ahead, identifying opportunities for incorporating display when completing medium-term planning.
- Gather resources.
- Save children's work.
- Choose an appropriate colour scheme for where the display is, say, in a dark corner, or which reflects the content of the work, such as blues and silver for work on water.
- Put up backing paper evenly and carefully.
- Either single- or double-mount children's work (named).
- Use a commercial border or produce one using a computer or photocopier.
- Use a variety of text (computer, stencils and handwriting which conforms to school guidelines) for titles and captions.
- Think about the height of displays (can children read them?).
- Remember that less is more: spaces between items are as important as those which are occupied.
- Include an explanation of the task for the benefit of parents, staff and any other visitors.
- Encourage interaction through questions and labels.
- Loosely pin up, then staple each corner; use drawing pins only to hold heavier articles in place.
- Maintain displays in good condition.

Figure 4.1 demonstrates several features of good practice. It focuses on enquiry, encourages interaction with the display and incorporates maps, photographs and artefacts. Children can also listen to a tape of music or rainforest sounds on a small cassette player. Commercial material can be used initially as a stimulus and then replaced with or supplemented by children's work as the unit of work progresses.

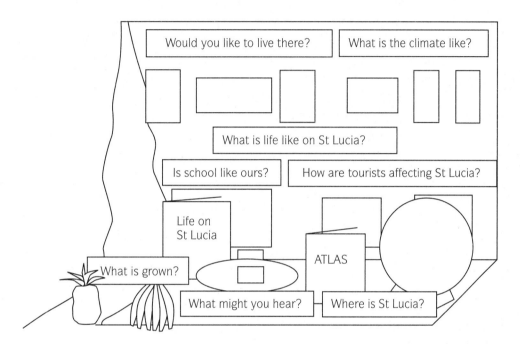

Figure 4.1 Display on St Lucia

Self-evaluation of Geography Teaching

The previous two chapters have focused on planning and organizing for effective teaching and worthwhile learning in geography. However, the processes of monitoring and evaluating, reflecting upon and refining one's practice are essential for improving teaching and consequently benefiting children's learning. Monitoring is basically a descriptive activity – in other words, recording what takes place, such as what the pupils did, what the teacher did and how resources were used. Evaluation, on the other hand, can be summative, at the end of the unit of work or, more usefully, ongoing and formative. It involves teachers considering not only individual lessons but also their approach to education and how that might be reflected in their geography teaching. It need not be a solitary experience: teachers at any level can benefit from working together, observing each other's practice in order to analyse and develop their practice. Parents, visitors and non-teaching staff can also be asked for their opinions and ideas or feedback if appropriate.

Beginning teachers may need guiding in the skills of effective practice and will be involved in trial and error and problem-solving as they develop. As they become more competent, in other words clearer about what they want children to learn and how they think they should go about helping them learn it, and successful in getting children to listen and do as they are told, their confidence will grow. Although becoming a teacher involves achieving a number of standards – a 'technician' model – this and a 'reflective practitioner' model do not have to be mutually exclusive. If teachers reflect intelligently on their practice, they can become more flexible, independent and creative in the long term, for example involving children in more open-ended enquiries. The quality of children's learning should also be improved as a result of the bank of effective teaching ideas which has been built up and the insights which have been gained from children's responses.

Numerous aspects of practice can be evaluated. At individual lesson level, a focus might be identified before the lesson. Alternatively, a session may go outstandingly well or be a near-disaster, in both cases it is worth reflecting afterwards why this was so. Teachers need to remember that the enjoyment children gain from a lesson is important, but this does not necessarily equate with learning, and they need to adopt a more critical attitude. A further skill is to identify criteria that indicate success and then, if necessary, decide what to do differently next time. For example, if most of the children remained on task for most of the time, this could indicate a high level of interest and motivation. The following questions indicate areas on which teachers might choose to focus.

Teachers' self-evaluation

- Did I plan in sufficient detail and anticipate any problems?
- Was I enthusiastic and were the children interested in what I had to say and motivated to complete the task?
- Did I involve the children in enquiry, encouraging them to ask as well as answer questions?
- Did I represent geography so the children could understand it and were my vocabulary and the task pitched at an appropriate level?
- Was the lesson well structured and paced and was adequate time allocated to each part?
- Did I choose an effective approach to achieve the learning objective?
- Did I group the children appropriately?
- Did I cater for the more as well as the less able?
- Did I have sufficient resources and were these used well?
- Did I make best use of adult support?
- Did I integrate ICT successfully?
- Did I reward children for their efforts?
- Was the lesson too demanding on my abilities or energy?

While being a reflective practitioner is one way in which teachers can improve their ability to teach geography, it is equally important to make use of other sources of information. OFSTED inspection reports provide details on geography teaching at both national and individual school level. National findings can indicate common strengths and weaknesses. Reports on individual schools can provide more detailed examples of good practice.

Teachers can also use the results of research into teaching and learning to improve their practice in geography. These may be accessed in summaries of research such as those in publications edited by Scoffham (1998) and Bowles (2000) and briefer accounts in, for example, the *Times Educational Supplement*, *Primary Geographer*, *Child Education* and *Junior Education* as well as in academic journals. The research may be specific to geography, for example concerning how children learn about physical features or about distant localities, or use and draw maps; or it might focus on a more general aspect of education which can be applied to geography, such as developing children's enquiry skills, teaching ICT successfully, effective questioning or developing group work skills.

Two final points are worth making. In the first place, foundation and primary practice has been influenced by a range of people and events. Some of these influences have become accepted as unquestionable characteristics of practice rather than as being features open to scrutiny and question (Clegg and Billington, 1994). It is important that teachers do not see 'good practice' as a set of rules for teaching and learning that cannot be challenged; good practice should always be the subject of debate. All teaching is underpinned by a personal theory of how children learn and, as Alexander (1992) pointed out, if the practice is introduced from a sense of obligation rather than conviction, then it is likely to have adverse effects on children.

Second, reflective teachers should be aware of ways in which educational processes are influenced by and contribute to wider social forces (Pollard, 1997). They should act as responsible professionals and be open-minded and willing to consider different evidence and arguments. They need to develop their own philosophy of education by searching for answers to questions such as those listed below. This will have implications for their geography teaching. Practitioners may, for example, see geography as a major vehicle for raising children's awareness of inequality and for developing their sense of environmental responsibility.

What is my philosophy of education?

- What is the purpose of state primary education?
- To what extent should it contribute to the creation of wealth by preparing pupils for economic production?
- To what extent should it contribute to achieving social justice and individual rights?
- What can be achieved through education?
- How do I think children learn?

Reflective Questions

- How do you plan to balance whole-class, group and individual teaching?
- How do you group children in different ways and for different purposes?
- How do you teach children the skills necessary for successful group work?
- How do you provide for differentiation in a variety of ways?
- Are you critical in your use of commercial worksheets?
- Are your worksheets well produced and do they encourage active learning?
- Are your resources organized in a way that makes them readily accessible?
- How do you plan to use space beyond the classroom?
- How do you involve other adults in your geography teaching effectively?
- How do you group children for ICT?
- Do you measure children's time on the computer by time or task?
- How do children know what their role is?
- How do children learn to use the software?
- How do you avoid a queue of children asking the following questions during a geography lesson: 'What do I do?' 'What do I do next?' 'Where is . . .?' 'How do you spell . . .?' 'Can I . . .?' 'Is this right?'
- Can you identify what makes a particular geography display effective?
- Do you evaluate your teaching on a regular basis and also use research and the opinions of others to improve your practice?
- In what ways does your geography teaching reflect your personal philosophy of education?

FURTHER READING

Cooper, H., Hegarty, P., Hegarty, P. and Simco, N. (1996) *Display in the Classroom.* London: David Fulton.

The Ideal Teacher (2000) www.tes.co.uk

McNamara, S. (1995) 'Let's co-operate! Developing children's social skills in the classroom', in J. Moyles (ed.) *Beginning Teaching: Beginning Learning.* Buckingham: Open University Press.

Office for Standards in Education: www.ofsted.gov.uk

Teacher Training Agency (1999) *Using Information and Communication Technology to Meet Teaching Objectives in Primary Geography.* London: TTA.

REFERENCES

Alexander, R. (1992) *Policy and Practice in Primary Education.* London: Routledge.

Bennett, N. and Dunne, E. (1992) *Managing Classroom Groups.* Hemel Hempstead: Simon & Schuster.

Bowles, R. (ed.) (2000) *Raising Achievement in Geography.* London: Register of Research in Primary Geography.

Clegg, D. and Billington, S. (1994) *The Effective Primary Classroom: The Management of Teaching*

and Learning. London: David Fulton.

Hart, S. (1992) 'Differentiation: part of the problem or part of the solution?' *Curriculum Journal* 3(2), 131–42.

Pollard, A. (1997) *Reflective Teaching in the Primary School*. London: Cassell.

Scoffham, S. (ed.) (1998) *Primary Sources: Research Findings in Primary Geography*. Sheffield: Geographical Association.

Vygotsky, L. S. (1978) *Mind in Society: The Development of Higher Psychological Processes*. Cambridge, MA: Harvard University Press.

5 Learning and Teaching Approaches in Geography

The apocryphal tale of the 'expert who couldn't teach' has a resonance with many teachers, and some have gone so far as to suggest that knowledge of learning and teaching approaches is all that is needed. This chapter does not take this position, but argues for a successful balance between subject knowledge, planning skills and knowledge of teaching and learning approaches. It examines some of the approaches that can be used in teaching geography, and illustrates these with examples from the Foundation Stage and Key Stages 1 and 2. The chapter makes reference to some of the ideas concerning children's cognitive development which inform a great deal of current practice in 3–5 and primary settings. It outlines effective learning approaches, discusses effective organization in the geography classroom, and summarizes suitable teaching strategies that allow the development of the four aspects of geography.

Effective Learning Approaches

The Early Learning Goals guidance (QCA/DfEE, 2000) gives practitioners very good advice about effective learning approaches, which can be applied to all learning in 3–11 settings. Whether current curriculum organization and assessment demand allow this effective learning to occur is another question, one which was discussed in Chapter 2.

According to QCA, effective learning involves a number of aspects.

Effective learning involves

- Children learn effectively by using stimulating resources that they can explore at their own pace. If resources are organized and located effectively, then teachers and practitioners can work alongside the children and interact appropriately. In such situations children can also learn from one another.
- Children should be active learners who use all their senses to learn. They bring prior understanding of concepts and ideas from previous learning experiences.

- Children need time to explore ideas and experiences, and there may not be a linear progression from learning objective to learning outcome.
- Children need to feel secure and have confidence in themselves and their teachers in order to learn effectively. They need to trust their teachers in order to take risks in their learning or try to solve problems.
- Children learn in different ways and at different rates.
- Children make links from unstructured play to the acquisition of concepts such as location.
- Children learn a great deal from creative and imaginative play. They use new and complex vocabulary within that play.

Teachers are effective when they

- Work in partnership with parents.
- Plan enjoyable but challenging activities.
- Model a range of positive behaviour.
- Use language that is rich and use correct grammar.
- Use conversation and carefully framed questions.
- Teach skills and knowledge directly.
- Allow children to teach each other.
- Intervene with and support children in a way that helps them to develop positive attitudes to learning.
- Plan the indoor and outdoor environment to provide a positive context for learning and teaching.
- Make skilful and well-planned observations of children.
- Assess children through planned and spontaneous activities.
- Work with parents in this process.
- Identify the next step in children's learning to plan how to help the children make progress.
- Use assessment to evaluate the quality of provision and your own training needs.

These checklists are a useful aide-mémoire for reflection on your own teaching and learning style. Review the checklists and consider the following questions:

1 How often do you communicate with parents about their children's geographical abilities?
2 How do you ensure that children have the opportunity to learn from one another in geography?
3 How have you used play to develop children's understanding of geographical concepts?
4 How have you approached formal and informal assessment of their geographical learning?

Effective Organization of Learning

This section gives examples of when teachers and students can use whole-class teaching, group work and individual learning in their repertoire of geography learning activities and lessons.

Whole-class teaching

Whole-class teaching has grown in importance over the past few years, not least because of the introduction of the literacy and numeracy hour in primary education. It has a place in effective organization of geographical learning in the following situations:

Introduction and plenary sessions at Key Stages 1 and 2

It is effective to teach the class together when you are beginning a geography lesson, especially if it is at the start of a unit of work. Often it will have been a week (or longer) since the last geography lesson. Whole-class teaching gives you the opportunity to revise the concepts and skills that were learned in the previous session, introduce new concepts through questioning, as well as getting the children to generate their own questions (perhaps with you acting as scribe at the whiteboard). Whole-class plenary sessions give you the opportunity to show that you value the children's work, and allow you to set up situations where the children are learning from each other – especially if during the session they have worked on a particular product such as a map or writing frame. Plenary sessions allow you to recap on the key ideas in the lesson and give you the chance to informally assess children's progress. Many teachers and students often find that the time for effective plenary sessions disappears as the main body of the lesson drifts on or breaktime looms. This is a shame, as much learning can be reinforced in this session.

Handling discussions and asking questions in introductory and plenary sessions

Be clear about what you want the children to learn, and plan for the questions and prompts that you will use to start the discussion:

- recall questions, some of which may be 'closed', requiring one-word answers and playing to the strengths of those with good memories;
- reasoning questions, likely to be 'open-ended' in nature, offering children the chance to demonstrate understanding and thinking skills as well as creating opportunities for them to express a point of view or opinion, and make use of geographical evidence in doing this;
- speculative questions, requiring the children to move beyond the evidence and start to employ their structural imagination (see p. 96) (e.g. Why is the character of the street changing?);
- personal response questions that draw on pupils' feelings and introduce the notion of empathy in geography (see p. 96) (e.g. What does it feel like to be in this place?).

Think of definitions, explanations, clarifications and exemplar material that you might need.

Receive pupil contributions in a positive manner and be sensitive to the feedback from the children (including non-verbal feedback). Use this to gauge any possible mismatch between content and capabilities as well as the pace and timing of the discussion to avoid over-dwelling.

Aim to be inclusive of all children, not just those sitting at the front and centre of your position.

Use of audio-visual resources

Television, video and slides generally demand that the whole class has the same experience at the same time, often in a room other than your classroom. Preparation is the key to effective learning in these situations. Prepare the children for what they are going to watch and set expectations about what they should do whilst watching it. Giving them some key questions which you will be asking after the programme is a useful prompt. 'Sharing the learning objective' with them may impress your tutor or a visiting OFSTED inspector – but make sure it is in language the children can understand. Knowing your children and their ability to navigate from the classroom to the television room without incurring the wrath of the headteacher or harming others in the class is important; often an exciting geographical experience can be marred by the need to discipline particular children.

Demonstrations: direct instruction

Marjory was introducing her Year 6 children to the magnetic compass in preparation for an orienteering activity in the school grounds. They would be following a compass trail to decipher a 'secret code' to reveal a message about the next activity. Marjory had borrowed an extra-large demonstration compass and used this with the whole class to show them how to set a bearing and walk on this bearing. After the whole-class demonstration Marjory worked with a group of less able children to reinforce her whole-class work.

Although the children in this example could be said to be passive during the demonstration, Marjory's use of a striking artefact (a three foot by two foot compass complete with movable needle) held their attention and made small group practice more familiar after the whole-class demonstration. Demonstration does have a place in early years and primary settings, as long as it is followed up with active learning experiences pitched at the right levels for the children.

Learning in groups

Enquiry and problem-solving

Much learning theory suggests that most people learn well if they can discuss what they are learning with their peers and collaborate to come to a shared understanding or solution to a problem. Children working in groups to solve a problem or work through a section of a geographical enquiry may come up with learning approaches and actual answers to the enquiry question that would not have been possible had the same individuals been working alone.

Collaborative learning is a whole-school issue. It is something that is taken for granted in early years settings but is subject to wide variations in primary schools. Some children become very confident in group work in science, design and technology, and geography at an early stage owing to the learning ethos in the school; others in different schools (or even individual classes) do not get the chance to succeed in effective group work.

Learning in pairs

Exchange and evaluation of products

Year 5 children in a Barnsley school working with Catherine Hopkins drew up a checklist of what they valued in their school environment. They then shared the results of this list with a partner and justified their choices. There are many examples in primary geography of effective learning occurring in pairs – often based on exchange and evaluation of a geographical product. Children can exchange their views on a particular place, comment on a photograph or artefact together, set each other routes to follow on a play-mat or 1:10,000 Ordnance Survey map, as well as setting each other problems using the Roamer or swapping enquiry questions at the start of a unit of work.

Individual learning

Analytical writing – 'Why is that place like that?'

It is a general criticism (Hackett, 2000) that primary children's writing skills have not developed as well as their reading, speaking and listening. Planning time for drafting and writing answers to higher-order questions to do with the impact of geographical processes, or why a place may change in the near future, is essential, as is considering the use of a geographical writing (or thinking) frame (see Figure 5. 1, p. 97). The final stages of geographical writing are often best completed by individual pupils as this gives them time to reflect on what they have learned (or failed to learn) in their group or class.

Effective Learning Activities

This section discusses some effective learning activities that enhance children's geographical learning. Many are not geography specific, but are simply good early years and primary practice. They can all be seen as active learning and build on the key learning concepts discussed at the beginning of the chapter. The section starts with a general discussion of evidence-based learning and creative and imaginative approaches, then offers specific activities to enhance geographical learning with children aged 3–11.

Evidence-based learning in geography

The use of geographical evidence in all its forms is a vital part of the geography curriculum. Evidence-based approaches to the teaching of geography involve introduction of maps, images, information and objects representing different localities or themes as a way of extending children's geographical knowledge and skills. The geography curriculum encourages the understanding of artefacts, systems and environments from different places and cultures. Not only is the introduction of such materials into the classroom highly motivating for children, it also fits well with theories of how children's learning can be enhanced through first-hand experiences, particularly, though by no means exclusively, with younger pupils.

Good practice in helping the youngest children to formulate some early ideas about place, geographical patterns and the environment is informed by the same principles of good practice that inform all learning in nursery and reception settings. Children benefit from time to explore and manipulate their environment. High levels of high-quality interaction between children and adults make a major contribution to learning. Although there is no subject called geography in the Early Learning Goals, there are many opportunities for early years practitioners to introduce to children ideas about geography through the use of evidence. Early years practitioners work from the familiar in using evidence-based approaches by focusing upon the home, the family and the locality. They help children by modelling observation and examination techniques and by introducing and reinforcing descriptive language.

Helping very young children gain geographical experience

Children at Collegiate Crescent Nursery gained useful geographical experiences by planning a visit to the shops on nearby Ecclesall Road. They used geographical evidence such as photographs of the possible route to the shops and shopping lists made by other children who had visited the shops. The end purpose was to visit the shops to buy the ingredients for an afternoon snack and then cook it; this led to numeracy work when paying for the goods, as well as widening their understanding of their locality through a purposeful walk to the main road.

Creative and imaginative approaches to geography

The idea of introducing creative and imaginative approaches into the teaching of geography fits well with current understandings of how children learn. Bruner's suggestion that there is a social dimension to cognitive development, whereby a child's learning is influenced and affected by experiences that involve interaction with others, offers support for play, while his arguments in favour of the importance of language and communication lend weight to the use of story.

Ultimately it could be said that all approaches to teaching and learning in geography are evidence based. It is hard to envisage how children could engage effectively in creative and imaginative approaches to geography without access to some evidence with which to inform their work.

However, it is perhaps a mistake to see the relationship between evidence-based and imaginative approaches as hierarchical with non-permeable boundaries between the two. The impossibility of visiting all the localities studied means that understanding distant localities requires acts of imaginative reconstruction, albeit based on evidence, in order to make sense of the world. The use of creativity and imagination in geography can take a number of forms and requires children to make use of their cognitive, emotional and communication abilities.

When trying to establish what imagination and creativity in geography might involve it is useful to draw on the work of Campbell and Little (1989), who outline three aspects to the use of imagination in the related humanities subject of history. **Structural imagination** draws on children's cognitive abilities and involves 'filling in the gaps', and creating generalizations about the places in order to highlight the significance of events, to see things as a whole and thus to make greater sense of the world. Examples of geographical generalizations could include being able to imagine what common features any village might have after learning about several real examples. Structural imagination must, however, be tempered with caution, particularly over the application of generalizations to people in distant places. Just because one family in Lima lives in a shanty town it does not follow that all the citizens of Lima have a similar lifestyle.

Ornamental imagination draws on children's communication skills as they seek to set the scene, flesh out geographical details about children's lives in other places, and organize a narrative or create an image. A creative account of what it might be like to go to school in Mumbai, India, based on stimuli from a television programme, would use ornamental imagination.

The third aspect, **empathy**, introduces the idea that feelings as well as thought can impel behaviour. The notion of empathy is open to criticism from those who regard the purpose of geography as being to give an objective explanation of spatial patterns. It is certainly the case that caution needs to be exercised when putting oneself into someone else's shoes. It is never possible truly to understand how and why children aged 10 in Indonesia are at work simply by imagining what it would be like to work in a sweatshop. That said, there is no shortage of evidence of the power of emotions to motivate behaviour and learning (Hyson, 1994). Memory and learning can be enhanced in creative and imaginative approaches to geography that heighten children's interest and enjoyment, and can offer children opportunities to experiment with and try out feelings and behaviours in an attempt to make sense of them. Through story and play children can begin to reinforce their understanding of the actions and behaviour of real people in real places.

Effective Teaching and Learning Strategies in Geography

1. Enquiry	6. Using fieldwork
2. Using, making and interpreting maps	7. Using play and role-play
3. Using photographs	8. Using physical modelling
4. Using visitors	9. Using stories
5. Using ICT	

1. Enquiry

There is mounting evidence that the stages of geographical enquiry are taught, not caught (Roberts, 1996; Martin, 1999; QCA, 2000), so it is important to scaffold the development of children's enquiry skills. The phrase 'children should be taught to' gives teachers much direction, and the QCA Key Stage 1 and Key Stage 2 Schemes of Work are all enquiry based with key questions focusing the learning objectives.

Good learning activities that develop children's ability to become independent enquirers include the following learning activities.

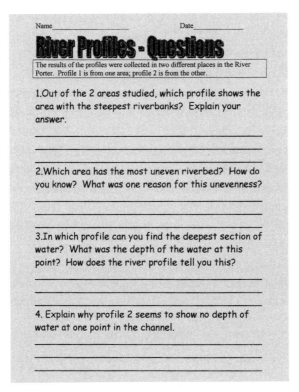

Name_____ Date_____

River Profiles - Questions

The results of the profiles were collected in two different places in the River Porter. Profile 1 is from one area; profile 2 is from the other.

1. Out of the 2 areas studied, which profile shows the area with the steepest riverbanks? Explain your answer.

_____

_____

2. Which area has the most uneven riverbed? How do you know? What was one reason for this unevenness?

_____

_____

3. In which profile can you find the deepest section of water? What was the depth of the water at this point? How does the river profile tell you this?

_____

_____

4. Explain why profile 2 seems to show no depth of water at one point in the channel.

_____

_____

_____

Figure 5.1 A geographical writing frame

Learning activities

- Always frame your learning objective for any lesson as a question.
- Choose key questions that are open and require the use of a range of geographical skills to investigate the other three aspects of geography (e.g. Where is this place? How is it connected to other places?).
- Use resources such as photographs, artefacts, video evidence or maps to stimulate questions from the children. Make a display of the questions they ask and use the questions to evaluate what they have learned at the end of the enquiry.
- Model enquiry by taking your children through each stage before asking them to choose enquiry questions. Decide on which geographical skills to use and what mode of reporting to use.
- Make sure there is a progression in the types of geographical skills you ask the children to use (e.g. from measuring distance in non-standard units to measuring in metres and centimetres).
- Ensure a progression from enquiries with a simple 'answer' to those with a range of interpretations.
- Use a writing frame, prompt sheet or set of oral teacher questions to scaffold the children's analysis of the data they have collected.
- Ensure that there is an audience for the finished enquiry work.

2. Using, making and interpreting maps

Children are natural mappers (Blades and Spencer, 1998). This, however, does not absolve practitioners and teachers from the responsibility of nurturing this natural skill. Research into children's mapping abilities suggests that children as young as 3 can use an aerial photograph as a map, and that children aged 5 who have been taught effectively perform as well as children aged 8 who have not been taught. Other findings are that gender has been an issue since the 1980s (Matthews, 1992), and that orienteering is a very effective way of introducing and developing map reading skills (Boardman, 1989). Wiegand (1991, 1993) has analysed the extra difficulties posed by using atlas maps and from this has designed atlases suitable for Key Stage 1 and Key Stage 2 children, as well as investigating how children collaborate using electronic maps (Wiegand, 2000).

Effective learning involves using maps, atlases and globes for way-finding, location and in the context of enquiries by:

- creating play maps of the classroom, school/nursery or locality and using them for navigational games and developing directional language;
- Key Stage 1 children locating the most littered areas on a teacher-prepared map of the school grounds as part of an enquiry into school environmental quality;
- Key Stage 2 children designing a sustainable development trail around their locality.

Children can be helped to learn how to interpret maps, atlases and globes by developing their understanding of:

98

Perspective: viewing an object or landscape in plan view

- By drawing around three-dimensional shapes to produce a plan-view drawing.
- By viewing model landscapes from above and drawing the resultant plan view.

Symbols: using lines, points or areas of colour to represent features on the ground as print on a map by:

- Key Stage 1 and foundation children making up their own picture symbols.
- Key Stage 2 children using iconic symbols based on Ordnance Survey symbols.

Location: where an object or person is located using language, a landmark or a grid system

- 'The wheel-toys are always kept next to the fence at the bottom of the play area'.
- Using an alpha-numeric grid, then four-figure grid system, then latitude and longitude coordinates on an atlas map.

Direction: showing which way to go using language and compass directions by:

- describing 'Rosie's Walk' using directional language;
- using compass directions to explain what the land use is like in the four quadrants of a village.

Scale and distance: measuring *how far* on a map and knowing *how much* land is shown on a map:

- By using a piece of string to measure relative distance.
- By using linear scales to measure distance.
- By plotting shapes (triangles, polygons) at different scales on squared paper.

Understanding atlas conventions:

- By using the index.
- By using the key.
- By checking the scale.   (After Wiegand, 1993)

Children can be helped to develop locational knowledge by focusing on

- Events in the news – a volcano erupting, a sporting event, a drought: these are real and often dramatic, and consequently resources (newspapers, video clips of the news, the World Wide Web) are readily available. However, the news is often of disasters. It can paint a negative picture, particularly of countries in the South, without indicating that lack of equality (poverty, lack of access to health care and clean water, etc.) often compounds the problem. You need to point out that every country has certain problems and that these may be comparatively short-lived.
- Holidays. Avoid the assumption that most children go on package holidays to Spain or Florida. They don't! Holidays or day trips can provide real experience to talk about and children may bring back postcards and other souvenirs. You may feel that this might be divisive with older children (one-upmanship), in which case you could talk about your holiday.
- Origins of goods such as food and clothing: an excellent way to develop children's locational knowledge. Make sure that the children do not gain the impression that some countries exist solely for the convenience of Western consumers (although in the case of certain cash crops this is true to some extent).

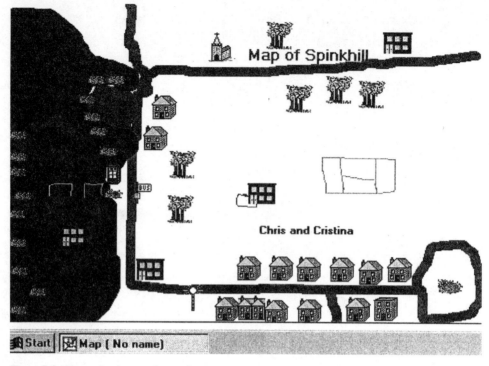

Figure 5.2 Using a simple mapping package

3. Using photographs

Geography is a visual subject. BBC24 and other news stations bring images from around the UK and around the world to anyone with a television set or Internet connection. Children are used to analysing pictures and photographs in art, English and history as well as geography. They are asked to create pictures, drawings and photographs in a variety of subjects as well as use them for a variety of purposes. However, it is important to remember that pictures, drawings and photographs in geography will be used as sources of evidence for the distinctiveness of a place and its people, illustrate geographical features or show spatial patterns.

Children's learning and photos

Research done over the past decade shows that children can read oblique photographs more easily than vertical aerial photographs, that children as young as 3 can successfully navigate around a vertical photograph of a familiar environment (Blades and Spencer, 1990), and that the way children read photographs develops with age (Mackintosh, 1998). Children up to the age of 14 also seem to respond best to photographs that contain people rather than 'blank landscapes' (Jones, 1998). This research evidence can helpfully inform teaching and learning activities in the following ways. Children need to be taught to see, read and interpret photographs (Mackintosh, 1998).

Teaching them to see photographs involves:

- Sorting/selecting: e.g. physical/human features, coastal/inland, children's daily lives, evidence of weather/climate; which ones could or could not have been taken in the UK? why?
- Similarities and differences: encourage children to identify similarities with people in unfamiliar localities, emphasizing common needs such as food and shelter.
- Sequencing: e.g. the banana trade in St Lucia – from plantation to dockside.
- Captioning: matching captions with photos; writing captions, e.g. for a tourist brochure.
- Labelling: e.g. annotate a black-and-white photocopy.
- Describing: describe a photo for a partner to draw.

Teaching them to read photographs involves:

- Where is it? Children search for clues (e.g. housing, clothing, vegetation, physical landscape) as to where a place might be and what it might be like.
- Questioning: write questions around a photo stuck on a large piece of paper.
- Likes, dislikes, surprises.
- Speech/thought bubbles.

Teaching them to interpret photographs involves:

- Issues: what is happening? Why? What/whom does it affect? How can it be solved?
- Linking: children describe orally or write a letter to a person in the photograph, describing their own locality.
- Cropping: draw or describe the rest of the photo.
- Story writing/drama: what is happening in the photo? What might happen next?

4. Using visitors

The use of factual accounts and personal geographies through the introduction of people who can talk about their experiences of how things are in a distant place (or give a different view on how things are done in a local one) can be very stimulating for children. To get the maximum educational benefit from using human sources of evidence in this way, visitors to the class need to be briefed and the children too need to be prepared. They should already know something about the topic, and should have prepared questions to ask. Inform the visitor beforehand about the areas that the children are going to raise so that they can give their answers some forethought and perhaps gather some concrete evidence such as artefacts or photographs with which to support their account.

Chambers and Donert (1996) (presumably urban dwellers) describe the teacher using the 'village idiot' or 'agent provocateur' approaches in order to support the adult who may not be used to talking with young children. In 'village idiot' guise the teacher asks very simple questions so that all the children will understand the answers, whereas the 'agent provocateur' rigorously questions the visitor to show there is more than one point of view on the issue that is being put forward. Do inform your visitor of the role you are going to take.

An inspector calls . . .

A teacher invited her husband (a local policeman) to visit her class to give evidence about the traffic problems experienced on the local high street. He described what he had seen from the police helicopter above the street, and listened as the children made presentations about the traffic problems from their point of view. He then answered their questions and let them know what the police were doing in terms of traffic management in the area.

5. Using ICT

The use of information and communications technology in the nursery or classroom offers considerable potential for enriching and enhancing the geography curriculum, as well as providing opportunities for interactive learning, the promotion of fine motor control, personal and social development and the development of reasoning skills. Using ICT in a variety of ways and contexts will also aid children in becoming increasingly familiar with it, and confident and positive about their skills as users. ICT can provide valuable tools for reinforcing first-hand and practical geographical experiences, for example through the use of writing packages. Children's abilities at recalling, selecting and organizing geographical information, as well as communicating their knowledge and understanding in a variety of ways (DfEE/QCA, 1999), can all be enhanced and enriched through the inclusion of ICT. Similarly, ICT can play a part in widening pupils' geographical knowledge and understanding as well as offering yet another context within which to engage in geographical enquiry.

Student teachers are also required to meet specific standards in ICT in order to gain QTS. The following checklists summarize the ways in which ICT can enhance learning in primary geography. The range and management of ICT resources will be discussed in Chapter 6.

ICT allows children to learn more effectively when they can:

- Use an animated presentation from a CD-ROM, e.g. to show river processes in action.
- Create graphs quickly so that they can concentrate on analysing the data from an enquiry on road use.
- Choose the most appropriate chart type to show their data when presenting the results of an enquiry.

- Use a much wider range of primary and secondary information, e.g. a CD-ROM, an atlas, an encyclopedia, the Internet, to learn about St Lucia.
- ICT allows data to be changed easily; a *My World* or *Local Studies* map can be updated after fieldwork, or used for different purposes such as a place investigation, or to improve understanding about symbols and scale. Children's work or photographs can be scanned and the text or images altered or annotated.
- The interactive nature of ICT can be exploited by children collecting data and using spreadsheets to ask 'What if?' questions; for example, when investigating water use in the home.

Effective use of ICT by teachers in relation to objectives in geography

- Ensure that ICT-based work focuses on well-defined geographical questions (e.g. Figure 5.3 about France).
- Ensure that ICT-based work develops children's enquiry skills, or knowledge of places and themes.
- Ensure that ICT is the best way of meeting their teaching objectives. For example, using a paper atlas rather than a CD-ROM would be the best tool to develop children's skills in using contents and index pages to find places.
- Ensure that children are aware of how ICT is helping them learn in geography – for example, how using graphing software gives them more time to analyse the data from an enquiry.
- Ensure that children can justify why they used a particular chart, colour of display, or object on a *My World* screen – for example, explaining why they chose particular colours on a map using *Local Studies*.
- Ensure that children are aware of the role played by ICT in geographical aspects of everyday life – for example, weather forecasting and communicating with friends and family in distant places.

For those aspects of lessons where ICT is used, teachers should identify in their planning:

- How ICT will be used to meet geographical learning objectives.
- Key questions to ask and opportunities for teacher intervention.
- How the children's geographical progress will be assessed and recorded.
- Assessment criteria that ensure that children's progress and attainment are not masked because ICT is used.
- The impact of the use of ICT on the organization and conduct of the geography session and how this is to be managed.
- How the ICT used is appropriate to the geography learning objectives and allows access to the least ICT-capable and most ICT-capable children.

All about France

Using *Microsoft* Encarta or *Microsoft* World Atlas answer the following questions.
Here are some suggested key words to help you search…

- France
- Great Britain

Remember to use the outline for the two articles above to help you to scan for information. The outline is found on the left-hand side of the screen.

1. Imagine you are planning a holiday to France. You want to avoid wet weather. What months of the year should you avoid?

2. What is the total population of France?

3. How does this compare to the population of Britain?

4. Name some rivers flowing through France.

5. How could you get to France from England?

6. Where is the highest land in France?

7. What are the natural resources of France?

Figure 5.3 Example of ICT-based worksheet

Geography lessons can contribute to the development and consolidation of children's ICT capability by:

- Developing children's ICT skills first so that the geographical learning objectives can be met – for example, by teaching the children how to insert clip art or images so that they can successfully complete an enquiry report that includes their drawings or sketch maps.
- Using appropriate ICT vocabulary and co-ordinating ICT in geography with ICT in other subjects – for example, by using a desktop publishing package in geography and English for different learning objectives.

Teachers should monitor children's progress by:

- Purposeful intervention to ensure children are focused on answering a geographical question – for example, when using a CD-ROM or web browser.
- Asking focused questions about children's understanding – for example, What have you learned about tourism in Castries from the World Wide Web?
- Asking children to explain the advantages and disadvantages of using ICT – for example, email communication with children in another school.

Teachers should recognize standards of attainment in geography when ICT is used by:

- Designing assessment criteria that always focus on identified geographical teaching objectives.
- Being alert to the ways in which ICT can affect the assessment process.
- Noting whether work was done in a group or by individual children.
- Designing assessment criteria that distinguish between outcomes that are the result of an automatic function of the computer and those which reveal children's geographical knowledge and understanding, for example, children can find useful secondary data on a distant place and paste it into their work without understanding it; a graph can be drawn automatically but children may not understand the relationships between the variables.
- Designing activities that focus on using ICT-related data to answer a framework of geographical questions.

6. Using fieldwork

David Job (1996) has presented a pithy introduction to the range of fieldwork options available to teachers. He puts forward a typology of fieldwork, which can be summarized as follows:

- **The Cook's tour:** teacher-directed field visit where the learners often play a passive role and the teacher 'tells the story' of the place or environment.
- **Hypothesis testing:** the teacher chooses a statement (e.g. all villages are the same) and sets off the learners as data collectors who will collect evidence to prove or disprove the hypothesis.
- **Discovery learning:** the children are exposed to experiences in the field from which they learn a variety of things not necessarily determined by the teacher.
- **Earth education:** the children are 'immersed' in the environment and learn about ecological concepts through well-structured games and role-play.
- **Enquiry-based learning:** children use the enquiry approach to answer geographical questions, collecting data in the field.

Many 3–11 teachers are influenced by the fieldwork that they experienced as secondary school students. This may be no bad thing: it may propel them to share this powerful way of learning with their children. But the 'big project' approach to GCSE and A-level fieldwork (mirrored in fieldwork-focused units of work) is not the only option, and in many cases may not be appropriate, especially with younger children. Equally, teacher-directed 'nature study' (as described by Blyton, 1933) has had a strong influence on activities outside the classroom in the early years and primary settings. The 'cross-curricular' *trip* in which the children and teachers visit a museum or even (during 2000) the Millennium Dome is now often seen as a reward for hard work revising for Key Stage 1 or 2 SATs, or a good use of a summer day in the nursery. Fieldwork, enshrined in the geographical education community as a benchmark of quality provision, is often viewed by non-geographers as 'our day out' (Russell, 1984). Good fieldwork has to be planned. It does not just occur whenever the children are not inside their 'classroom'. Equally, high-quality fieldwork learning can occur metres from the classroom window.

All effective teaching and learning related to fieldwork has three main stages. In the **preparation phase**, the teacher must identify skills the children will use, knowledge they will gain, concepts involved and attitudes that may be fostered. It is good practice to involve the children in planning the activities to be carried out in the field; encourage them to hypothesize, suggest enquiry questions and subsidiary questions. You will need to practise the skills needed for the fieldwork at school, e.g. using the compass or tallying. You will need to decide on methods of recording, e.g. use of digital camera, palmtop computer, sketching, mapping. At Key Stage 1, use adults as scribes; at Key Stage 2, if appropriate, provide a booklet containing information and tasks. The **fieldwork stage** itself should be focused on the safety and management issues (to be discussed in Chapter 6). The children should be briefed and reminded of the expectations of their behaviour (litter, noise, manners and safety), and children should be visible to adults at all times. The **follow-up phase** should take place at the earliest opportunity and allow the children to discuss the visit, display results, make models, dramatize events, create artwork and conclude and evaluate the enquiry.

Fieldwork

Final-year geography students, working with an experienced geography co-ordinator at Junior School Lowry Sheffield, planned very effective fieldwork for Year 5 and Year 6 children as part of a unit of work that investigated river features and processes. The students prepared the children for the fieldwork by activities such as labelling photographs of rivers to name the particular features shown that they would experience at the River Porter. The fieldwork experience involved using geographical skills such as drawing a sketch-map and field-sketch to record evidence of what river features were present at the site, and measuring depth, width and velocity at a specific site using measuring metre sticks and a stopwatch and ping pong ball (Figure 5.4). The children worked in groups of six, each with an adult who had been fully briefed on questions to ask and teaching points to make. The follow-up phase involved the children drawing a cross-section of the section they had surveyed, and attempting to explain how the processes of erosion and deposition had formed the features they had recorded. The students' evaluations noted the fact that it was essential that the children had chart-drawing ability (learned in mathematics) in order to draw the cross-section. The challenge for the least able children was as much mathematical as it was geographical.

Lowry Junior School

Names:	Group:

River Porter – Stream Study

Activity 2	Rate of flow

Measure the rate of flow of the water in two different locations along the stream. If possible try a **straight section** and a **section around a meander**.

Measure a 10m stretch of water. Mark with a line across the stream at the start and finish.

Drop a ping pong ball into the stream, time its journey between the two lines.

Try each one ten times!

Does it make the same journey each time? Why?/Why not?

Find the average time for the ten journeys.

Multiply the average time by 100 to calculate the speed per kilometre.

Remember to mark the locations on the map.

You will need: 2 lines, long tape measure, ping pong balls, stopwatch, calculator, 4 tent pegs, hammer.

Try	Location A	Location B
1		
2		
3		
4		
5		
6		
7		
8		
9		
10		
Average		

Speed per kilometre:

Location A	Location B
per kilometre	per kilometre

Figure 5.4 Fieldwork on river processes

7. Using play and role-play

Tina Bruce (1991) sees play as central to young children's learning. It enables the integration of their learning, making it deeper, broader and more relevant than might otherwise be the case. In geography, first-hand experience through play offers the chance to manipulate, explore, discover, practise and apply knowledge and ideas. Exploratory play of this sort can help children to gain a deeper understanding of geography through first-hand experience of artefacts and model geographical environments (the travel agent's, the market). Other forms of play offer children opportunities to increase their understanding and their ability to express thoughts and feelings. Although most children will play spontaneously, in an educational setting teachers will need to structure some play opportunities to make the most of the potential for geographical learning. In some cases it will be necessary to establish a physical environment to promote play, including the provision of props (i.e. geographical artefacts), and to provide time. Teachers may need to act as mediators, intervening sensitively to advance children's play by modelling, explaining and promoting co-operation and consideration. Teachers may also find it useful to engage in more active participation as co-players, offering suggestions and information that will help to sustain the play. Finally, teachers are charged with making assessment of children's learning in geography and therefore will have to act as assessors and communicators, using observations and data to make judgements about pupil development and learning, and recording that information (Jones and Reynolds, 1992).

Although play is not as prominent in many primary settings as it is in the Foundation Stage, it is important to remember that older pupils too can gain an

Table 5.1 **Types of role-play in primary school geography**

Type of role-play	Examples
Hot-seating	Taking on a role and being questioned. The managing director of Nike being asked about conditions in factories alleged to use child labour.
Recreation/reconstruction	The public enquiry – 'Do we need a new cycle path?'
Non-costumed role-play	Acting out scenes in role, booking a holiday to St Lucia at the travel agent in the play area.
Role-cards	Role-cards give information on character including name, age, status, etc. Children take on the role in a debate, e.g. those who stood to gain/lose/were unsure about changes. Role-cards also support the teacher who is apprehensive about using role-play.
Costumed role-play	Experiencing the Antarctic weather whilst observing the penguins.
ICT simulation	Some packages offer children a simulated experience requiring children to engage with the imaginary world on screen. *Sim City 2000* and *My World* fit in this category. They ought not to be regarded as a substitute for first-hand experience, rather as an addition, an approximation. To the extent that simulations are a form of role-play there is also the possibility of offering opportunities for children to engage in empathy.
Predicting what happened next, or would happen if . . .	Teacher tells part of a geographical story and pupils produce what they consider to be the likely ending or what could be an alternative ending.

understanding of people and places by acting out and taking on the persona of individuals from particular localities. Planning drama and role-play scenarios with a geographical theme (Table 5.1) offers older children opportunities to extend their ability to empathize with people and the everyday decisions they have to make. Such activities can also underpin geographical enquiry as children are offered an exciting and stimulating context within which to draw upon and apply their previous learning based on the evidence of literature, visits, artefacts, ICT and interactions with the teacher. Geographical drama and role-play activities can take place in school or in the field.

Preparation matters, and teachers ought to have a clear focus for role-play activities in geography. In addition, it is important to give some thought to where the children will locate the information (i.e. evidence) with which to inform their role-play. Watching geographical activities (perhaps at a visit to the post office) can offer children useful pointers by helping them to picture the past and build mental images that will aid their understanding and help retention of learning. Role-play works best with those pupils who are used to working in this way. Consequently, if such an approach represents a departure from normal practice, it is best not to make unrealistic demands of the children. What skills/previous experiences/games would help them to work in this way? Finally, what resources, such as costumes or props, will the children need to make the most of the opportunity for play?

On yer bike . . .

A group of PCGE students altered an exemplar role-play situation (what to do with a local quarry – GA, 1997) to fit with a local issue at Firs Hill School in Sheffield. Community leaders had called for a new cycle path to be established along the busy street that bounded the school grounds. The students drew a map of the locality showing the school and key roads and then designed role-cards that illustrated the views different people around the school may take about the cycle path. For example, the headteacher (an exciting role to play . . .) believed that the cycle path should be built, but the owner of a local shop did not, as she would lose parking space in front of her shop.

Year 4 children took part in role-play based on a public meeting held to discuss the issues. They voted, then considered whether the winners of the vote (the 'build the path coalition') would actually get their way in reality.

8. Using physical modelling

Geographical patterns and processes present many potential problems for the geography co-ordinator. The geography team at QCA felt it necessary to explain in the Programme of Study exactly what a geographical pattern and process was, as teachers had found these concepts difficult in the past (geographical space and astronomical space having been confused in the 1990 curriculum). Research into children's understanding of physical features (Harwood and Jackson, 1993; Platten, 1995) showed that children's understanding of the vocabulary associated with 'simple' landscape features such as hill, valley, cliff and coast as well as physical processes (evaporation, erosion, deposition, flooding) could be very confused. Modelling these features in the classroom of school grounds can be very effective to change some of the children's misconceptions.

Children can model:

- river processes by using a sand tray, sand of different sizes and small pebbles and rocks;
- coastal processes by building a 'coast' of more resistant and less resistant materials (e.g. plasticine and clay) in the wet-play area and observing the impact of waves on this coast;
- settlement features by using 'small world' materials and rebuilding the road and shop layout of a familiar area.

9. Using stories

The use of story is a common occurrence in 3–11 settings and offers good links between literacy and other areas of the curriculum such as geography. Stories can be extremely powerful vehicles for examining different places and environments. Even the youngest children can find their understanding and awareness of people and places, their geographical vocabulary and their understanding of geographical themes being enhanced through the use of story. Stories offer a familiar medium through which to encounter unfamiliar worlds by introducing children to situations and events beyond their own experiences. For this reason, stories constitute a powerful way of making geography accessible to young children, as they offer a means of helping children to:

- identify similarities and differences between places and environments;
- acquire locational information and so develop a more complex sense of place;
- examine geographical evidence;
- understand concepts such as change and interdependence; and
- draw parallels with their own experience, i.e. stories about children.

Geographical fiction can provide children with information on a wide variety of topics including dress, transport, food, the built environment, the natural environment and society. It can also introduce higher-order concepts such as change and continuity over time, as well as offering opportunities to discuss the distinction between fact and fiction. Stories can also provide teachers with opportunities to help children challenge stereotypical attitudes and assumptions, and to respect and understand the similarities and differences that exist between people. Teachers therefore need to give careful consideration to the stories that they employ to ensure that they support a positive approach to diversity rather than undermining it. Chapter 6 reviews some of the fiction resources that can be used with children aged 3–11.

'Did I Learn It Wrong?': Challenging Misconceptions

Children's 'alternative conceptions' in geography may arise through misunderstanding what has been taught or through the influence of, for example, films, literature, television or holidays. Once embedded, they are difficult to change and may act as a barrier to further learning. It is important for students and teachers to be aware of and anticipate these alternative conceptions in order to plan appropriate learning activities. Some common alternative conceptions are listed below.

Many features are seen as only having one **form**, **type** or **scale**:

deserts	are hot, with sand dunes, cacti and camels
beaches	are sandy
islands	are small
mountains	have pointed summits
rivers	are made by people; don't flow through cities; mountain streams invariably flow faster than lowland rivers; the Nile flows North to South
cities	people don't live in cities
countryside	people don't live in the countryside

stereotypical images (poverty and problems) of people and places in less economically developed countries

'being in two places at once' (nested hierarchies; e.g. Rome and Italy) is often difficult for young children to grasp

the ***greenhouse effect*** is often seen as a result of the hole in the ozone layer

(After Dove, 1999)

Problems also arise when children fail to understand the relative scale of feature in photographs and do not appreciate the direction from which they have been taken.

Addressing alternative conceptions

Most alternative conceptions can be addressed through the following strategies:

- fieldwork: undertaking an enquiry into a river's speed of flow;
- practical demonstration: a stream tank to demonstrate erosion;
- practical tasks: building a model to understand contours;
- the use of different contexts: identifying different types of deserts through the use of a variety of photographs and videos;
- the use of clear and accurate vocabulary;
- using positive images;
- teaching children how to 'read' photographs; and
- careful questioning, using open-ended questions.

The next chapter discusses the resources needed to make effective use of these teaching and learning opportunities, and explores the safety management issues present in many of the teaching and learning activities discussed.

Reflective Questions

- How do you think children learn? Is it in the same way as you learn as an adult, or in a different way?
- Would you choose whole-class teaching or small group teaching as your preferred teaching style? Why?
- How have you used play as a learning strategy in geography?
- How do you use maps and photographs in the enquiry process with your children?

FURTHER READING

Carter, R. (ed.) (1998) *The Handbook of Primary Geography*. Sheffield: Geographical Association.

Milner, A. (1996) *Geography Starts Here! Practical Approaches with Nursery and Reception Children*. Sheffield: Geographical Association.

Scoffham, S. (ed.) (1998) *Primary Sources: Research Findings in Primary Geography*. Sheffield: Geographical Association.

Wiegand, P. (1992) *Places in the Primary School*. London: Cassell.

Williams, M. (ed.) (1996) *Understanding Geographical and Environmental Education: The Role of Research*. London: Cassell.

REFERENCES

Blades, M. and Spencer, C. (1990) 'The development of 3–6 year olds' map-using ability: the relative importance of landmarks and map alignment', *Journal of Genetic Psychology* 15 (1), 181–94.

Blades, M. and Spencer, C. (1998) 'The development of children's ability to use spatial representations', *Advances in Child Development and Behaviour* 25, 157–97.

Blyton, E. (ed.) (1933) *Modern Teaching in the Infant School Vol 2*. London: Newnes.

Boardman, D. (1989) 'The development of graphicacy: children's understanding of maps', *Geography* 74 (4), 321–31.

Bruce, T. (1991) *Time to Play in Early Childhood Education*. London: Hodder and Stoughton.

Campbell, J. and Little, V. (eds) (1989) *Humanities in the Primary School*. London: Falmer Press.

Chambers, B. and Donert, K. (1996) *Teaching Geography at Key Stage 2*. Cambridge: Chris Kington.

DfEE/QCA (1999) *The National Curriculum: Handbook for Primary Teachers in England, Key Stage 1 and 2*. London: QCA.

Dove, J. (1999) *Theory into Practice: Immaculate Misconceptions*. Sheffield: Geographical Association.

GA (1997) *Geography Teacher's Handbook*. Sheffield: Geographical Association.

Hackett, G. (2000) 'Literacy targets hinge on writing', *Times Educational Supplement*, 22 September.

Harwood, D. and Jackson, P. (1993) 'Why did they build this hill so steep?: problems in assessing primary children's understanding of physical landscape features in the context of the UK national curriculum', *IRGEE* 2 (2), 64–79.

Hyson, M. C. (1994) *The Emotional Development of Young Children: Building an Emotion-Centred Curriculum*. London: Teachers College Press.

Job, D. (1996) 'Geography and environmental education – an exploration of perspectives and strategies', in A. Kent, D. Lambert, M. Nash and F. Slater (eds) *Geography in Education: Viewpoints on Teaching and Learning*. Cambridge: Cambridge University Press.

Jones, E. and Reynolds, G. (1992) *The Play's the Thing*. London: Teachers College Press.

Jones, S. (1998) 'The interpretation of geographical photographs by 11 and 14 year old students in international research', *Geographical and Environmental Education* 7 (2), 122–39.

Mackintosh, M. (1998) 'Learning from photographs', in Scoffham, S. *Primary Sources – Research Findings in Primary Geography*. Sheffield: Geographical Association.

Martin, F. (1999) 'The enquiry approach: what, why, how?', *Primary Geographer* 38, 4–8.

Matthews, M. H. (1992) *Making Sense of Place*. Hemel Hempstead: Harvester Wheatsheaf.

Platten, L. (1995) 'Talking geography: an investigation into young children's understanding of geographical terms, part 2', *International Journal of Early Years Education* 3 (3), 69–84

QCA/DfEE (2000) *Curriculum Guidance for the Foundation Stage*. London: QCA.

Roberts, M. (1996) 'Teaching styles and strategies', in A. Kent, D. Lambert, M. Nash and F. Slater (eds) *Geography in Education: Viewpoints on Teaching and Learning*. Cambridge: Cambridge University Press.

Russell, W. (1984) *Our Day Out*. London: Methuen.

Wiegand, P. (1991) 'A model for the realisation of a school atlas', *Geography* 76 (1), 50–7.

Wiegand, P. (1993) *Children and Primary Geography*. London: Cassell.

Wiegand, P. (2000) 'Children's collaboration using electronic maps', in A. Kent (ed.) *Geographical Education: Research Forum 2: Information and Communications Technology*. London: International Geographical Union with the Institute of Education, University of London.

6

Resources in Primary Geography:

Using the Classroom, Using the Outdoor Environment and Using Information and Communications Technology

Bringing the world into the classroom requires a wide range of resources and perhaps an acquisitive nature. In order to make people and places that children may experience only vicariously seem real, you need to be constantly vigilant for resources that are topical, eye-catching and challenging. Bringing the local into the classroom is perhaps more straightforward than creating a wide range of distant places resources, but even this is becoming easier with the increased focus on global education, world citizenship and sustainable development.

However, collecting and managing geographical resources is only one side of the coin. Teachers need to consider their resources from a critical standpoint. Does the photopack they have chosen to use really represent all the features of life in Nairobi or Cairo? Does the local tourist office represent all sides of the nearest town, or only the aspects it wishes to publicize? Teachers can encourage children to see geographical resources not as the 'truth' about places, but as just one view by involving them in the process of resource creation, especially when focusing on local issues.

This chapter will detail which geographical resources can support pupils' learning in geography and consider their management and safe use. It will also look specifically at ways of making effective use of ICT resources. Finally, the chapter will examine the use of environments and resources beyond the classroom to develop children's geographical learning.

The Learning Environment within the Classroom

How can you organize your classroom to support the learning of geography? Geography is a resource-based subject and yet competes with the rest of the curriculum for funding and storage space. The role of the geography co-ordinator is crucial in developing, organizing and maintaining geographical resources in the school (see Chapter 10).

One way in which the co-ordinator can maximize the impact of geography in the school is by setting high standards for geographical classroom displays. The display environment is important in enhancing geographical learning, and can be used to complement other geographical resources in the following ways. Work on continuous units of work (see Chapter 3) can be highlighted throughout the year. QCA units such as 'Where in the world is Barnaby Bear' and 'What's in the news?' can be displayed. These units give the children opportunities to develop their local, national and global locational knowledge whilst actively using map, atlas and globe resources. UK and world maps visible on the wall and a globe available in the classroom can be used in discussion of key events. The Sydney Olympics and floods in Kent and Sussex (to take two examples of events from 2000), even the location of Britney Spears' concerts, are real events that can be used to develop locational knowledge. A 'places in the news' display can be used for geography and English, and as inspiration for desktop publishing in ICT. Many early years settings have a semi-permanent display featuring the immediate local area and the locations of children's homes or routes to school, using a simple street map and photographs, created by the teacher and children. As is the case with all displays, they should be interactive, use questions and involve the children in their creation, appreciation and active use.

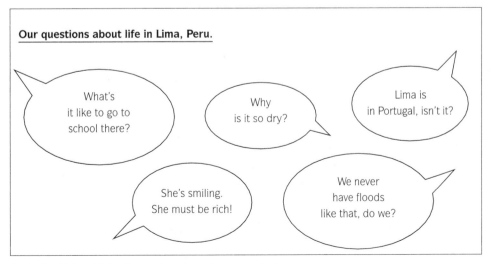

Figure 6.1 Using children's questions for a classroom display

Displays also enhance work in blocked units of work at Key Stage 1 and Key Stage 2, or topics in the Foundation Stage. Starting a unit of work on a distant place by asking what the children already know about the place and its people can create an instant display based on the children's prior knowledge, questions and possible misconceptions.

This display can form the basis of enquiry-based work and can be used to review the learning gained in the unit. Have the children's questions been answered by the end of the unit? What misconceptions have been challenged? What new questions could the children raise at the end of the unit? Access to water, sand, play-mats and other wet and dry play equipment can also enhance learning in geography. Using a wet play area for modelling river or coastal processes in a stream tray or sand tray can be very effective but also has safety implications (see next section). Equally, having a role-play area in the classroom allows much useful activity around journeys (e.g. setting up a travel agent's) or modelling an environment (e.g. creating a 'rainforest' corner).

The computer area is discussed in the following subsection but it is worth seeing how this area can be exploited for geography. Are there instructions or guidance for the geography applications? Are there suggestions as to how generic software can be used for geographical learning? Are there key geographical Web sites bookmarked or recorded as a display?

Organizing a safe learning environment

Teachers have a duty to establish a safe learning environment in which children can feel secure and confident, and in which they can operate safely. An important consideration in geography is the use of artefacts, equipment and visual resources in the classroom. Teachers are expected to be familiar with the likely actions of their pupils in a given situation and are expected to be able to exercise a degree of foresight. Failure to prevent injury or harm to a child in the classroom when the dangers could reasonably be foreseen constitutes negligence.

A major problem for teachers trying to exercise this foresight is that no environment, and certainly no 3–11 setting, can be made entirely risk free. It is inevitable that children will fall over, trap their fingers or mishandle objects from time to time. Risk avoidance, risk awareness and, ultimately, risk management are important skills for children to acquire, given that they cannot be supervised 24 hours a day. However, children's abilities in these areas develop over a long period and teachers therefore need to make every effort to ensure their pupils' safety and not behave in a thoughtless fashion, thereby exposing them to unnecessary hazards. Foresight therefore requires an understanding of the children themselves. Teachers need to make judgements about the extent to which their pupils:

- are mature enough and dextrous enough to handle geographical equipment (e.g. a clinometer or compass);
- can be expected to take responsibility for themselves and their actions; and
- can understand and observe early years setting/school rules and conventions (e.g. no running).

These assessments form an important part of the decision-making process when establishing a safe learning environment. Once these issues have been thought through, teachers can then employ their common sense to reduce risks to acceptable levels when deciding on what artefacts and resources to introduce into the nursery or classroom and by thinking carefully about the organization of space and resources. Storage areas containing geography resources ought to be correctly labelled using words and pictures, and children should be encouraged to refer to the labels and take some responsibility for organizing their own learning when selecting and handling these resources. Teachers need to encourage pupils to make choices, to select equipment and materials, to take responsibility for keeping the classroom tidy, and to develop their own resource management skills.

Some geography activities – for example, those requiring children to examine photographs, maps or artefacts, seek out information or role-play aspects of life in a place – may be quite noisy and dynamic, while others, like painting and model-making, are potentially messy. As a result, teachers will need to plan and establish a mixture of clearly defined areas and general-purpose spaces in the nursery or classroom, where there should be sufficient space for different activities. Furniture can be used to mark out and define areas, such as quiet areas and ICT areas in which children may seek out geographical information, although it is important to make sure that these arrangements do not hinder a teacher's ability to observe and monitor children's learning.

In addition to teachers' common law duty to care for their pupils, they are also bound by the provisions of the Health and Safety at Work Act 1974. Under the provisions of this Act, it is forbidden for any employee, including a teacher, to meddle or interfere with anything provided for the purpose of ensuring people's health and safety. Employees must also have a care for their own safety at work and the safety of others that might be affected either by their actions or by their failure to act. Teachers are required to co-operate with other members of staff who have duties under the Act such as the school's health and safety representative or the first aid specialist.

Schools and nurseries have health and safety policies (often based on LEA policies) and staff are expected to be familiar with the content of these policies. For example, activities involving potentially hazardous material need very careful supervision and in some cases will necessitate adult involvement, for example using sand and gravel in a stream tray to model river processes. Children must understand the importance of safety and, where necessary, teachers may restrict usage of some resources to adults only.

Teaching and Learning Resources for Geography

Geographical resources should be as up to date as possible to reflect the changing nature of the world both at local level and globally. They should also be evaluated carefully to ensure, for example, that a photopack portrays a balanced picture of life in a particular locality and avoids stereotypical images (see Chapter 8).

A full set of Ordnance Survey maps is unnecessary but having a range of maps is important. The local authority or local library can often help obtain maps of the local area, as they will have a licence from the Ordnance Survey for using them in an educational context. Geography advisers should be able to provide further details. Large-scale maps related to local planning issues can be collected: if the area around the school is part of a traffic-calming scheme, then this will be mapped and the local planning department will have copies. Local tourist offices, shopping centres and transport interchanges have a range of maps and plans drawn from many different perspectives. A wide-ranging collection of map styles can be built up quickly and relatively cheaply. The resources in Boxes 6.1 to 6.5 would enable the effective delivery of the geography curriculum.

Box 6.1   Maps

- large-scale Ordnance Survey maps (1:1250 in urban areas, 1:2500 in rural areas, 1:10,000 available for all areas)
- medium-scale Ordnance Survey maps (1:25,000, 1:5000)
- street and road maps, tourist maps
- school plan
- plan of the classroom (drawn by the teacher)
- atlases appropriate for Key Stages 1 and 2
- globes (blank outline, simple political and physical)
- plastic-covered maps (UK, Europe, the world)
- jigsaws
- play-mat with model buildings, people, vehicles, etc.

Satellite images are available from the Geographical Association as a resource pack which features St Lucia and UK locations (see Barnett *et al.*, 1994) and are increasingly available from the Internet (see pp. 129–30). Any type of image, whether it be from a satellite or from the school's camera, needs to be protected. Consider laminating all photos and decide whether it would be beneficial to mount them on large pieces of card, thereby allowing children to surround the image with questions or labels. Oblique aerial and vertical photos are often available through the local authority advisory service and are also becoming available on the Internet (www.multimap.com). Photopacks have been the mainstay of many schools' contrasting and distant locality studies for the past decade. Again, the materials within them need careful management. They could be kept in a ring binder or on display boards and checked regularly to ensure that photographs do not go missing.

Teachers can locate and collect resources to supplement these materials. St Lucia has perhaps the widest variety of published resources in this format, most of which are available through the Geographical Association and Worldaware, although resources on the Indian village of Chembakoli have recently been updated by Action-Aid. Many excellent television programmes exist such as the geography Landmarks series (BBC) and *Zig-Zag*. The BBC Education website also hosts materials to support the programmes.

Non-fiction texts such as the Wayland series 'Countries of the World' and biographies of children and families such as *Children Just Like Me* (Gavin, 1997) are useful to support geographical learning. Fiction texts with a geographical focus or theme have been in use for many years and have received extra attention through the use of big books in the National Literacy Strategy. Examples of geographical fiction include the Katie Morag stories by Marie Hedderwick, the Geographical Association's Barnaby Bear big books, and *Handa's Surprise* by Eileen Browne. Each text links very well with existing geography units such as 'An island home' and 'Where in the world is Barnaby Bear?', and they are exciting ways into the geography of Coll, Dublin, Brittany and Kenya.

Consider making up place boxes to support learning about particular localities. Large 'tidy-boxes' with lids can be filled with artefacts and materials that represent the local area, and the other national and international localities that are being investigated. These resources can also be used to create exciting environments in the home corner or role-play area.

Wildgoose Publications (www.wgoose.co.uk) produces a catalogue that provides all the fieldwork equipment that may be needed. Many of these resources may be available in the school to support science and technology teaching and most early years settings will have 'small world' resources already.

Obtaining and managing the resources is important, but using them intelligently in a critical way is also crucial. It can be all too easy for students and teachers to present resources about places as the single explanation of what life is like in that place. One photograph, artefact or story cannot hope to represent the totality of human and physical geography in a place. Place resources should be seen as evidence (as in a portrait or artefact used in history) or media (as in adverts, brochures and other texts examined in English). Using a wide range of resources is essential for children to gain a rich sense of place concerning the localities they are learning

Box 6.2   Photographs

- satellite images
- postcards, slides
- photographs of the local area (human features, physical features, evidence of change, etc.)
- aerial photographs (oblique and vertical views)
- video: moving images of places and environments as well as video footage shot by teachers and children
- photopacks for locality studies

Box 6.3   Primary and secondary sources

- topical newspaper extracts
- travel brochures
- artefacts (menus, stamps, currency, music, newspapers)
- samples of local rocks, soils and fossils
- goods: fairly traded goods such as tea and coffee; packaging from goods may reveal local as well as international place of origin

Box 6.4   ICT

- Roamer
- digital camera
- CD-ROMs
- email
- software for word processing, desktop publishing, data handling and spreadsheets
- data logging, mapping, graphing, games and simulations
- aerial photographs in electronic form
- maps in electronic form

Box 6.5   Measuring instruments and modelling equipment

- compasses, clinometer
- rain gauge, wind vane, thermometers, anemometer
- trundle-wheel
- stream tank/sand tray/guttering, sand, gravel, rocks of various sizes
- 'small world' resources: people, buildings, animals, Lego, Duplo track

about. Equally, giving children the chance to question the resources that they use can help to develop their thinking skills. Try the activities and questions below to hone your own critical thinking skills in preparation for using resources to support a unit of work.

Critical thinking and resources

- How many different sources will you use during the unit of work?
- Does the same publisher or agency produce them?
- What types of media will you use? Can you justify why you have used a range of media or stuck to just text, video or photographs?
- How does your medium-term planning allow for reflective, creative and critical thinking?
- Who chooses the enquiry questions?
- Are alternative interpretations shown?
- Does your class have the opportunity to evaluate the evidence gathered during the enquiry?
- Who draws the conclusions? You, the children, or both?

Critically evaluating locality packs

Try these activities on any locality pack you already use or are about to buy:

1 Who produced the pack?
   - A commercial publisher, a charity, a government organization?
2 What is its function?
   - Mainly to give information? To highlight injustice? To advertise a product?
3 What impact will it have on the individuals portrayed in the pack?
   - Will they benefit from the sales of the pack? Will their locality become inundated with visitors?
4 Question the information in the pack.
   - When was it researched? Who researched it? Who took the photographs, made the video, wrote the 'day in the life'? How many different viewpoints are represented? How does the pack present controversial issues?
5 How does it compare to the focus of your own locality pack?
   - Are the views of the people presented? To what extent does it rely on materials produced by the school, the tourist office or the local authority?
6 How is the information presented, aesthetically? Would you redesign it?
   - Do the text and images communicate their message clearly? Is it attractive to its chosen audience?
7 What feedback would you give to the creators of the pack?
   - What questions are left unanswered or not even raised? Do they acknowledge that the pack is only one view or do they present it as 'the truth'?

Using the School or Nursery Grounds

The Early Learning Goals and the geography Programme of Study for Key Stages 1 and 2 both implicitly and explicitly suggest that teachers should use the school or nursery grounds as a resource for fieldwork learning. In the Foundation Stage the children are likely to have access to a well-designed outdoor play space with appropriate wheel toys, play furniture and hard and soft surfaces. Teachers at Key Stages 1 and 2 may not be as well served by their school grounds, but a small amount of work can often provide an excellent learning environment for developing geographical skills, investigating environmental and sustainability issues, and observing physical processes working at a small scale. Teachers and students can maximize the use of the school or nursery grounds in the following ways.

Making use of the school grounds

- **Creating a map of the grounds**. It can be drawn from a 1:10,000 or 1:2500 Ordnance Survey map, or an architect's plan of the school. This can be used on A4 paper as a base map for fieldwork, for designing trails or for orienteering activities. The same map drawn on a play-mat can be used for modelling and indoor navigation.
- **Taking photographs of the grounds**. Photographs of the human and physical features in the grounds, and photos of children at work and play outside, can be used for sorting activities and to support way-finding and location activities in conjunction with a map of the area.
- **Painting a compass rose on the play area**. Children can use the compass rose to learn about direction and then use this information in enquiries. For example, would we want to sit outside on the north or the south side of the building today? Which direction is the wind coming from today?
- **Planning an environmental area**. Many schools and early years settings have created an environmental area in part of the grounds. Children can be involved in planning and maintaining such an area. This is a large-scale, medium-term project that is not to be undertaken lightly. Often much help can be gained from the local authority, who will support such developments through Local Agenda 21 initiatives, or urban development schemes funded from the Single Regeneration Budget (SRB).

Organizing and Managing Safe Fieldwork

The impact of geographical fieldwork experiences and other learning outdoors can stay in a learner's mind for a lifetime. The excitement of visiting a new place, travelling on the train or bus with friends, following a trail or completing a survey in a group can all be remembered decades after the actual experience. However, for teachers the experience of organizing, leading and following up fieldwork can be fraught. Well-publicized accidents that have occurred to children when in the care of their teachers out of school are a sombre reminder that fieldwork experiences have the potential to endanger children. As with any other aspect of geography teaching, planning and preparation are essential in order to gain the maximum educational benefit from fieldwork, and to ensure the health and safety of the children.

Teachers need to weigh up the appropriateness of potential fieldwork sites for their pupils. Younger children may benefit more from sites closer to the nursery/school, whilst older pupils may be better able to cope with a long journey and make more sense of the geography associated with a more distant location. A preliminary visit without the children is crucial in order to become familiar with what the site has to offer, and to assess potential hazards. Teachers will need to think through the logistics, health and safety, and housekeeping issues associated with outside visits – for example, conducting a risk assessment and making the arrangements for travel, toileting, feeding and sheltering the children. A preliminary visit may also provide valuable information for drafting letters to parents dealing with issues such as pocket money, clothing and footwear. Having visited a site will enable a teacher to talk from experience when matching pupils to adults and issuing reminders about standards of behaviour and risk avoidance.

It is also important to establish clear purposes for the visit and share these with the other adults who will be accompanying the group. The fieldwork learning style (see p. 105) needs to be explained to the helpers. If the children are to act as 'geographical detectives' and use an enquiry approach, then adults need to be discouraged from providing all the answers. Using a briefing sheet such as that shown in Box 6.6 can help in this process. Think through, and write down, what will happen during the field visit. Where on the site will the children be recording data or participating in an activity? When will the class be together as a whole group and when will they be working with the other adult helpers? Where will they eat? Where exactly will you, as responsible teacher, be during the fieldwork? How often will you be checking the location of each group? How will you manage the safe use of any fieldwork equipment? How will you draw the fieldwork to a close? What will happen after the visit? What follow-up work will the children engage in? Remember that with young children the chance to talk about their observations and experiences fairly soon after the visit is likely to aid retention and learning.

Whenever pupils are taken beyond the confines of the nursery/school, staff have to consider the health and safety implications. Teachers should always conduct a risk assessment prior to visiting a site, copies of which should be given to adult helpers with a further copy remaining on file in the school. It is important to bear in mind that when assessing risk there is a need to give consideration to *likelihood* as well as *severity*, and to take steps to minimize the risks to the children. Completing a fresh risk assessment pro forma, such as the one shown in Figure 6.2, serves a number of important functions in the preparation of successful fieldwork.

Box 6.6   Briefing sheet and notes for parent helpers

Site: Ecclesall Road

Year group: Y3

Unit of work: Investigating our local area

Purposes of visit:

- To identify land use in a small area of the road (e.g. houses, shops, roads, services, parkland, school) and record on a map of the area.
- To record images of the land use using a camera.

Parent activities

1 Show the children how to match up the map with the buildings around you.
2 Remind the children how they can record land use on the map.
3 Rotate the use of the camera so all children take at least two photographs.

Suggested questions for the children

1 Which buildings are used as shops?
2 Which buildings are used as houses?
3 Show me where the park is on the map.
4 Show me where we are standing on the map.
5 Do any buildings have more than one use?
6 How can you tell that a building may have more than one use?
7 Why do you think there are so many fast-food shops [or similar land use] in this section?

Names of children in your group

1 Aimee Weaver
2 Shahida Roshni
3 Philip Staniforth
4 Billy Wazcek
5 Hayley Price
6 Leon Sharpe

First, it acts as a checklist or aide-mémoire in the planning process. Consistent completion of such a form is a major step towards a well-planned and safe visit. It requires teachers to be focused about teaching and learning activities and to identify hazards (such as traffic) and the level of risk (low, medium or high), and to state the action to be taken to limit exposure to such hazards. Provision for children with special needs is taken into account, as are emergency procedures and the need for the teacher to be contactable by mobile phone.

Visit planner / Risk assessment

Year group   Y3

Number of children   28

Details of adult helpers

Class teacher and leader Cherie May

Other adults Philip Peascod (student teacher), Kim Brown, Terri Sharpe, Frances Fisher (all parents)

Destination Ecclesall Road and Endcliffe Park

Transport Supervised walk from school

Date 14/06/2001

Timing 0930–1200

Preliminary visit made (YES)/ NO

Adult helpers briefed (YES)/ NO

Learning objectives

- To identify land use in a small area of the road and record on a map of the area
- To record images of the land use using a camera

Activities

- Land use mapping
- Land use interpretation
- Photograph taking

Resources

- One camera per group of six children
- One base map of area per two children
- Clipboards
- Land use key (designed by children in preliminary work)

Hazards	Level of risk (high/medium/low)	Action taken
Traffic	Medium	Children briefed about dangers of stepping onto road and required not to leave group; children only cross road at crossing with their teacher or adult.
Pets in park	Medium	Children and adults instructed not to touch animals and to check potential sitting areas for dog mess.
Other pedestrians	Low	Adults briefed to avoid obstructing other pedestrians when with group.
Weather	Low	Forecast obtained. Children and parents wearing appropriate clothing and footwear. Adults have spare hats and water if sun is strong.

Pupils with special needs likely to affect safety   Catherine McGowan: asthma

Action required   Inhaler with class teacher

Mobile phone number 08708 1232134   **School telephone number** 0114 555 34344

Mobile and medication held by   Cherie May

Signed	Date	Emergency procedures
Cherie May	12/1/01	• Secure safety of group • Contact emergency services if necessary • Contact teacher responsible (Cherie)

Figure 6.2 Visit planner/risk assessment

Second, although this process may seem daunting, it gives you written evidence of your fieldwork planning. This is useful both for planning future visits to the same site or other locations, and for providing evidence of your safe planning in the now unlikely situation of an accident. Conducting a risk assessment is therefore much more than just a paper exercise as it is an integral part of fieldwork preparation. Equally, vigilance does not stop after the completion of a risk assessment. The teacher shown in Figure 6.3 is continually posing questions to herself throughout the development, actual visit and follow-up of a fieldwork experience.

No child can be taken out of nursery/school without the parents' permission. Have I sent letters to parents informing them of the details of the visit such as appropriate clothing, dates and times?

What are the procedures in the event of an emergency or accident, for example a fire alarm? Do I have an emergency kit (sick bags, 'wet wipes', spare clothing)?

Have I briefed accompanying parents/adults about the visit and their role? Which children are they to accompany? What should they wear? Have I explained why the children are going, and what the learning purposes of the visit are?

Do any of the children have special needs? Have I planned for this?

Have I explained to the children where they are going, who with, why and what's expected?

Where will the children eat, sit, keep dry and go to the toilet?

Have I checked the site beforehand?

Have I checked the route? What are the safest crossing points, and are there any toilets en route just in case? Do I know the bus times, stopping places and alternative routes in the event of a non-arrival? Have I told the bus company that we are making the visit?

Have I got enough adults to supervise the children adequately? (For example, a ratio of 3:1 in nursery, and 6:1 with infants ensures a high margin of error.)

Are there any particular hazards to avoid?

Figure 6.3 Planning a visit

Information and Communications Technology as a Resource for Geography

Information and communications technology (ICT, including computers, calculators, video, tape recorders, etc.) has had a profound effect upon our lives and its growth in recent years has been exponential. The presence of computers in nurseries and schools has increased considerably since the 1980s. Many bases and classrooms have more than one machine and some primary schools have dedicated ICT suites. However, the provision varies from school to school, as these comments from students and OFSTED (posted on Student email Conference November 2000) reveal.

> School A is a brand new school with a purpose-built ICT suite and a full-time assistant who is responsible for the smooth running of it. Each class is allocated a 40-minute slot per week and the IT lady liaises with the class teacher to discuss what the focus will be, gives ideas of resources on the Web and gets it set up ready for the class before they arrive . . . very good for time management as I found when I took the class myself! They also have a wide range of software that is catalogued and kept in the ICT suite. Each class also has its own computer which I thought wasn't used to its best advantage because they tend to rely on the weekly visit to the computer suite. There are also classes for parents to come in and get some expert tuition from an outside tutor. I was very impressed!

> School B was visited by OFSTED inspecting the partnership provision provided by primary schools and a higher education institution. After visiting the school the inspector commented that the ability of students to use ICT effectively was marred by the presence of broken computers and out-of-date software.

The final section of this chapter will focus on the resources students and teachers can use if they are working in a setting that has adequate hardware provision such as a PC in each classroom, as well as access to the World Wide Web and email from at least one location in the school or nursery.

Opportunities for using ICT in Key Stage 1 and Key Stage 2 geography

Analysis of the ICT opportunities in the original sixteen QCA geography units (Table 6.1) gives a clear picture of the resource implications for geography teaching. Children need to have access to simple and more complex chart-drawing facilities, to word processing applications and desktop publishing, to a database and simple simulation software such as *MyWorld*. They need access to the Internet for email and ideally to publish pages on the school Web site. They need to use reference materials on CD-ROM and search engines such as Ask Jeeves for Kids for Internet research. Access to simple mapping software such as *Local Studies* and the use of the school video camera is necessary.

Table 6.1 **ICT opportunities in the QCA units of work**

Unit no.	Unit title	ICT used
1	Around our school – the local area	Children can draw simple charts of how children in the class come to school.
2	How can we make our local area safer?	Children create, describe and explain charts of parked cars in a street, and use the evidence to locate a crossing.
3	An island home (Struay)	Children can design their own island using a simple drawing package, mapping package or use the *MyWorld* screen entitled 'Island'.
4	Going to the seaside	Children use a simple database and create charts showing the results of a school survey ('What is the most popular place visited?').
5	Where in the world is Barnaby Bear?	With teacher assistance, the children publish a class newspaper on the school Web site showing where Barnaby has been.
6	Investigating our local area	Children use different types of software to present their results – mark on base map, database, simple graphs, simple pie charts.
7	Weather around the world	Children research chosen holiday destination (CD-ROMs). Use a concept keyboard or multimedia resource to find out about life in that locality (similarities and differences).
8	Improving the environment	Children use graphs to demonstrate movement around the school. Graph to show the weight of rubbish collected.
9	Village settlers	Children use mapping software to make a map of a village showing physical constraints on development.
10	A village in India	Children use CD-ROMs and the Internet to find diverse images of India.
11	Water	A spreadsheet is used to display the use of water at home.
12	Should the high street be closed to traffic?	Spreadsheets and graphing software are used to display data concerning traffic issues.
13	A contrasting UK locality – Llandudno	Create a map of a coastal location using a simple mapping package and use the World Wide Web.
14	Investigating rivers	Enter and store data in a data file. Use ICT to provide a project folder on a local river using CD-ROMs and simple desktop publishing software.
15	The mountain environment	Use CD-ROMs for research, and Internet weather forecast services.
16	What's in the news?	Use word processing and desktop publishing to report a local or global issue. Create a radio or video news report.

ICT resources for geography learning

Geography-specific software

Some packages set out to provide information in support of specific places and themes within the geography curriculum such as the Worldaware *Village Life in India* CD-ROM or support specific geographical skills such as Softeach Education's *Local Studies* mapping package and *Weather Reporter* package. *Mapventure*, produced by Sherston Software, allows the children to learn about scale through a ride in a hot air balloon. CD-ROM atlases include the *Ordnance Survey Interactive Atlas of Great Britain* and the *Oxford Talking Infant Atlas.* It can be unwise to purchase too many geography-specific packages as the enquiry-based nature of the subject fits well with using generic open-ended software as discussed in the next section.

Generic software

Generic software is not specifically related to any particular geography topic, but can be used to extend and enhance children's efforts to communicate through geographical enquiry. Word processing packages include *Textease* (Softease Ltd), which is a simple-to-use word processor and desktop publisher, and *Talking First Word* (Black Cat Software). *Junior Pinpoint* (Longman Logotron) is an excellent database and chart-drawing package that can support much enquiry-based work, whereas *Graph_IT* (Sherston Software) is a simple tool to produce bar, pie and scatter graphs. *Dazzle* (Semerc Software) allows Foundation, Key Stage 1 and Key Stage 2 children to 'paint' and draw on the computer, and *MyWorld* (also Semerc) is a very popular package in which children can move objects to create villages, make weather forecasts and learn to read maps.

Communications technologies: email and the Internet

Numerous Web sites exist with a geographical content. Many are not suitable for direct use by children, although some schools have started to produce their own Web sites in which geographical topics feature. Those sites that are not appropriate for children as a result of the subject matter or the level at which the text is written can still offer teachers a considerable source of information with which to inform their teaching (see the list below). Children can search using search engines such as Ask Jeeves for Kids which censor the questions they ask and sites that are returned to them. The Central Bureau for Educational Visits and Exchanges (www.centralbureau.org.uk) provides a service to link schools across Europe and beyond. Such links provide a real context for email use as well as enabling children to use email to contact other schools or ask 'experts' geographical questions.

Other new technologies

The use of digital cameras is growing in schools as the price of all computing hardware comes down. Nurseries and schools have used them to record products the children have made and to record fieldwork evidence, as well as provide images that can be edited and altered in a graphics package such as *Paint* (available on all PCs). On the 'technology horizon' is the use of global positioning systems (GPS) in primary schools, the wider use of speech recognition software and increased access to video conferencing.

Useful geographical Web sites for teachers

- The Geographical Association: the source for resources, links and professional development
  http://www.geography.org.uk

- Schemes of work for Geography
  http://www.standards.dfee.gov.uk/schemes/geography

- Programmes of Study for Key Stages 1 to 3 and level descriptions
  http://www.nc.uk.net/servlets/NCFrame?subject=Gg

- Staffordshire Geography Guidance: an award-winning site with lots of useful links and information for primary school teachers and children
  http://www.sln.org.uk/geography/

- Enhancing geography with ICT
  http://vtc.ngfl.gov.uk/resource/cits/geog/index.html

- United States Geological Survey: great ideas for teaching using maps and images
  http://rockyweb.cr.usgs.gov/public/outreach

- Ordnance Survey: some free images and information about all OS products.
  http://www.ordnancesurvey.co.uk

- ESRI Schools and Libraries page: free software and a great introduction to GIS (Geographical Information Systems)
  http://www.esri.com/k-12

- Internet aerial photography: a portal for overhead imagery from all over the world. Includes UK images.
  http://www.terraserver.com/

- UK StreetMaps: interactive map of the British Isles, searchable by postcode.
  http://uk.multimap.com/map/browse.cgi

- Geography World: lots of useful links at the teacher's and children's level on all aspects of geography
  http://members.aol.com/bowermanb/101.html

- Geography Discipline Network: a geography in higher education site that is a good starting point when searching for research articles
  http://www.chelt.ac.uk/el/philg/gdn/

ICT, the teacher and resource organization

Currently, the standards for initial teacher education require geography specialists to be able to demonstrate that they can review, select and effectively organize ICT resources for use in an early years setting or school. Beginning teachers and students need to be able to answer the following questions based on their practice working with children aged 3–11. These questions highlight the fact that the teacher is still indispensable in ICT-based learning. To conclude this section it is worth reflecting on the three key principles (TTA, 1999) that should govern the selection and use of ICT resources in geography. The first principle is that ICT should be used only to support good practice in teaching the subject. The second is that resources selected should be directly related to the teaching and learning objectives of a particular teaching session. The final principle is that using ICT should allow the learner to achieve something that could not be achieved without it.

The most effective organization of classroom ICT resources to meet learning objectives in geography

- Does a large monitor, TV screen or display need to be used for whole-class teaching when discussing the advantages and disadvantages of using *Local Studies*?
- When should the children be working away from the computer(s) – for example, when discussing what to include in a desktop publishing report on a local issue?
- When can children work in the classroom with ICT for a short time – for example, listening to a weather forecast, asking a question using Ask Jeeves for Kids, or entering their group's data into a class graph, answering a particular question using a CD-ROM?
- How can you ensure that the computer-based work does not distract the other children in the class (e.g. limiting the sound level when using the *Talking Infant Atlas*)?

Choose and use the most suitable ICT to meet teaching objectives, by critically reviewing a range of generic and geography-specific software

- What is its potential to enhance children's learning in geography? For example, do the animations in a CD-ROM help the understanding of coastal physical processes? Does the software help develop the skills associated with map reading, e.g. *Mapventure*?
- Do materials show bias – for example, in how people in distant places are portrayed, or how roles of men and women are shown?
- Are the geographical vocabulary and concepts used oversimplified or too complex for Foundation, Key Stage 1 or Key Stage 2 children?

In conclusion, although geography is a strongly resource-based subject, it is still the practitioner or teacher, and the other children in the class, who are the most important resources. Without interaction between the children, and between the children and teacher, learning will be limited and enthusiasm for learning unused. It is only the practitioner's or teacher's skilful use of resources that can unleash the children's natural curiosity about people and places around the world.

Reflective Questions

- Do you use geographical questions to structure your geography displays?
- How do you locate the geographical resources in your classroom? What is accessible to you and what is accessible to the children?
- How do you use globes, atlases and wallmaps in your continuing geographical work?

- What percentage of your resources was bought in the past five years?
- What geographical resources have you created or collected yourself?
- How do you use the school or nursery grounds to support geographical learning?
- What fieldwork locations do you and your colleagues use? Why were they chosen?
- How do you use the base or classroom computer to support geographical learning?
- How do you use the Internet to develop your own subject knowledge and professional skills in geography?

FURTHER READING

Barnett, M., Kent, A., and Milton, M. (1994) *Images of Earth: A Teachers' Guide to Remote Sensing in Geography at Key Stage 2. Sheffield: Geographical Association.*

Bowles, R. (1999) *Resources for Key Stages 1 and 2*. Sheffield: Geographical Association.

Rachel Bowles has created a directory of every possible resource needed for primary geography, complete with information on where to obtain the resources and how to use them. A must for every geography co-ordinator.

Fieldwork in Action Series (1993–8), published by the Geographical Association:

1 *Planning Fieldwork*. May, S., Richardson, P. and Banks, V.

2 *An Enquiry Approach*. May, S. and Cook, J.

3 *Managing Out-of-Classroom Activities*. Thomas, T. and May, S.

4 *Primary Fieldwork Projects*. May, S. (ed.)

5 *Mapping Land Use*. Richardson, P. and Walford, R.

6 *Crossing the Channel*. Richardson, P. and Whiting, S.

Humanities Education Centre (1996) *Storyworlds: Ideas for Teaching Primary Geography Using 10 Popular Children's Stories*. London: Humanities Education Centre.

Milner, A. (1997) *Geography through Play*. Sheffield: Geographical Association.

Norris Nicholson, H. (1994) *Place in Story-Time: Geography through Stories at Key Stages 1 and 2*. Sheffield: Geographical Association.

Pickford, T. (1999) *ICT and Geographical Enquiry*. Sheffield: Geographical Association.

GEOGRAPHY RESOURCE SUPPLIERS

ActionAid, Chataway House, Leach Road, Chard, Somerset TA20 1FA. www.oneworld.org/actionaid

BBC Education: www.bbc.co.uk/education

BECTa Publications, Milburn Hill Road, Science Park, Coventry CV4 7JJ. www.becta.org.uk

Central Bureau for Educational Visits and Exchanges, 10 Spring Gardens, London SW1A 2BN. www.centralbureau.org.uk

Development Education Association, 29–31 Cowper Street, London EC1A 4AP.

Environment Agency, Head Office, Rio House, Waterside Drive, Aztec West, Almondsbury, Bristol BS12 4UD. Tel: 0645 333111.

Field Studies Council, Preston Montford, Shrewsbury SY4 1HW.

Geographical Association, 160 Solly Street, Sheffield S1 4BF.
www.geography.org.uk

MJP Geopacks, 92–104 Carnwath Road, London SW6 3HW.

Ordnance Survey, Education Department, Romsey Road, Southampton SO16 4GU.
www.ordnancesurvey.co.uk

OXFAM, 274 Banbury Road, Oxford OX2 7GZ.
www.oxfam.org

Wayland Multimedia, 61 Western Road, Hove, East Sussex BN3 1JD.
www.wayland.co.uk

Wildgoose Publications, The Reading Room, Dennis Street, Hugglescote, Leicestershire LE67 2FP.
www.wildgoose.co.uk

Worldaware, 31–35 Kirby Street, London EC1N 8TE.

REFERENCES

Gavin, J. (ed.) (1997) *Children Just Like Me*. London: Dorling Kindersley/UNICEF.

Teacher Training Agency (TTA)(1999) *Using Information and Communications Technology to Meet Teaching Objectives in Primary Geography*. London: TTA.

7 Monitoring and Assessing Children's Learning in Geography

In recent years, assessment in education has become increasingly important. Governments have been concerned to 'measure' educational outputs in order to enable comparisons between schools to be made and to inform parents about schools' performance. Assessment has also been seen as a means of raising the standard of pupils' achievements.

Teachers, meanwhile, have developed their expertise in using different forms and methods of assessment. Successful teachers use their subject knowledge effectively and develop a range of skills. These skills include the ability to employ a variety of assessment strategies in order to plan, teach and promote children's learning.

This chapter begins by considering the different purposes of assessing children's learning in geography and what teachers should focus on in their assessments. It then looks at various forms of assessment and a number of ways in which children's progress in geography can be assessed. The chapter focuses on formative assessment. This involves identifying what children have achieved in order to plan the next stage and is seen as the most important form of assessment in terms of children's learning (Blyth and Krause, 1995). Finally, suggestions are made as to how teachers can record their assessments and how they might report to parents on children's progress. The chapter emphasizes that systems for assessing and recording children's work in geography and for reporting on their progress need to be simple, straightforward and manageable.

Why Assess Children's Learning in Geography?

Assessment can take place before, during and following teaching. The process involves gathering, and sometimes recording, then interpreting and using information gleaned from children's responses to educational tasks for a variety of purposes. Assessment should be integral to the planning process and, through a spiral approach to the curriculum, enable children to revisit aspects of geography at progressively greater levels of refinement and understanding. The focus of the curriculum on the core subjects accompanied by target-setting and the publication of the results of Standard Assessment Tests (SATs), means that most teachers now prioritize statutory assessment of English, maths and science. Nevertheless, irrespective of legal requirements such as reporting on children's attainment to parents, assessment lies at the heart of promoting their learning in any subject (TGAT, 1988), and there are a number of reasons why assessing children's learning in geography is worthwhile, for teachers, pupils and a wider audience (Table 7.1).

Table 7.1 **Purposes of assessment in geography**

Purpose of assessment	Example of what a teacher might do
To identify what children can/cannot do	Ask children to draw a plan of the classroom
To identify what children know/do not know	Initiate a brainstorm at the beginning of a topic on a contrasting locality
To identify what children understand/do not understand	Ask children to explain how certain coastal features have been formed
To find out how well children have achieved what was intended	Ask children to list similarities and differences between two localities
To inform planning for groups and individuals	Elicit children's (possibly stereotypical) images of a locality to be studied
To extend children through appropriate intervention	Observe children, then take on the role of customer in an estate agent role-play
To check whether children are ready for the next stage in a particular progression of learning	Consider how successfully children interpret oblique aerial photographs
To consider whether a child has made satisfactory progress	Compare Year 2 and Year 4 end-of-year reports on geography
To provide feedback to pupils about their progress	Mark and comment on children's interpretations of weather data they have collected
To help pupils devise personal targets	Ask children to evaluate their use of mapping software
To motivate pupils	Provide constructive feedback based on assessment
To summarize children's attainment	Produce an end-of-unit record or yearly report for parents
To place children against different descriptors of achievement	Make a summative assessment at the end of a Key Stage
To identify how children are performing relative to others of a similar age	Compare achievements of children in a parallel year group undertaking the same activity
To record whole-class progress	Produce records to pass on to the next teacher
To illustrate the school's standards of attainment in geography	Level a range of children's work for inclusion in the school's geography portfolio
To evaluate the effectiveness of one's own practice	Determine whether the use of a compass was explained sufficiently clearly in a lesson
To evaluate the geography curriculum provided by the school	The geography co-ordinator reviews teachers' end-of-year records

What to Assess in Geography

Assessment should focus initially on children's achievement in individual lessons or activities, in other words the extent to which they have met the learning objective, which will have been drawn from the National Curriculum (2000) Programme of Study for geography or Early Learning Goals. These assessments will contribute to identifying their progress in the four aspects of geography:

- geographical enquiry and skills (for example, can they suggest questions to research about children's lives in a contrasting locality? Can they locate features on a map using four-figure grid references?);
- knowledge and understanding of places (for example, can they identify similarities and differences between housing in the local area and in a contrasting locality?);
- knowledge and understanding of patterns and processes (for example, can they explain how certain features of a local stream have been formed?); and
- knowledge and understanding of environmental change and sustainable development (for example, can they suggest how their school grounds might be improved?).

An activity may often relate to more than one of these. For example:

- Key Stage 1: children draw a map to show where litter can be found in the playground (skills and patterns).
- Key Stage 2: children produce a poster identifying views for and against plans to construct a wind farm in the local area (skills, places and environmental change).

However, there are also other, cross-curricular elements of children's learning (as well as their interest in geography) on which teachers can comment. These include how well they co-operate with each other when they are engaged on geographical tasks, their attitude towards the environment, other people and places, and their understanding of what it means to be a global citizen. In addition, the work children produce may demonstrate their creative abilities as well as their geographical understanding – for example, through writing stories and poems, drawing, using ICT or producing a display.

It is worth remembering that assessment is not an exact science and that it is more difficult to assess some areas of children's geographical learning than others. For instance, assessing whether children can describe the location of a feature by using a four-figure grid reference is relatively straightforward. Determining to what extent they are developing a sense of environmental responsibility or a sense of place is more problematic. Moreover, children may appear to have grasped, for example, a new skill but be unable to use or apply it in a different context. Furthermore, much of the knowledge and understanding of very young children is fleeting in nature and they need constantly to revisit and revise their experiences. Because their thinking is extensively driven by cues in the context, it is often very difficult to be sure what they have learned (Edwards and Knight, 1994).

Assessment and monitoring of children's learning in geography should take place within the context of the school assessment policy. This should indicate, for example, how and when children's attainment is to be assessed. Opportunities for assessment should be identified in the school's scheme of work for geography wherever it might be appropriate to check on the development of particular skills, knowledge or understanding within the four aspects of geography.

Forms of Assessment

In order to acquire information on children's learning, teachers can undertake different forms of assessment, both formal and informal, summative and formative, criterion and norm referenced. These may be carried out in various combinations: for example, intervening in what children are doing as part of everyday teaching is informal and formative; matching children's work to a particular level is summative, criterion-referenced assessment. Similarly, summative assessments can be used formatively by subsequent teachers. It can be difficult for assessment to serve several possibly conflicting purposes, and thus clarifying its purpose enables the appropriate form of assessment to be chosen.

Informal and formal assessment in geography

Informal assessment takes place as an integral, unplanned part of everyday teaching. A teacher, for example, may look at the work on which a child is engaged, praise his or her efforts so far, and assess his or her needs and respond appropriately with a question, a suggestion, an explanation or a slight adjustment to the task. This type of assessment can provide instant feedback to children and thus motivate them. It can help teachers deal there and then with any misunderstandings which have arisen or develop teaching points further if necessary.

Teachers store much of this information in their heads and these assessments are not usually recorded unless they are of particular significance. Once teachers get to know the children in their class, they are usually able to anticipate their needs. However, it is always worth considering alternative ways of explaining a task or presenting information should this prove necessary, as well as ensuring that there are worthwhile extension tasks planned for those who may need them.

Extension tasks and alternative presentation of information

Danny (Reception) had confidently and accurately completed a task which involved him sorting pictures of different clothing into those that he would wear in winter and those he would wear in summer. His teacher praised him and suggested that he now drew two sets of pictures showing the kinds of things he might do in winter and summer.

Shahida (Year 4) had not started a written task which involved describing how the local environment was being improved, following fieldwork the class had undertaken: 'I don't know what to write.' Her teacher referred her to the display of photographs which the children had taken and wrote down some cue words such as *traffic*, *litter* and *dogs* to help her.

Formal assessment, on the other hand, has a specific purpose, criteria for success and a method for collecting evidence which are all established before the lesson takes place.

Formal assessment

After a residential visit to a village in the Peak District, children in a Year 3 class were asked to complete a table in order to demonstrate whether they could identify similarities and differences between the village and their local area. Less able children were given specific headings, such as shops, schools and transport. The more able were asked to provide reasons for the differences: this would provide evidence of achievement at a higher level.

Formative and diagnostic assessment in geography

Formative assessment, either formal or informal, is an integral part of the planning–teaching–learning process. Teachers initially enable children to demonstrate what they know, understand or can do and match their achievements against specific learning objectives and criteria for success in the short term, and broader learning objectives in medium-term planning. They can then plan to support children's future learning by providing appropriate 'scaffolding' (Vygotsky, 1978) in order to extend, challenge or reinforce as appropriate. Diagnostic assessment also informs teachers' planning, but this focuses on identifying children's learning difficulties.

Formative assessment allows for individual children to be targeted, for example if a child has clearly misunderstood something, as well as indicating the next stage for larger groups. Formal formative assessment can provide detailed feedback on a child's progress.

Formative assessment

As she was playing outside, Claire (aged 4) was asked to name certain features in order to ascertain the geographical vocabulary she needed to be taught.

A Year 3 class of children began a unit of work focusing on the local area with a task which involved interpreting a picture map. Their teacher wanted to find out whether they were ready to progress to using Ordnance Survey maps.

The results of formative assessment can be shared with children and it can incorporate opportunities for self-assessment. Unlike summative assessment, it can take into account other factors which might affect individual children, such as their lack of experience of other places. It also makes possible a value-added element, in other words how far an individual child has progressed from his or her starting point. Teachers need to be as objective as possible in their assessments, which can sometimes say more about their expectations than about a child's progress (Marsden and Hughes, 1994). They also need to ensure that they are assessing what they set out to assess – that is the geographical content – and do not give undue weight to, for example, a child's presentational skills.

Summative assessment in geography

Summative assessment in geography is not part of everyday classroom activity. It requires teachers to use their ongoing records to summarize children's attainment and may take place at the end of a unit of work, year or Key Stage. It can involve deciding which level description a child's work matches best. Records of these assessments can be used to inform parents or subsequent teachers of children's attainment as well as assisting their class teachers in planning the next geography unit of work.

Self-assessment in geography

Teachers should aim to provide opportunities for all children to assess their own work. The High Scope approach, for example, involves children in early years settings in a cyclical process of planning, doing and then reviewing their activities (Pollard, 1997), and evaluation features as a cross-curricular skill in the National Curriculum (2000). Self-assessment has a number of benefits.

Benefits of self-assessment

- helping children to recognize their capabilities and understand what is needed for their future development;
- helping children to evaluate their learning strategies and achievements; and
- encouraging children to become more active, independent learners as they learn how to assess their own work and set their own learning purposes, and thus gain a sense of ownership of the learning process.

Self-assessment can take place in a number of different ways. The importance of a plenary has been reinforced by the national literacy and numeracy strategies. Here teachers can reinforce the lesson's learning objective, but children can also identify how far they think this has been achieved. In some schools, children compile their own portfolio or record of achievement (PRAE) which is culled and updated regularly. This can be a time-consuming process but it enables children to see how they are making progress by selecting a piece of work for inclusion, say at the end of a unit of work, which is dated and annotated and which shows evidence of their learning.

For self-assessment to be successful, teachers need to do the following.

Enabling successful self-assessment

- Ensure children understand a lesson or activity's learning objective and how it will be assessed.
- Discuss children's work with them: how and why they have done it, how far they understand it, how well they think they have done it.
- Encourage children to identify their 'best work' in terms of the geographical content.
- Encourage children to review their work with their peers, in pairs or in small groups.
- Encourage children to set their own targets (what they will be able to do or know about, for example).
- Let children help to report their progress, for example by writing part of the report to their parents.

Evaluative assessment

Evaluative assessment is slightly different in that it focuses on teaching rather than on individual children's attainment. Reviewing the geography curriculum provided by a school is one of the responsibilities of a geography co-ordinator, as will be explained in Chapter 10. Teachers can also use their assessments to evaluate the effectiveness of their own practice. This was explored in Chapter 4.

Methods of Assessment

The fact that there is no statutory assessment for geography at Key Stage 1 or Key Stage 2 can be seen as an advantage. Teachers do not feel obliged to 'teach to the test' and thus can have more flexibility in using a range of assessment methods as well as making assessment an integral part of planning the geography curriculum. They can plan appropriate tasks through which children can demonstrate what they know, understand or can do. These tasks can be accessible to all children but produce differentiated outcomes, enabling teachers to identify what particular children have learned. This section focuses on different methods that teachers can use to assess children's learning in geography formally, although some of these methods, such as observation, can also be used in informal assessment.

Beginning teachers need to be aware that collecting relevant information through assessment needs practice. It also requires certain skills such as observation, listening and being able to interact with children through discussion, as well as the ability to interpret the information that is collected and use it constructively.

Observation

QCA/DfEE (2000) emphasizes that systematic, focused observation of children's achievements, interests and learning styles should be a fundamental part of the process of teaching, particularly in early years settings. However, observation is not an end in itself: it can help teachers understand children's learning and development and reflect on the effectiveness of their provision, as well as having a formative and summative role. When observing children, it is important that teachers aim to be objective and non-judgemental and see what children are actually doing rather than what they think they are doing or even what they want to see. Unplanned, spontaneous observation can be useful when children are learning independently, but sometimes this provides only partial information which is inadequate for making judgements on children's learning. It is also impossible to record what is happening all the time. Thus it is worth teachers planning to undertake short, clearly focused observations. Observation can be made easier if teachers do the following.

Observation

- Plan for observation – who, what, how and for how long.
- Tell children what you intend to do and what you are looking for.
- Aim to carry out observations in as natural a way as possible, either being unobtrusive or interacting with the children.
- Ask the children not to interrupt; in other words, ensure they have 'getting on' strategies.
- Concentrate on the task in hand and try not to be distracted.
- Avoid the urge to intervene.
- Take notes, perhaps on a pre-planned form.
- Interpret these notes as soon as possible while they are fresh.
- Provide short and focused feedback to the children.

Suitable contexts for observation include the following:

- a child building a model according to a predetermined plan;
- a group using a play-mat with geographical features;
- a group engaged in fieldwork involving measuring and recording features of a stream.

Listening

Teachers may wish to listen to what children have to say to each other whilst engaged on particular tasks; what they say when talking about their work or during a presentation to the class or what they say to their teacher in discussion. As with observation, listening to children needs to be planned for carefully, taking the same points as are identified above into consideration, if the information gained is to be useful. Again, teachers can make brief notes, perhaps on a pre-planned form. Alternatively, children's talk can be tape-recorded, although it is not always easy to distinguish between individual children's contributions, and any background noise may be picked up.

Listening

A Year 4 class was undertaking a unit of work which involved investigating plans to demolish a local pub and use the land for housing. The children had been asked to work in small groups to present the different views of the people they had interviewed. Their teacher had deliberately set up a group of the more able children and he planned to listen to their discussion. He made brief notes on the contribution of all the children, to determine whether they could:

- explain their own views;
- explain the views of others;
- recognize how change might affect the lives of local people;
- recognize how change might alter the nature of the locality;
- recognize how change might be beneficial; and
- recognize how change might have drawbacks.

Questioning

Effective teachers will plan for questioning in geography rather than leave it to chance. Questioning can be a useful tool for diagnosing learning difficulties and developing insight into ways in which children learn and work, as well as for identifying what they know and understand. Questions can be oral or written and similarly require an oral or written response. They can range from questions which require lower-order thinking, for example to answer factual or closed questions, to those which require higher-order thinking, such as comparing, analysing, evaluating or solving problems (Table 7.2). Teachers need to ask both kinds of questions to enable children to make progress in geography: lower-order questioning will encourage children to remember facts, whereas higher-order questions should promote more complex thinking processes. Teachers may also need to provide a core of questions supplemented by further questions to extend the more able.

Concept mapping

Concept mapping involves children in mapping out what they have learned and how it appears to 'fit together'.

Table 7.2 **Questions which will reveal different features of children's geographical knowledge and understanding and their thinking processes**

	Required thinking	Example
Knowledge	Recalling facts or observations	What is the name of the river we saw? Where is Tocuaro? What was the weather like yesterday?
Comprehension	Comparing, contrasting, describing, explaining	What sort of food does the Horta family eat? How is the school in Tocuaro similar to yours?
Application	Applying knowledge to solve problems, relating knowledge to everyday lives	Can you follow this plan and put the model village back in the right place? Where [on a map] do you think all the houses that were flooded are?
Analysis	Drawing conclusions, making inferences, finding causes	Why do some people not want the supermarket to be built? Why does the stream flow faster here?
Synthesis	Solving problems, making predictions, proposing	How can we encourage children to walk to school? What will happen if the school in the village closes?
Evaluation	Judging, evaluating, deciding, appraising	Would it be a good idea to cut down that tree? What do you think of the new houses by the canal?

An example of concept mapping

A Year 5 class, unfamiliar with concept mapping, had just completed a river enquiry, focusing on river processes. To assess their understanding, their teacher initiated a brainstorm of aspects of the topic. The children then:

- wrote the words on small pieces of paper;
- arranged them appropriately and stuck them down on a larger piece of paper;
- drew lines to represent relationships; and
- wrote a few words expressing these relationships, explaining how they saw the links.

Testing

Testing can take place in a number of ways and be used for formative as well as summative assessment. The less threatening it is, the more children are likely to show what they have learned. In other words, it should be little different from any other teaching, perhaps taking the form of a series of oral questions, or a special worksheet.

How a test might be administered

A Year 5 class was given a short oral test to help ensure that basic information on a local issue (the construction of speed ramps in the local area) had been consolidated before they went on to discuss the issue in role:

- Who is proposing to construct the speed ramps?
- Why? What will the ramps do?
- Where?
- Who thinks they are a good idea? Why?
- Who thinks they are a bad idea? Why?
- Did all the local people the class interviewed agree?
- What do you think?

Children can also test each other, setting the questions and scoring the answers themselves. Older children can ask questions of a more interpretative nature such as 'What's he doing?' 'Why?' 'How will that help his family?' (referring to a photograph).

Planning for Assessment

As assessment should be part of the normal planning, teaching and learning cycle; opportunities for assessment should be incorporated at the planning stage. Children have different learning styles and so teachers should use a range of assessment methods to enable them to demonstrate their geographical competence. Particular methods will also be used depending on whether teachers want to assess the products of children's learning (written, made, drawn or oral responses) or the processes of learning, such as the ability to discuss ideas with others. In early years settings, observation, listening and questioning are of particular importance because of the emphasis on experiential and investigatory learning (Palmer, 1994).

It is important to plan specific and realistic learning objectives appropriate to the age and ability of pupils with clear criteria for success. Just as teachers need to use a range of assessment methods, so children should be able to demonstrate evidence of attainment through a broad range of activities carried out in a variety of contexts and including the use of ICT (Table 7.3).

Some activities do not fulfil the requirements for a valid geographical task. For

Table 7.3 **Assessment of children's attainments**

Type of work	Activities
Written/word-processed work	Report, diary, story, questionnaire, letter, newspaper article, poem, list, description, table
Visual work	Painting, poster, diagram, cross-section, video, photograph, graph, table, printout, map
Oral work	Presentation, role-play, debate, interview, description, discussion
3D work	Making a model
Practical work	Programming a Roamer, using a play-mat

example, colouring-in a picture does not aid children's progression in geographical understanding. Completion of a worksheet can sometimes appear to be the purpose of the activity for children rather than a means of enabling them to demonstrate their learning. Similarly, having children learn definitions off by heart is poor educational practice as it does not link knowledge with understanding.

The choice of type of assessment may be determined by a particular topic. Role-play and simulations, for example, can be an effective way to explore different views connected to an environmental issue such as the construction of a local bypass; completing a table can provide evidence of children's ability to identify similarities and differences between contrasting localities. Enquiry skills such as observation and collecting and recording evidence can be demonstrated through fieldwork. Sometimes teachers may want to assess whether children have remembered particular information. However, they should plan tasks which encourage children to apply their skills and understanding (enquiry-based learning) in new situations.

Designing valid assessment tasks

Designing valid assessment tasks involves identifying:

- what is to be assessed, for example geographical knowledge or the application of a particular skill;
- the criteria which will identify whether pupils have achieved the learning objective;
- the kinds of questions or tasks that will need to be set in order for pupils' responses to provide reliable evidence of achievement;
- matching tasks to the children's abilities and so giving them the opportunity to succeed and thus motivating them for the future;
- how the evidence will be collected (if possible, listening to children as well as watching them and looking at their work);
- the sort of responses expected (tasks or activities capable of producing a range of responses, whether written, oral, or formal, will prove more enlightening); and
- how the results of assessment will be recorded and used to help teaching and learning.

By sharing learning objectives and criteria for success with children, they are more likely to succeed and demonstrate their abilities.

Sharing learning activities and criteria for success

Today, we're going to finish off our work on St Lucia. Remember what you've found out over the past five weeks? . . . Today, I'd like you to imagine that you are on holiday in St Lucia. I want you to write a letter to a friend explaining why you would like (or not like) to live there. Of course, I'll be looking for neat writing and a letter that's set out correctly – you can use a writing frame if you've forgotten how. But I really want you to concentrate on all the similarities and differences between St Lucia and Sheffield that we've talked about. So, one of the things you might want to write about is the weather. What could you say? . . .

Baseline Assessment

Baseline assessments are conducted towards the end of the reception year in preparation for the start of Key Stage 1. Baseline assessment is intended to form both a summative record of pupils' attainment and a formative tool for future Key Stage 1 teachers. It can also be used to provide a benchmark against which pupils' progress can be measured. It is important that teachers involve parents in these assessments whilst reassuring them that any information they supply will be used to benefit their child. Collaboration gives parents the opportunity to provide information that might contribute to the assessment as well as enabling them to become familiar with the nature and purpose of assessment. Baseline assessments currently lean heavily towards personal and social development, literacy and numeracy but they are expected to consider the wider curriculum. This would include those aspects of the Early Learning Goals linked to a sense of place.

Box 7.1   Possible indicators of the development of a sense of place

The child can:

- gain information about the environment from simple maps, photographs, people and visits;
- create simple maps and plans, paintings, drawings and models of observations and imaginary landscapes;
- express his or her opinions on features of the environment, using appropriate vocabulary; and
- make suggestions for improving the environment.

Box 7.2   Possible indicators of skills useful in geography

The child can:

- ask questions;
- recognize similarities and differences;
- question why things happen and give explanations;
- see issues from other points of view;
- imagine and recreate experiences in play;
- use positional language; and
- use ICT for recording and finding out.

Early Learning Goals and Level Descriptions

Children in the Foundation Stage work towards the Early Learning Goals. It is intended that most children will achieve, and some will go beyond, these goals by the end of the stage. Much of children's geographical experience at this stage falls within the area of 'knowledge and understanding of the world'. So, for example, it is expected that most children, when developing a sense of place, will start by showing an interest in the world in which they live, then begin to comment, noticing differences and asking questions until by the end of the stage they can:

- observe, find out about and identify features in the place they live in and the natural world;
- find out about their environment, and talk about those features they like and dislike.

QCA/DfEE (2000) provides useful guidance as to what children might do as they progress through these 'stepping stones', as well as what teachers need to provide to support children's learning. For example, the use of words such as 'busy', 'quiet', 'noisy', 'attractive', 'ugly' and 'litter' could be introduced and encouraged, to help children express their opinions on their local park.

Level descriptions in the National Curriculum, on the other hand, are summative statements which describe the characteristics of attainment a child working at a particular level should demonstrate over a period of time. Each level description is a composite statement comprising enquiry, places, scale, themes and skills. Teachers are expected to exercise their professional judgement to weigh up children's strengths and weaknesses to decide what description best fits their performance using as a basis a range of their work (SCAA, 1996).

Figure 7.1 is an example of work from a child who is achieving at level 2 in geography. She has used photographs to describe and make observations about life on St Lucia. The worksheet in Figure 7.2 was produced by a child achieving at level 4. The class drew up a list of questions about the Nile and used secondary sources of evidence to answer these. This piece of work demonstrates an understanding of how physical and human processes affect places and the people who live there.

SCAA (1997) has produced guidance as to what should be expected of children at Years 2, 4 and 6 respectively in geography. This publication (part of a series on different subjects) seems to suggest that the level descriptions are norm-referenced – in other words, for comparing a child's performance with the average – rather than criterion-referenced assessment based on the attainment of particular standards. It has also been suggested that these levels do not relate to any accepted theory of learning and may not actually describe the nature of children's progress in geography, although lack of research means that this cannot be confirmed (Butt *et al.*, 1995). They fail to reflect the fact that knowledge and understanding are the keys to fostering

I think it is hot in st lucia because they grow bananas.

It rains quite a lot because everything is green.

They have short chlothes made of thin matirial.

Figure 7.1 Life on St Lucia

148

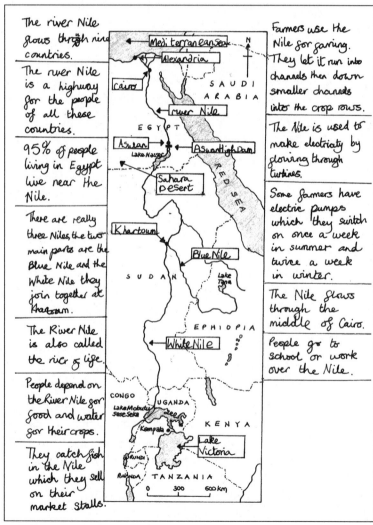

The river Nile flows through nine countries.

The river Nile is a highway for the people of all these countries.

95% of people living in Egypt live near the Nile.

There are really three Niles, the two main parts are the Blue Nile and the White Nile they join together at Khartoum.

The River Nile is also called the river of life.

People depend on the River Nile for food and water for their crops.

They catch fish in the Nile which they sell on their market stalls.

Farmers use the Nile for garing. They let it run into channels then down smaller channels into the crop rows.

The Nile is used to make electricity by flowing through turbines.

Some farmers have electric pumps which they switch on once a week in summer and twice a week in winter.

The Nile flows through the middle of Cairo.

People go to school or work over the Nile.

Mediterranean Sea
N
Alexandria
Cairo
SAUDI ARABIA
river Nile
EGYPT
Aswan
Lake Nasser
Aswan High Dam
Sahara Desert
RED SEA
Khartoum
Blue Nile
SUDAN
Lake Tana
EPHIOPIA
White Nile
CONGO
UGANDA
Lake Mobutu Sese Seko
KENYA
Kampala
Lake Victoria
RUNDI
Rwanda
TANZANIA
0   300   600 km

Figure 7.2 The Nile

higher-level intellectual skills and that levels should essentially be related to development of these skills.

It is not intended that these levels should be 'unpicked' to produce atomized ticklists or used for everyday assessment. However, for practical purposes the different aspects of geography can be identified within the levels and, as well as acting as a tool against which to match children's work, they can assist teachers to:

- understand children's progression in geography more clearly;
- identify more purposeful learning objectives, derived from the Programme of Study;
- generate broad learning objectives within the medium-term plan;
- design and select tasks to meet individual children's needs more effectively; and
- be aware of the wide range of learning activities needed for children to make progress and demonstrate achievement.

Geography Portfolio

Any system of 'levelling' pupils' attainment is to some extent subjective and relies on a shared interpretation and understanding of the characteristics and differences between levels. For example, what is the difference between 'appropriate vocabulary' at level 2 and at level 4? This should support consistent judgements being made on pupils' work across a school. One way of achieving this consistency is through discussing and moderating examples of children's work and then compiling a portfolio of annotated work which demonstrates the levels they are achieving. As well as assisting in assessment, this portfolio can also, for example, help teachers understand children's progression in learning in geography, help new colleagues to develop appropriate expectations, and exemplify how 'best fit' judgements can be made. This is one of the responsibilities of a geography co-ordinator and will be discussed in more detail in Chapter 10.

Marking

Marking children's work is usually a significant feature of teacher assessment and needs some thought if it is to be useful. Effective marking has a number of functions.

Uses of marking

Effective marking can:

- indicate children's strengths and weaknesses to them;
- provide children with constructive feedback;
- provide a record of pupils' attainment and progress;

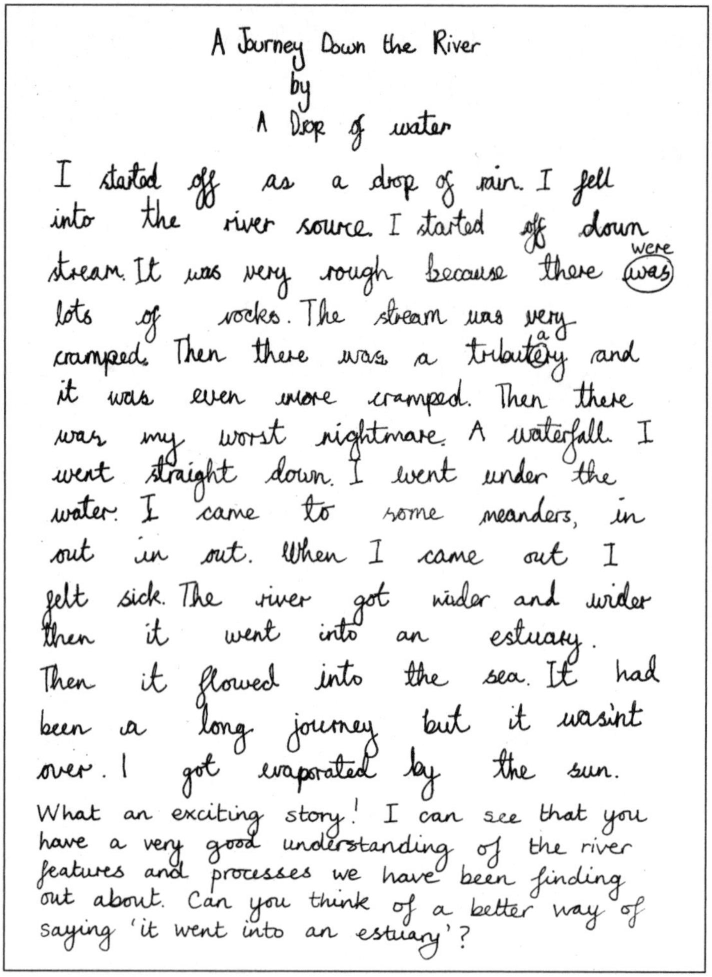

> ### A Journey Down the River
> ### by
> ### A Drop of water
>
> I started off as a drop of rain. I fell into the river source. I started off down stream. It was very rough because there ~~was~~ were lots of rocks. The stream was very cramped. Then there was a tributary and it was even more cramped. Then there was my worst nightmare. A waterfall. I went straight down. I went under the water. I came to some meanders, in out in out. When I came out I felt sick. The river got wider and wider then it went into an estuary. Then it flowed into the sea. It had been a long journey but it wasint over. I got evaporated by the sun.
>
> What an exciting story! I can see that you have a very good understanding of the river features and processes we have been finding out about. Can you think of a better way of saying 'it went into an estuary'?

Figure 7.3 Marking a story about river processes

- reward children's efforts;
- set targets and encourage children's progress; and
- help parents understand strengths and weaknesses in children's work.

Teachers' comments on children's work are sometimes limited to congratulatory statements such as 'well done!' or 'you have tried hard', or comments related to the presentation of the work. Thoughtful feedback, whether through marking or discussion, should be a feature of good practice because it helps pupils make progress. Thus, whilst effort and presentation are important, teachers should also make subject specific comments which focus on progress as well as achievements in order to support future learning (Butt *et al.*, 1995).

It is useful if there is a common system of marking across a school as this helps children understand the standards, for instance in terms of presentation, that are expected. Guidelines could encourage teachers to make comments that

- relate to planned learning objectives;
- recognize children's achievements;
- indicate the next steps in children's learning.

(SCAA, 1997)

Marking that takes place in the presence of the child means that, for example, any misunderstandings can be clarified immediately and assessment can be diagnostic if necessary rather than evaluative. Targets can also be set with the child. This becomes more difficult as children produce a greater quantity of work, and it could be argued that teachers may be able to give a more considered response to a piece of work away from the hustle and bustle of the classroom. In this case it is important that children are given time to reflect on marking and how they will respond to it.

When marking children's work, teachers need to consider the purposes of their comments. Are they, for example, to inform future work and/or to correct or improve the task in hand? Are children expected to read them when their work is returned? Figure 7.3 shows how a teacher marked a story which a Year 6 boy had been asked to write, incorporating what he had learned about river features and processes.

Recording the Results of Assessment

Much of the assessment that teachers undertake is informal and the results are not recorded unless they are of particular significance. However, it is impossible for teachers to remember all the results of more formal assessments. Schools are also required to keep annually updated records of their pupils' attainment and thus of the progress they are making (QCA, 1999). This means that the results of formal assessments in geography need to be recorded in some way. The format for recording pupils' attainment is for schools to decide and should be developed as part of the school's assessment policy. The geography scheme of work will detail the content and progression in what is taught, which should avoid any repetition. Thus, coverage of the subject does not need to be recorded unless for some reason it has diverged significantly from the scheme.

Teachers can use records of children's learning in geography for a number of different purposes including the following.

Uses of records of children's learning

Records have the following uses:

- identifying who is making better and worse progress than expected and who needs support or extension;
- setting individual and group targets for improvement;

- indicating whether aspects of teaching need refining;
- tracking the progress of individuals and groups;
- confirming end-of-year assessments;
- discussing pupils' progress with their parents;
- providing information to headteachers, governors, geography co-ordinators, special needs education co-ordinators, OFSTED and future teachers on children's attainment and progress; and
- filling in any gaps in skills or knowledge before the end of a Key Stage.

QCA (1999) emphasizes that record systems should not be complicated, extensive, bureaucratic and time-consuming, nor record everything a pupil does; essentially they should assist teachers to help pupils to progress. It is far more important that they:

- are manageable and concise, recording significant progress;
- are useful, accurate, consistent and easy to interpret;
- are fit for their purpose;
- provide a significant contribution to teaching and learning; and
- help teachers and parents track children's progress.

Teachers need to keep records at three levels:

- for individual lessons/activities;
- half-termly or termly; and
- annual.

It should be possible to make comments on pupils' achievements in at least three of the aspects at the end of a unit of work focused on geography which will feed into a summative end-of-year report.

Teachers often assess informally the extent to which the learning objectives from a lesson or activity have been met to assist them in planning or refining the next step, but much of this informal assessment is not recorded. However, they may find it helpful to make brief notes, particularly of ephemeral evidence, annotate a lesson plan, maintain a mark book, and make comments on pupils' work in exercise books or folders. Beginning teachers may find it useful to complete a simple matrix which indicates the extent to which children achieve the learning objective of a lesson or activity (Figure 7.4). It includes space for recording unexpected outcomes or concerns, such as lack of interest. It also indicates the aspect of geography that the learning objective is linked to. This makes it relatively straightforward for teachers to produce a summative record of children's attainment (Figure 7.5). It is not necessary to keep detailed collections of evidence: individual teachers as well as schools will need to decide how much evidence they want to keep to enable them to make a professional judgement on pupils' progress. Much of the evidence for younger children's learning is likely to be ephemeral and so teacher notes will form an important part of the evidence base. Keeping children's records on a database enables them to be updated quickly, with records that have been superseded by subsequent progress of the pupils being deleted.

Subject: Geography **Unit of work:** How can we make our local area safe? **Year:** Y2

name	can carry out a traffic survey (E&S)	can analyse results of survey (E&S)	can compare features of two roads (P)	can identify parking problems (P&P)				comments

X absent; ○ not achieved/understood; ● partial understanding/ability; Y fully understands/can do

Figure 7.4 Class record sheet for a unit of work

Subject: Geography   **Class**: Y2   **Year**:

	Level 1	Level 2	Level 3
Enquiry and skills (E&S)	Make observations express views use resources and observations to ask and respond to questions	Describe features, make observations, select information from resources; express views, ask and respond to questions, begin to use appropriate vocabulary	Describe and make comparisons, respond to a range of geographical questions, begin to use appropriate vocabulary to communicate findings
Places (P)	Recognize and make observations about human and physical features	Describe physical and human features, recognize features that give places their character, show awareness of places beyond own locality	Describe and compare physical and human features of different localities, show awareness that different places may have similar and different characteristics, offer reasons for some of the observations
Patterns and processes (P&P)	Recognize and make observations about human and physical features	Describe human and physical features	Describe and compare physical and human features of different localities, offer explanations for locations of some features
Environmental change and sustainable development (EC)	Express views on features	Express views on the environment, recognize how people affect the environment	Recognize how people seek to improve and sustain environments, offer reasons for some judgements and views

Name	E&S	P	P&P	EC	E&S	P	P&P	EC	E&S	P	P&P	EC	Comments

Figure 7.5 End of year or key stage summative class record sheet

Reporting to Parents on Pupils' Progress

In nurseries and primary schools where there is daily contact between teachers and parents, a considerable amount of informal reporting is likely to take place:

> 'Wesley drew some really careful sketches of different types of houses when we went out this afternoon'; 'Kelly spent ages playing with the farm this morning, making a model of where she'd stayed on holiday – I've never seen her so interested in anything.'

These informal discussions also enable teachers to find out about places children may have visited, experiences they might have had, or any interests related to geography they might have. When more formal verbal reporting takes place, as at parents' evenings, it is worth discussing examples of children's work to indicate, for instance, how their ability to draw accurate maps is developing. Teachers can also suggest how parents can support their child's learning in geography by, for example, reading stories which take place in other localities with them.

Parents are regarded as partners, with teachers, in the education of their child. However, schools are accountable for children's progress and parents of all pupils are entitled to an annual written report. This must include 'brief particulars' of a child's progress in all the National Curriculum subjects. It can also indicate targets for the child and comment on his or her interest in a subject. Again, it is useful for teachers to focus on the four aspects of geography whilst ensuring that the language they use is appropriate for their audience.

There is no requirement to report a level for geography either yearly or at the end of a Key Stage.

Report to parents (Reception)

Knowledge and understanding of the world
Fahd can draw simple maps and paint pictures of real and imaginary places.
He can talk about what he likes and doesn't like in the local area and he is developing a good vocabulary to describe the world around him.

Annual report to parents (KS1)

Geography
Kate can answer questions about other places by using photographs and simple reference books. She worked hard on the environmental topic and made some thoughtful comments on improving the school grounds. She needs to develop her observational skills in order to improve her drawing and mapping abilities.

Annual report to parents (KS2)

Geography

Mark shows a real interest in geography. He has an extensive knowledge of other places and uses ICT confidently in his enquiries. He has shown a good understanding of the environmental issues he has studied. His ability to interpret maps is developing but he needs to take more care when he is drawing maps.

Reflective Questions

- Do you use a variety of ways of assessing children's learning in geography?
- Do you assess their learning in all the four aspects of geography?
- Can you devise appropriate assessment tasks for different purposes?
- Do your assessments inform your teaching?
- Do you plan tasks which are appropriate and accessible for all children while having the potential for yielding differentiated outcomes?
- How do you elicit what children already know? How do you use this information?
- How do you assess children who have English as an additional language?
- How do you involve children in assessing their own work?
- Are your assessments valid (that is, do they assess what they are intended to assess)?
- Do you understand the level descriptions? Can you collect a range of one child's work and arrive at a 'best fit' judgement? Which pieces of work are most useful?
- Is your marking encouraging and constructive?
- How do you record children's attainment so that it is manageable, easily accessible and useful? Do you make use of ICT?
- Do you avoid technical and educational jargon in your reports to parents? Are you positive but also suggest how children can improve?

FURTHER READING

Qualifications and Curriculum Authority (1998) *Assessment and Reporting Arrangements.* London: QCA.

School Curriculum and Assessment Authority (1995) *Consistency in Teacher Assessment.* London: SCAA.

School Curriculum and Assessment Authority (1996) *A Guide to the National Curriculum.* London: SCAA.

School Curriculum and Assessment Authority (1997) *Expectations in Geography at Key Stages 1 and 2.* London: SCAA.

REFERENCES

Blyth, A. and Krause, J. (1995) *Primary Geography: A Developmental Approach.* London: Hodder & Stoughton.

Butt, G., Lambert, D. and Telfer, S. (eds) (1995) *Assessment Works: Approaches to Assessment in Geography at Key Stages 1, 2 and 3.* Sheffield: Geographical Association.

Edwards, A. and Knight, P. (1994) *Effective Early Years Education.* Buckingham: Open University Press.

Marsden, B. and Hughes, J. (eds) (1994) *Primary School Geography.* London: David Fulton.

Palmer, J. (1994) *Geography in the Early Years.* London: Routledge.

Pollard, A. (1997) *Reflective Teaching in the Primary School.* London: Cassell.

QCA/DfEE (2000) *Curriculum Guidance for the Foundation Stage.* London: QCA.

Qualifications and Curriculum Authority (QCA) (1999) *Keeping Track: Effective Ways of Recording Pupil Achievement to Help Raise Standards.* London: QCA.

School Curriculum and Assessment Authority (SCAA) (1997) *Teacher Assessment in Key Stage 2.* London: SCAA.

Task Group on Assessment and Testing (TGAT) (1988) *Report.* London and Cardiff: DES/Welsh Office.

Vygotsky, L. S. (1978) *Mind in Society: The Development of Higher Psychological Processes.* Cambridge, MA: Harvard University Press.

Geography and Equal Opportunities

Geography offers teachers of pupils in the 3–11 age range excellent opportunities to begin to raise children's awareness and understanding of values such as fairness, respect and equity. Those teaching 3–11 pupils play a key role in fostering positive attitudes in children towards diversity. The social and cultural diversity that exists in Britain today needs to be viewed as an asset and not a problem to be evaded. To pretend that such differences do not exist, that children are not exposed to ideas about these differences and to fail to encourage respect for diversity is to imply that there is something wrong about it. However, for these ideas to be dealt with adequately, teachers must ensure that their message is not undermined and contradicted by their day-to-day practice in the nursery or classroom.

This chapter will outline the context within which early years and primary teachers need to think about equality of opportunity, including legislation such as the Race Relations Act 1976 and the Sex Discrimination Act 1975, and will attempt to define some of the terms involved. (Special educational needs also raise issues of equality and entitlement which will be dealt with separately in Chapter 9.) The chapter will begin by outlining some of the terms involved when discussing equality of opportunity. It will then consider the development of an inclusive geography curriculum by ensuring that the breadth of geographical study presents positive and non-stereotypical messages about people and cultures in local and distant localities, focusing on aspects of class, race and gender. Finally the chapter will examine ways of developing an equal opportunities approach to teaching and learning in geography by addressing the classroom ethos and the teaching methods selected.

Defining Inequality

The Race Relations Act 1976 and the Sex Discrimination Act 1975 place an onus upon schools to work actively towards the elimination of discrimination and the promotion of equal opportunities and positive relations between staff, pupils and parents. The two Acts make direct or indirect discrimination, whether on the grounds of race, colour, ethnic and national origins or gender, illegal (www.qca.org.uk/overview/key_principles.htm).

Working to attain equality of opportunity is a complex and sometimes difficult challenge facing teachers. Caring and fair-minded teachers do not wish to promote inequity in their nurseries and classes. Yet the majority of nursery and primary teachers are drawn from a relatively narrow section of society, tending to originate from white, middle-class backgrounds and holding beliefs, attitudes and values based on their experiences (Marsh, 1998). What is more, teachers themselves as part of their own education may have experienced a geography curriculum that gave scant attention to certain events and certain groups of people. Establishing equality of opportunity in the classroom therefore may necessitate reflection upon one's own beliefs, assumptions and behaviour.

Inequality: 'race' and geography in a textbook from the 1920s

Although yellow men have been leading settled civilised lives quite as long as the white men elsewhere, they have not made the great strides that the white man has made in modern times, so that although they are almost as numerous as the White Race they have remained in their original homelands, leaving the New World to be developed by the white peoples. But the awakening and rapid progress of the Japanese in the last half century have shown that the yellow man is not essentially inferior to the white man, and the possibility of a similar awakening in China, which holds about a quarter of the world's people, may lead to some difficult problems in the future.

(Thurston, 1926, p. 33)

Thurston's geography focuses on difference – especially difference based on skin colour. A move towards economic and cultural equality is seen as a potential threat rather than a positive global change. Such a negative view of 'race' and a concern about threats from 'the yellow peril' or other non-white groups permeated school resources throughout the nineteenth and twentieth centuries.

Inequality: race, gender and geography in children's attitudes, 1998

Year 4 children were shown a photo of a woman working in Jamaica and a man working in Australia. They were asked what the people would be doing after work. This is what one child replied:

Jamaican photo:
'When she finished work she had a drink of water then she was ill because the water was dirty. Then she went to bed fast asleep.'
Australian photo:
'When he finished work he went home and he watched television and had his lunch.'

(Din, 1998, p. 44)

These comments were representative of the study. Children quickly absorb mainstream views about what living in a Southern country might be like, what characteristics people from different places may have, and what roles men and women may take. This leads to the question 'To what extent are teachers responsible for promulgating Thurston's views or holding the same views as Din's children?'

The prospect of concluding that one's geographical knowledge, practices and attitudes might actually be detrimental to equality of opportunity would be deeply worrying to most teachers. In response, some teachers might be tempted to adopt the position of 'treating everyone the same', ostensibly as a way of fending off accusations of discriminatory practices. One by-product of such an approach, however, is that it also results in the avoidance of having to confront and possibly challenge previously held truths and beliefs. A second by-product of such an approach is that far from ensuring equality of opportunity, it could well result in greater inequality (OFSTED, www.ofsted.gov.uk), as such policies ignore and fail to tackle the individual needs and differences of children. If one aspect of good practice in nursery and primary settings is to draw on the children's experiences, then clearly the children will have different geographical experiences and links with different local and distant places.

It is also a mistake to think that children themselves are ignorant of the differences between them. Even the youngest pupils may have their attention drawn to these differences by others both inside and outside the school or nursery. Children are learning all the time; what they see and do not see, hear and do not hear, do and do not do, all inform their ideas about the world around them, their attitudes and their behaviour. Even quite young children can be conscious of the physical differences between themselves and others and will begin to ask questions concerning them. The attitudes and behaviour of other family members will have a profound impact upon the attitudes and behaviours that the children themselves exhibit. The wider world around them will provide still more cultural information and reinforcement on the role and place of different people in society – for example, images of black or ethnic minority peoples in the media, and implied messages about the roles of men and women in the home, in everyday life and in employment. Becoming increasingly effective in offering equality of opportunity in the classroom may mean therefore facing up to some uncomfortable truths about our own, and our children's, prejudices, assumptions and experiences of difference.

Geography is full of examples of prejudice and discrimination of all kinds (Hicks, 1981). Equally, geography in terms of both its content and its processes can be a vehicle through which children can be empowered to challenge discriminatory behaviour and prejudiced attitudes that they see around them today. Where such issues are not raised, the geography curriculum runs the risk of appearing to legitimize such things, reinforcing prejudicial beliefs and offering justification for discriminatory practices and attitudes. Teachers of primary geography therefore

159

need to consider how the content of the geography curriculum can be used to dispel notions of innate superiority and inferiority, and of how the process of studying geography can equip pupils with critical skills and open-mindedness.

Box 8.1 Some useful terms and definitions

Prejudice is defined as unfavourable feelings, opinions or views formed in advance and/or without knowledge or reason.

> The reasons for people being prejudiced are complex and varied, but they include our different histories and the legacies they leave, different economic and social situations, different power relationships between people and groups, and ignorance and misinformation.
>
> (Lane, 1999)

Prejudice is an interpersonal matter between individuals or between individuals and groups. Prejudice is not the preserve of white people or men; anyone can be prejudiced.

Stereotyping involves ascribing characteristics perceived in one person to all apparently similar people.

Discrimination is rooted in prejudice but involves the translation of attitudes and beliefs into behaviour and action. As a result, people are treated less well because they are of a different colour, gender, religion or class. The treatment in question may range from verbal abuse to harassment, violence, or restricted access to services. **Direct discrimination** is considered to have occurred in any instance where an individual is overtly treated unfavourably. **Indirect discrimination** relates to those instances where individuals are ostensibly being treated equally, but where the outcome is actually discriminatory in nature.

Racism and **sexism** are examples of discriminatory behaviour and can have an institutional dimension. They are rooted in subordination, and result in groups of people finding themselves kept in less powerful, less important positions in society as a result of their colour or gender. Such doctrines, when expressed indirectly, can be hard to see by those who are part of the dominant groups as inequality becomes embedded in society and accepted as the norm (Lane, 1999). Racism and sexism can permeate the thought, speech patterns and actions of whole groups to such an extent that they are perceived as normal or natural.

Direct racism:
'A group of young Asian girls had to be escorted into their school by the headteacher, during which time they had to suffer racist taunts and spitting from white parents.' (OFSTED, 1998)

Indirect sexism:
Ostensibly the geography curriculum in school A is the same for all pupils. However, an examination of some of the older geography resources in use reveals the normalization of discriminatory language, such as 'man and his environment' or 'women's work'.

Box 8.2   *Cultural separatism*

Peter Jackson cites Lord Tebbit as believing that multiculturalism is a divisive force in UK society. In 1997 Tebbit argued for

> immigrants to be taught that the Battle of Britain is part of their history. The alternative, Tebbit warned, is the kind of ethnic and cultural division that led to the break-up of the former Yugoslavia. His words recalled earlier interventions from right-wing politicians, including Enoch Powell's 'rivers of blood' speech in 1968 which warned of the inevitability of violent conflict if immigration was permitted to continue unchecked.
>
> (Jackson, 2000, p. 277)

Tebbit's statements reflect the view that there is somehow a specific English history and geography that should be transmitted to all learners so that they conform to a distinct 'British' identity.

Separatism in the primary classroom

The chairman of governors at a village school in the south-east of England was very worried that a class would be focusing on Europe as part of their geography work. Would the teacher be encouraging the children towards closer union with mainland Europe? Would they want to use the euro instead of the pound? Would the parents who were involved in farming object to the children learning about food production in France? The geography co-ordinator had to justify her planning with reference to the children's National Curriculum entitlement.

Curriculum planners in a predominantly white suburban Midlands school were keen for the children to learn about life in St Lucia as part of a geography unit of work. The classroom displays showed the black Harvey family at school, work and play in Castries. However, when an 'exchange' was organized for the children to visit a predominantly black Birmingham school, many of the parents refused permission for their children to participate. Why were they happy for the children to learn about a black community in the Windward Islands but unhappy about local learning?

Cultural pluralism

A more considered view of UK geography could take the position that the existence of separate ethnic or national cultures is now in doubt. Jackson (2000) maps the balance between the acceptance of multiculturalism in the UK (through the commodities of music and food) and continued evidence of intolerance (expressed as racial violence and religious intolerance). This view is not a romantic 'melting pot' notion but rather a cautious analysis of how communities are developing into the twenty-first century. The idea that different places and localities could be considered as pluralist in nature would seem to allow the primary teacher and early years practitioner to value the contribution of all groups in creating the place that they live in (the home locality) or when studying a contrasting locality (e.g. London).

Infant children learning about their locality

Year 1 children complete a unit of work entitled 'Special places'. It links geography and religious education as well as being an important vehicle for PSHE. The children identify the contribution of different ethnic groups in the area to the 'townscape' through locating, mapping and then contributing to a display focusing on the area's religious buildings. The children visit the buildings and learn about the different faiths represented and the links from the community to the wider world.

Local and National Geographies

Not surprisingly, an important part of the geography National Curriculum concerns studying the local and national. It is undeniably important for children growing up in England and Wales to know something of their country's geography and develop a sense of place at a local and national scale. It is equally important for teachers and children to have an inclusive and accurate, rather than exclusive and partial, appreciation of what the social make-up of places in the UK is like, and to have an idea of all those who have contributed to that sense of place. One view of UK places is essentially a white English view in which minority cultures and groups have played little or no part in the creation and development of that place. An alternative view sees the nature of UK localities as diverse and complex, resulting from thousands of years of continuous movement and interaction of different groups, as well as present-day flows of information and movement of people. Massey makes this point when describing a street in London:

> When, on Saturday mornings I walk down Kilburn High Road to do my shopping, the IRA graffiti and the Irish pubs, the Indian sari shop and the notices for Muslim gatherings, as well as the constant snarl of traffic which tells that this is the main route from the centre of London to the M1, all make it impossible to think of Kilburn without linking it on to centuries of the history of the British Empire and places half a world away. The very feel of Kilburn, my sense of it as a unique place, is in part constructed precisely out of its global (as well as wider national) connections.
>
> (Massey, 1997, p. 147)

Box 8.2 discusses two of the key concepts underlying how geographers have viewed the multicultural nature of UK and world geography. The separatist approach has its roots in the geographies of empire constructed in the nineteenth century, and the regional geographies of the mid-twentieth century that sought to classify areas as First World and Third World, and countries as economically developed and economically developing. The pluralist approach stresses the interdependence of different places and cultures, and acknowledges the impact of globalization (see p. 9).

Global Geographies: Learning about Distant Places

As well as making children aware of the contributions of individuals and different ethnic and cultural groups to local and regional geographies in the UK, the geography curriculum also offers opportunities to give proper consideration to the geography of other nations and civilizations around the world. At Key Stage 1 children must learn about a contrasting locality (which may be anywhere in the world) and at Key Stage 2 children must choose their overseas locality from a specified list of 'less economically developed regions'. This leads to an interesting question. Does this choice give a broad and balanced view of the world to junior school pupils? It could be argued that the children are introduced to the difference between places and gain an introduction to the inequality that undoubtedly exists in the world. However, the choice of localities and choice of resources can lead to problems for children and parents who have a link with the places studied. If your 'home' region was portrayed as poor, and people you identified with were photographed doing manual agricultural tasks or using 'old-fashioned' technology, then you might well feel stereotyped as 'Third World' or a 'charity case'. Much well-meaning visual material used to inform children about distant places has caused offence to the people and cultures represented in the material.

Children's attitudes to distant places

Research evidence is growing about the impact of geography on children's existing attitudes towards people living in other countries. Children can express negative reactions to particular ethnic groups from as young as 2½ (Derman-Sparks, 1989). Their ideas become more entrenched as they get older. Harrington (1998) cites Hibberd's (1983) study of 3000 US students in which a carefully planned course on the 'Third World' hardly altered their attitudes.

Harrington's own research highlights the importance of establishing children's existing perception of distant places and people and challenging these existing ideas through appropriate choice of resources and teacher intervention. Harrington tested 28 children in Years 4 and 5 before and after they had learned about Nairobi, Kenya, using the ActionAid photopack *Nairobi, Kenyan City Life* amongst other resources. Before the unit of work, elephants, deserts and the hot and sunny environment dominated the children's images of Africa. Sixty per cent of the children thought Africans lived in houses made of straw, mud or twigs owing to poverty. Their attitudes to Africa and its peoples were in general negative, although children were much more positive about the people than the environment. The unit of work had a positive effect on children's knowledge, understanding and attitudes about Nairobi. The attitudes of the children to the people featured were almost wholly positive and they recognized that a wealthy urban environment could exist in Africa. This research has been used to highlight the importance of learning about distant places and their people at Key Stage 1 through the use of appropriate resources.

Gender and Geography

A selection of gender stereotypes?

Do you find Table 8.1 offensive? Check your geography resources and activities (see the evaluation sheet shown in Table 8.2) and see if these static stereotypes are being laid to rest. Who are the 'people who help us' in your Foundation or Year 1 integrated topic? What roles do the 'small world' figures have that you use as people moving around the play-mat or duplo circuit? Throw away the male dustbin man and the female lollipop lady! What gender are your visitors? Have you invited the male planner to come in and talk about the changes to the local area? Is a woman talking to the children about being a nurse in Sudan?

Geography is the study of people and places. Fifty per cent plus of these people are women, yet when the role and contribution of women does feature in geography it is often in the context of their roles as workers, wives or mothers, and just as often the crucial importance of these roles economically, socially and culturally is underestimated. There are plenty of geographical examples where work both inside and outside the home has been characterized by a degree of sexual differentiation, but that does not mean we should ascribe primacy to the work of men over the work of women. Similarly, family life is more than just a private matter: families play a vital part in the social and economic fabric of any society.

The geography of women and gender-related issues has grown over the past twenty years. Development geography now recognizes the central role of women in the development process, whether it is issues of health care, the feminization of the workplace or the geography of water supply and demand. Feminist geography is also a strong aspect of contemporary human geography. The Institute of British Geographers (IBG) has a Gender and Geography research group, and many geographers, such as Gill Valentine, Sophia Bowlby and Doreen Massey, have written influential books and papers to promote a female interpretation of geographical events and theory. Geography, a subject that for many is synonymous with Empire, exploration and 'chaps with maps', is now moving towards becoming a more inclusive and representative discipline.

There are a number of ways in which teachers can begin to build and implement a more inclusive and equitable approach to teaching and learning in geography when in the classroom. The rest of this chapter will focus upon the ethos of the classroom and the selection of teaching methods.

Classroom Ethos

The ethos and philosophy of early years and primary settings is informed by the Education Reform Act 1988. Under the Act, all children have a right to expect that their

Table 8.1   **Male and female stereotypes**

Male stereotypes	Female stereotypes
Playing or working outdoors	Playing or working indoors
Having innate need for adventure	Having innate need for marriage and motherhood
Competitive	Gentle
Decisive, problem-solving	Confused
Mechanical	Inept
Leader, innovator	Follower, conformer

Source: Derman-Sparks (1989, p. 141)

Table 8.2   **Women's work? How men and women spend their time (hours per month) in Sri Lanka**

	Peak season		Slack season	
	Male	Female	Male	Female
Agricultural production	298	299	145	235
Household tasks	90	199	60	220
Fetching water and firewood	30	50	130	60
Social and religious duties	8	12	15	15
Total work hours	**426**	**560**	**350**	**530**
Leisure/sleep	294	160	370	190

Source: Momsen (1991), cited by Pearson (1992)

Note: *Sri Lankan women have much longer work times in both the peak and the slack seasons and consequently less time for leisure or sleep.*

teachers will provide them with every opportunity to achieve their full potential irrespective of their gender, race, ability or class. They are entitled to an education that will enable them to participate fully in society, an education that prepares them for the opportunities, responsibilities, choices and experiences of adult life (NCC, 1990).

Adult attitudes and behaviour

Adult conduct is central to the task of establishing a learning environment in which the ethos is supportive of all pupils. When working to identify and address the individual needs of children, teachers need to be careful not to fall into the trap of making stereotypical assumptions about children concerning their intellectual, emotional, social and physical attributes (Adams, 1989). Staff expectations can have a powerful influence on children's achievement and self-esteem. Establishing a positive ethos and environment in the classroom also necessitates reflection upon teachers' own ideas and behaviour. The majority of nursery and primary teachers are drawn from a relatively narrow section of society. However, many of the children in nursery and primary schools do not share this kind of background.

> ### Box 8.3 A model of progression in teacher behaviour to promote equal opportunities
>
> - **Tolerance:** enduring rather than embracing. The first step on the road to more equal treatment. To move beyond this, try to find out about the experience of groups and peoples different from your own in order to make connections and to develop compassion.
> - **Acceptance and respect:** a recognition that equality of opportunity is something to be striven for even if you don't know quite how to go about it. Start to reassess the curriculum; look for multicultural, non-sexist approaches.
> - **Affirmation:** Teachers are now more self-confident and knowledgeable and are thus willing to debate and disagree openly.
>
> (Nieto, 1992)

Raising confidence and tackling discriminatory behaviour in others

Discriminatory behaviour, either by other adults or by pupils, must be opposed by teachers as it creates barriers and obstacles that disadvantage and exclude children. In part, providing an entitlement curriculum concerns access – for example, ensuring that girls as well as boys have experience of the CD-ROM atlas. However, promoting equality of opportunity also means addressing the expectations and attitudes that some pupils have acquired. Children can form strong opinions about boys' things and girls' things, black and white, at a very early age, and as they get older these attitudes can become linked to job aspirations and life choices in a very limiting way. Some children who are capable of high standards in geography may be tempted to underperform in order not to attract attention, owing to social pressure to conform to stereotypes that undervalue their talents.

Self-confidence is an important factor in overcoming underachievement. The essential confidence to investigate or be creative comes from curiosity and ambition based on self-confidence.

Alternatively, if ethnic minority pupils or girls are failing to fulfil their potential in geography owing to a curriculum that appears irrelevant to them, then that could constitute a form of indirect discrimination. Equally, there may be other pupils whose behaviour is overtly discriminatory. Examples could include children calling out whilst others put their hands up; children who scoff and ridicule incorrect answers to questions; children who engage in verbal abuse of others when they give the correct answer; and children whose behaviour in practical sessions is aggressive and possessive (for example denying peers opportunities to handle fieldwork equipment).

- Tackle discriminatory behaviour head-on. Remember that, at times, equality of access will require active intervention on the part of the teacher. Be aware of how black and white pupils, and boys and girls, may interact in your geography lessons.
- Have high expectations of girls as well as boys, black as well as white children in geography. Teach the children that there are no gender-limited or racially limited subjects.
- Look for ways to broaden the geography curriculum to include black and female characters as positive role models, and provide a variety of learning materials in order to appeal to all children.
- Demonstrate that you value and respect diversity and individual differences by using pupils' first language where possible and by showing respect for non-English traditions, cultures and protocols.
- Help children to recognize and challenge discriminatory practices and behaviour when they find them in geography – for example, stereotypical gender images in geography resources which depict men as active, women as passive, black and Asian peoples as inferior to white Europeans.
- Help children to begin to understand ideas such as fairness, justice and diversity.
- Guide children in the adoption and use of non-discriminatory language and procedures.
- Give frequent positive and encouraging feedback to both boys and girls, black and white, for their achievements in geography, and for non-discriminatory behaviour in geography lessons.
- Evaluate and reflect upon your own teacher/pupil interactions. Do you treat children fairly by treating them differently on occasion?
- Seek to involve parents in your geography teaching and raise and broaden parental expectations of all pupils in geography.

Building Equal Opportunities into the Geography Curriculum

Opportunities exist throughout the Programme of Study for geography and the Early Learning Goals to incorporate equal opportunities into teaching and learning.

Knowledge and understanding of the world

The teaching and learning of geography offers the chance to introduce children to some fundamental ideas about fairness and justice. Studying geographical issues enables children to test out their views and values. Group work, if properly used, can offer some children a supportive and more secure approach to developing their geographical understanding and capability, through the provision of role-play and empathetic experiences. A key to effective group work is the establishment of conventions or ground rules – for example, we listen to others, we deal with bad behaviour,

---

Box 8.4 *People who help us . . .? How do women feature in your early years geographical work?*

- When you talk about the families in a place do you talk of mum, dad and the children or use other family structures?
- How does shopping feature in your local area work? Is mummy doing the shopping in role-play activities? What gender are the shopkeepers?
- Do you show the work of women as experts, e.g. when considering local planning issues?
- Who inhabits the world of paid work?

---

we co-operate, we resolve conflicts and disagreements through discussion and reasoned debate, we respect the differences between people and recognize the similarities.

Children can be made aware that people come to live in new areas and countries for a variety of reasons. There will be people in the area of the school whose families originated in many different parts of the world. Children can be encouraged to explore their own geographies in relation to countries and localities with which their parents and wider family have links. Through this, children can also begin to explore different cultures from around the world through involvement in a variety of anniversaries, celebrations and special events. The following extract from a nursery inspection report shows what is possible:

> The broad cultural diversity of the staff, and of the city of Sheffield in general, is reflected in an excellent range of cultural and religious activities. The home corner is changed regularly to become a home from any of a large range of cultures throughout the world, including a British or a Pakistani home, or even a Bedouin tent. Many festivals are celebrated, including Harvest Festival, Eid and Chinese New Year, and visitors such as a Native American and an Inuit were invited to the Centre to speak in their own languages and to talk about their cultures and histories. The children sing songs in different languages and they are introduced to different scripts from around the world through books, captions and artefacts with letters engraved on them.
>
> (OFSTED, 1997, p. 1)

Geographical enquiry

It is quite possible that socio-cultural factors have an impact upon people's preferred learning styles (Marsh, 1998). Awareness of how these socio-cultural factors may impact on pupil learning and behaviour is the starting point for considering how curriculum delivery and teaching methods might be made more relevant to pupil experiences and expectations. Children brought up not to touch things until given permission may have difficulty adjusting to situations in nursery and school in which they find themselves encouraged to handle and investigate artefacts such as a globe or a product from a distant locality. Children brought up not to question adults until given permission may be reluctant to seek clarification from their teachers, and may need support in geographical enquiry. A child used to adult instructions delivered in the imperative may feel confused by instructions featuring courtesies such as 'please' or 'would you mind . . .?', as such courtesies might suggest that there is the option not to obey. At the same time, a child who would be reprimanded or punished for 'eyeballing' a parent at home may be extremely reluctant to engage in eye contact with a teacher, potentially giving rise to teacher assumptions about lack of attention, disrespect, insolence and defiance.

Although not all children will necessarily thrive in an enquiry environment at first, it is important not to generalize. Far better to be aware that such differences may exist and to try to evaluate individual pupils as to their preferred learning styles and start from there.

When planning for geographical enquiry, teachers can encourage children's interest in finding out more about different places and peoples, appreciating and respecting aspects of other cultures. Children can seek out links between countries and cultures from around the world, using a wide variety of techniques. Geographical enquiry is based on open-mindedness and critical thinking, exploring the distinction between fact and opinion prior to making judgements. Thinking aloud with pupils provides opportunities for reasoning, investigating and solving simple problems verbally. Children should be praised for questioning and sharing their ideas.

Geographical skills

There are many research studies that have focused on gender and mapping skills. Boardman (1990) reviewed the literature concerning spatial ability and gender. He found that in surveys carried out some twenty or thirty years ago, males performed better than females after the age of 8 or 9. Boys performed better at tasks such as way-finding, recalling and representing their home area on a sketch map and interpreting contour sketch maps. Reasons put forward for these variations included hereditary factors and the ways in which boys and girls were encouraged to 'roam' around their local area or were discouraged from doing so, or given jobs such as running errands. Recently the twin threats of increased traffic and 'stranger danger' may have limited the mobility of young children, so it is instructive to read more recent studies. Taylor surveyed 263 children between the ages of 4 and 11. She gave the children the following challenge:

> You are organising a party and people are coming to your house from all over town. To make sure that everyone gets to your house on time, you decide to draw a map to send out with the invitations. Try to cover as wide an area as possible, and do not forget to include any features which may help your guests to find their way.

(Taylor, 1998, p. 14)

Taylor noted the following differences in the results. Boys' maps generally covered a larger area than the girls'. In all age groups girls showed a greater awareness of shops and services. The boys were consistently more accurate below age 8, but the girls were more accurate after that. The ability to draw to scale increased with age, with boys and girls performing similarly. In every age group the boys' plan view representations were more sophisticated. The girls used colour more prominently. Of the nine children who used a grid, eight were male. Taylor's results show that boys can perform better than girls in certain aspects of spatial ability and that a motivating task may be the key to developing girls' mapping skills. All authors stress the importance of early practice using the local area and devising practical, relevant navigation tasks as crucial in giving equal access to geographical skills.

Learning about places – a sustainable approach

Developing a Global Dimension in the School Curriculum (DfEE/QCA, 2000) highlights the opportunities in the current National Curriculum to develop a global dimension in children's learning, which should 'secure commitment to sustainable development at a personal, national and global level' (p. 2). Securing a commitment to sustainable development at a personal level would have to include giving children equality of opportunity and also allowing them to learn about inequality at local, national and global scales. Asking the question 'Is it fair?' when focusing on how children live in local and distant places can be a starting point in this process.

Inequalities

Year 6 children calculated how much water they used at home over a weekend. They identified who used the water and for what purposes. They then learned about water supply in Nepal, and found out who obtained and transported the water, what it was used for and how much time was spent on securing such a vital resource. They were able to learn lessons about inequality in access to water at a global scale, as well as the role of women in the water collection process, and could question the fairness of such an arrangement.

Hudd (1998) investigated how Year 6 children from an economically impoverished area of Sheffield viewed three specific instances of inequality. These were their own social well-being compared with that of people from an economically prosperous area of Sheffield, the phenomenon of homelessness in the UK, and the existence of inadequate primary education in specific countries of the South. He found that they did not perceive that they lived in an area the local authority had described as an area of multiple deprivation, but that they were aware of injustice in the experiences of children in the South. This small-scale research project raises some interesting questions. Is it easier to position inequality in distant places and ignore it at home? If you do acknowledge inequality at a local level, how will you deal with the children knowing they are disadvantaged or privileged? Should such questions be raised at school or do they belong in the political rather than the educational domain? Teachers need to clarify their values in relation to such questions before focusing on local and distant locality studies.

Finally, many settings and schools teach about places using published locality packs. It is worth examining such resources from an equal opportunities standpoint. Great strides have been made since Hicks (1981) and Wright (1985) reported on racism and sexism in geography resources, but locality packs still cause offence to Asian students and teachers in the way localities in Pakistan and Bangladesh are presented. Use the evaluation matrix shown in Figure 8.1 to assess the locality packs that you use. Finding evidence of bias or stereotyping does not necessarily mean that you must abandon the resource, rather that it can be used as a stimulus to explore how and why different people and places are not represented fairly in the UK.

Title:					
Authors					
Illustrations	Male only	Female only	Black only	White only	Mixed
Photographs					
Technology: What level of technology is shown in the photographs?					
Role of people in illustrations	Male roles	Female roles	White people's roles	Black people's roles	
Sketches					
Are the sketches lifelike or stereotyped?					

Language (use of sex-specific terms in general situations)	He	She	Her	His	Man

Role-play	Male roles	Female roles	White roles	Black roles
	Total	Total	Total	Total
Class issues (number of families or case studies from each group)	Professionals, e.g. doctor	Managers	Manual/agricultural workers	Unemployed/ in poverty

Any omissions?

How are women depicted as an identifiable group?

How are black people depicted as an identifiable group?

Are there any people with physical disabilities shown? In what situations?

Figure 8.1 Resource pack evaluation matrix (after Connolly, 1992)

Using artefacts

Examining and evaluating artefacts can offer good opportunities to assist children in becoming more aware and respectful of diversity whilst simultaneously enabling them to see the similarities between the lives of people all over the world. Any artefact (i.e. an object designed and made by people) will be the product of a variety of factors and considerations. Children can be asked to think about the materials, skills and technologies available; economic factors such as the efficient use of energy and resources; and the design, including fitness for purpose, aesthetic considerations and the potential social or religious significance. Some or all of the above factors will have been taken into account when an object was produced, depending upon the purpose of the object, when, where and how it was made and who made it. By helping children to evaluate artefacts from different cultures and places in the light of these factors, they can be assisted in empathizing with the maker and the user of an object.

Teachers need to be alert to the danger of reinforcing evaluations that are culturally biased or negative. It can be dangerous to judge other cultures based on your own values. Different cultures set greater or lesser store by different things; this does not necessarily mean that one culture is correct, the other incorrect; one culture more advanced than (and hence by implication superior to) another.

Assessing artefacts

Year 4 children were given the task of selecting artefacts for a 'place-box' to represent their locality. They had to choose one object each that represented their place and people. Their teacher led a discussion of the artefacts in which she highlighted how difficult it was to show the many facets of a community through just one object. She then borrowed Egyptian artefacts from her local development education centre, and the children were able to view them as just one selection of representative objects, rather than solely showing Egyptian life.

Communication and recording skills

Providing a wide range of communication and recording techniques and offering children the chance to describe and explain their ideas about places in a variety of ways is one way of promoting equality of opportunity in this aspect of the geography curriculum. Ensuring that displays, labelling and written communication with children and their families reflect the diversity and variety of young children's backgrounds and traditions is also helpful.

For some, English is an additional language. These children may be bilingual or even multilingual; at the same time, however, they may be at the very earliest stages of English acquisition. Failure to appreciate this could result in teachers concluding, wrongly, that these children are less intelligent than their English-speaking peers. Providing a learning environment in which children feel able to utilize the full range of their linguistic repertoire demonstrates that their first language has legitimacy in the classroom.

It is important to realize that recognizing and supporting the breadth of their language skills and understanding will make a positive contribution to their learning of English and their success in education generally (Dodwell, 1999). At the same time, it is essential for all children to make progress in mastering English in the interests of their future achievements in school and their future opportunities as adults. The use of bilingual teachers and support staff to facilitate the geography work of pupils with English as an additional language can be a valuable way of helping these children to comprehend the spoken word, and provides skilled assistance enabling them to express themselves more clearly and appropriately. Such support can help children overcome feelings of isolation and frustration when much of what goes on in the nursery or classroom passes them by. Bilingual adults can provide useful models of how to use the English language appropriately, how to listen, and how to respond.

Reflective Questions

- Do you provide a variety of learning materials and ensure that all pupils have opportunities to develop their skills and confidence in using these materials through hands-on experience?
- Do you ensure breadth of curriculum content likely to appeal to all pupils?
- Do you challenge stereotypes of the sort sometimes found in geography books and other resources by promoting positive images of women and of peoples who in the UK are minority ethnic groups?
- Do you provide geography resources that actively and positively promote the diversity of culture and gender roles in society?
- Do you use attractively and professionally presented displays that incorporate objects, ideas, and visual and written material from a range of cultures and geographical locations?
- How do you ensure that the principle of equality of opportunity permeates planning and teaching and that the curriculum is enriched and enhanced by positive reference to diversity?
- Do you introduce and discuss notions of right and wrong, fairness, inequality and social justice when teaching geography?

FURTHER READING AND INFORMATION

Adams, J. (1997) 'She'll have a go at anything: towards an equal opportunities policy', in L. Abbot and R. Rodger (eds) *Quality Education in the Early Years*. Buckingham: Open University Press.

Barrett, H. (1996) 'Education without prejudice', in P. Bailey and P. Fox (eds) *Geography Teachers' Handbook*. Sheffield: Geographical Association.

Claire, H., Maybin, J. and Swann, J. (eds) (1993) *Equality Matters: Case Studies from the Primary School*, Clevedon: Multi-lingual Matters.

Commission for Racial Equality: www.cre.gov.uk

Equal Opportunities Commission: www.eoc.org.uk

Women and Geography Study Group of the RGS/IBG (1997) *Feminist Geographies: Explorations in Diversity and Difference*. London: Longman.

REFERENCES

Adams, P. (1989) *All Kinds: Who Cares about Race and Colour?* Swindon: Child's Play.

Boardman, D. (1990) 'Geography revisited: mapping abilities and gender differences', *Educational Review* 42 (1), 57–64.

Connolly, J. (1992) 'Geography: equal opportunities and the National Curriculum', in K. Myers (ed.) *Genderwatch*. Cambridge: Cambridge University Press.

Derman-Sparks, L. (1989) *Anti-bias Curriculum: Tools for Empowering Young Children*. Washington, DC: National Association for the Education of Young Children.

DfEE/QCA (2000) *Developing a Global Dimension in the School Curriculum*. London: The Stationery Office.

Din, S. (1998) 'What images and perceptions do children have of people from two contrasting localities in the North and South?', unpublished dissertation, Sheffield Hallam University.

Dodwell, E. (1999) '"I can tell lots of Punjabi": developing language and literacy with bilingual children', in J. Marsh and E. Hallet *Desirable Literacies: Approaches to Language and Literacy in the Early Years*. London: Paul Chapman.

Harrington, V. (1998) 'Teaching about distant places', in Scoffham (ed.) *Primary Sources: Research Findings in Primary Geography*. Sheffield: Geographical Association.

Hicks, D. (1981) 'The contribution of geography to multicultural misunderstanding', *Teaching Geography* 7 (2), 64–7.

Hudd, A. (1998) 'An unfair world? Injustice seen through the eyes of primary school children', unpublished dissertation, Sheffield Hallam University.

Jackson, P. (2000) 'Cultures of difference', in V. Gardiner and H. Matthews (eds) *The Changing Geography of the United Kingdom*. London: Routledge.

Lane, J. (1999) *Action for Racial Equality in the Early Years*. Wallasey: National Early Years Network.

Marsh, J. (1998) 'Schools, pupils, and parents: contexts for learning', in A. Cashdan and L. Overall *Teaching in Primary Schools*. London: Cassell.

Massey, D. (1997) 'Questions of locality', *Geography* 78 (2), 142–4.

National Curriculum Council (NCC) (1990) *The Whole Curriculum*. London: NCC.

Nieto, S. (1992) *Affirming Diversity: The Sociopolitical Context of Multicultural Education*. New York: Longman.

OFSTED (1997) *The Inspection of Nursery Education Inspection Report: Sheffield Children's Centre*. London: OFSTED.

OFSTED (1998) *Nursery Education Inspection Guidance on Equality of Access and Opportunity*. London: OFSTED.

Pearson, R. (1992) 'Gender and development', in T. Allen and A. Thomas (eds) *Poverty and Development in the 1990s*. Oxford: Open University Press.

Taylor, S. (1998) 'Working with young children and their familiies', in S. Scoffham (ed.) *Primary Sources*. Sheffield: Geographical Association.

Thurston, C. B. (1926) *A Progressive Geography*, Book 4: *Eurasia*. London: Edward Arnold.

Wright, D. (1985) 'Are geography textbooks sexist?', *Teaching Geography* 10 (2), 81–4.

Geography and Children with Special Educational Needs

In recent years, moves towards the inclusion of children with special educational needs (SEN) in mainstream schools and nurseries mean that most teachers are likely to encounter pupils with widely differing needs. Schools are required to provide relevant and appropriate learning challenges within a broad and balanced curriculum for all pupils (DfEE/QCA, 1999). This can prove demanding for teachers, who may need to undertake tasks ranging from drawing up an individual education plan (IEP) to planning for non-teaching assistant help and liaising with parents and educational psychologists. However, geography, with its focus on the relationship between people and places, has much that is relevant and interesting to offer children who in some way need special provision to make it accessible.

This chapter begins by summarizing the statutory requirements that teachers need to be aware of. It then outlines some of the special educational needs that nursery and primary teachers may encounter which arise from physical disability, learning difficulties and emotional and behavioural problems as well as the particular needs of gifted and talented children. It indicates how these needs might be manifested and identified and suggests ways in which the health, welfare and progression of these children can be ensured. Finally, strategies which are designed to promote the geographical learning of children with SEN are put forward.

Statutory Requirements

The publication of the Warnock Report (DES, 1978) and subsequent education Acts have all moved towards the inclusion of children with SEN into mainstream schooling. Underlying these developments is a belief that inclusion will benefit all children in terms of both personal and social development and academic achievement, as well as equip teachers with new skills. Current practice in respect of children with SEN is determined by a

Code of Practice introduced in 1994 and subsequently revised. This aims to ensure a consistent approach by schools and LEAs to meeting the needs of pupils with similar difficulties. The code describes how children's needs can be met through a series of stages and lists the responsibilities of different agencies and individuals (including the class teacher) within this process. It stresses the importance of schools and LEAs working in partnership with parents, and the part that children should play in making decisions. It also emphasizes that using better teaching strategies or greater differentiation within classes, for example, may be more effective than extra support staff or one-to-one teaching.

All pupils have needs, but those with SEN have additional needs. The notion of SEN covers a wide range of learning and behavioural difficulties where special provision has to be made for a child to learn successfully because he or she:

- finds it more difficult to learn than most other children of the same age;
- has a disability which affects his or her learning experience; or
- has a level of behaviour or achievement significantly different from that of most other children of the same age (this includes gifted or talented pupils).

Children with English as an additional language (EAL) do not automatically have SEN.

It is worth remembering that legislation may support inclusion but it cannot change attitudes, beliefs and values regarding disability and SEN. Integration is not inclusion and schools need to ensure that children do not face discrimination, for example by enforcing anti-bullying policies, developing positive images of disability within the school and encouraging children to feel valued and have a sense of belonging. Individual teachers should also consider their own preconceptions regarding children with SEN and what they think they are capable of achieving.

Identifying Children with Special Educational Needs

Early intervention is essential if children with SEN are to make progress, yet identifying these children is not always easy or straightforward. Some children may have a sensory or physical disability or medical condition which is easily identifiable. Others, however, may experience impairment, such as a loss of hearing, which is not immediately obvious or which may be intermittent. Similarly, some children will have been diagnosed as having a specific learning disability such as dyslexia, while others find it noticeably harder to achieve than their peers for reasons which are not instantly apparent. Whatever these needs or their origins are, early identification and intervention are essential in order to avoid possible frustration, low self-esteem, underachievement, and a cycle of 'learned helplessness'.

Nursery and primary teachers play an important role in identifying and assessing children with SEN and then providing and monitoring appropriate learning experiences. However, they are not amateur therapists, child psychologists or social workers and they should be able to look to the SEN co-ordinator (SENCO), headteacher, governors, LEA, and outside services and agencies for support, encouragement and practical advice. It is also important that the contribution of colleagues is valued: a Child Care Assistant, Non Teaching Assistant or nursery nurse may gain insight into a particular child by spending more time working more intensively with him or her than anyone else. This is particularly true in an early years setting, where teamwork is important in collecting and collating information, as well as in making appropriate provision for children with SEN.

Teachers should view children with SEN as individuals and not as a homogeneous group: the range of SEN is considerable and complex in nature, and some children may experience SEN that are multiple. Some children with learning difficulties may also have behavioural problems, perhaps as a means of concealing their shortcomings or of attracting attention. Some children have needs associated with physical, mental or emotional difficulties which may not adversely affect their learning. Nevertheless, this need can become educational if an appropriate environment and resources for learning are not provided: a disturbed but academically capable child, for example, may misbehave and not co-operate and consequently fail to make progress. It may be difficult to help certain children in circumstances, such as an unsettled home life, which are beyond teachers' control.

It is important for new teachers to familiarize themselves with the Code of Practice and the school's SEN policy. The policy will identify the SENCO, who will have information on children on the SEN register, their stage, copies of their IEPs and any statements.

What to do if a child appears to have SEN

If teachers think that a child has SEN they need to:

- initiate a registration of concern;
- identify not what the child knows but what he or she finds difficult to learn after suitably differentiated teaching has taken place within the normal classroom environment;
- identify whether there is a pattern to the child's difficulties;
- consider the cause of the difficulty and the consequences for teaching; and
- consult the SENCO for general and subject-specific advice (SENCOs are required to liaise with curriculum co-ordinators).

What Geography Has to Offer Children with Special Educational Needs

The National Curriculum (2000) stresses that all pupils have an entitlement to learning, to experience success in learning and to achieve as high a standard as possible. In order to provide this, schools have a responsibility to:

- set suitable learning challenges;
- respond to pupils' diverse learning needs; and
- overcome potential barriers to learning and assessment for individuals and groups of pupils.

This means that teachers need to be flexible, for example by choosing knowledge and skills with content appropriate for older/younger children, from an earlier/later Key Stage. However, much of what can be done to make the geography curriculum more accessible to children with SEN is of value to all children.

Ways of making the curriculum accessible to children with SEN

- Use a variety of activities, resources and teaching and learning approaches to enable all children to participate and demonstrate what they have learned.
- Similarly, use appropriate forms of differentiation and assessment.
- Develop children's self-esteem through high expectations and praise and by emphasizing what they can do rather than what they cannot do.
- Encourage children to set their own targets.
- Plan activities which are real and relevant; build on children's interests and take account of their experiences.
- Break down tasks into small, achievable steps and set attainable yet challenging targets for learning which are subsequently reinforced.
- Display children's achievements and record them systematically.

Differentiation is unlikely to be one-dimensional: teachers will probably need to use a combination of differentiated outcomes, tasks, delivery and resources as well as appropriate intervention. They will also need to be sensitive in their approaches. This could mean, for example, that as some children may need to use resources such as picture maps that their peers have long grown out of, it is advisable for more able children to use these resources on occasion to demonstrate their acceptability.

A structured approach to learning is particularly important for children with SEN. This can provide both teacher and child with clear evidence of progress which can inform the next stage (Blyth and Krause, 1995). It will involve using a range of teaching and learning strategies such as:

- common tasks sufficiently open-ended to challenge the more able;
- stepped tasks, where the first activities are accessible to all children;

- grouping children by capabilities and need, which allows for the use of tailored resources; and
- using teaching or support staff to respond to group or individual needs.

Much of the geography curriculum is particularly appropriate for children with SEN because its emphasis on practical and locally based activities provides a wealth of relevant, immediate and concrete experiences. It is also concerned with many aspects of children's worlds, such as homes, journeys and the weather, and thus gives them the opportunity to draw on their own experience and reflect on that of others. Children with SEN sometimes have more limited experiences than their peers: geography can extend their horizons, even if only by a small amount, as well as their sensory skills and language. An enquiry approach, as well as making learning more interesting, can be used across the full ability range, with teachers selecting an appropriate level of challenge. Geography has extensive links with cross-curricular elements and can encourage 'learning skills' such as those involved in enquiry. It also has links with PSHE, and can develop skills which encourage independence, such as way-finding, going to the local shops to collect data, experiencing different forms of transport, and working safely in new environments. Citizenship involves looking at roles and responsibilities, perhaps associated with a local environmental issue, and this may be particularly pertinent for pupils with emotional and behavioural difficulties (EBD), for whom addressing responsibilities and value systems is a major priority.

Physical Disabilities

Table 9.1 gives an overview of some of the more common physical disabilities that teachers may encounter. Not all pupils with disabilities have special educational needs: a child in a wheelchair, for instance, may simply need physical or technological access to the curriculum. Nevertheless, the impact of absences, hospitalization and possible reluctance to avail themselves of available aids may impede their educational progress. Children are often less distracted by another child's disability or illness than are some adults, but they can feel concern, for instance if a child has an epileptic seizure and they have not been made aware of the situation. They are also usually receptive to suggestions such as facing a friend who is hearing impaired while talking, or learning sign language. 'Buddy' systems can be appropriate for some activities as long as a child does not become over-dependent on a peer.

Table 9.1 Key characteristics of some physical disabilities

Disability	Characteristics
Hearing impairment	Children experience hearing loss when something interferes with the conduction of sound through to the inner ear (conductive hearing loss) or cells within the ear are damaged (sensori-neural hearing loss). Hearing devices can be used to amplify sounds for children with sensori-neural problems but they can distort sounds, and bombard children with sounds during fieldwork. Some children may feel self-conscious about wearing a hearing aid and 'forget' to bring it to school. Children with hearing loss may have: • problems understanding instructions or questions; • poor articulation and a limited vocabulary; • poor listening skills; • problems with reading and spelling.
Visual impairment	Visual impairment can have a number of causes, and vision can be impaired in a variety of ways (e.g. colour vision, near/distance vision). A child's eyesight may also improve or deteriorate. As with hearing aids, children can be reluctant to wear glasses. Signs of visual impairment can include: unhealthy appearance of eyes; • poor hand–eye co-ordination; • squinting; • headaches, tiredness and dizziness; • making omissions when reading or writing; • bringing a task close to the face.
Arthritis	Some children suffer from a form of rheumatoid arthritis. They may be under medication or have to have physiotherapy. Excessive physical activity can cause considerable discomfort and anxiety.
Asthma	Asthma appears to be becoming increasingly common in children. A narrowing of air passages in the lungs makes breathing difficult. Triggers for attacks range from temperature changes and allergic reactions, to infections and excessive physical exertion. Some children have only mild attacks, whereas for others it can be more serious and even life-threatening. Serious cases may result in frequent absences from school and can restrict children's involvement in more physical activities.
Diabetes	Diabetes results from a deficiency of insulin and a consequent inability to metabolize sugar and starch. Children with diabetes often have to have insulin injections and eat at regular intervals. Falls in blood sugar as a result of lack of food can happen quite quickly and produce headaches, irritability, lack of colour, sweating, palpitations or anxiety. Biscuits or sweets are sometimes used to rectify the situation. Excessive blood sugar levels can be far more serious: the onset is slower and if not dealt with can result in vomiting and diabetic coma. This is rare, but hospitalization is essential when it occurs. Older children are often capable of recognizing when a problem is arising.
Epilepsy	Epilepsy is a neurological disorder caused by temporary changes in the brain's electrical activity. Most forms of epilepsy can be controlled with drugs. Seizures can be brought on by illness, emotional and physical stress, or a lack of medication. Minor seizures often appear as momentary lapses of attention. Major seizures can result in facial or whole body spasms, loss of consciousness and loss of bowel or bladder control. Teachers need to remain calm, reassure the rest of the class and not attempt to restrain the child. The child should then be placed in the recovery position, with breathing and pallor checked, and medical help sought if the seizure has lasted longer than five minutes.
Cerebral palsy	Cerebral palsy results from brain damage. It can be barely noticeable or the child's movements may be awkward and jerky, and at rest the body may experience irregular and uncoordinated motion. This condition can also produce problems with balance and co-ordination. Some children may need wheelchairs; others may find their fine motor control impaired, or experience difficulties in speech and articulation.
Cystic fibrosis	Cystic fibrosis is an incurable genetic disorder that produces a thick mucus in the child's lungs. This can result in lung and stomach infections, and daily treatment (physiotherapy, medicines and special diets) is necessary to ameliorate the effects of the condition.
Spina bifida	Some children with spina bifida and other malfunctions of the spinal cord can have slight mobility problems. For others, the condition can result in specific learning difficulties, for example in judging size, direction and shape, in fine motor control, and in personal organization.
Muscular dystrophy	Muscular dystrophy is an incurable wasting disease that affects motor skills rather than the brain. As the condition worsens, the child may not be able to attend school. Working with families needs to be done with sensitivity, as ultimately the condition is fatal.

Supporting the geographical learning of children with physical disabilities

Fieldwork can present difficulties for children with physical disabilities. Teachers should complete a comprehensive risk assessment form (see Figure 6.2) to ensure the health and safety of all children. This might include, for example, identifying possible triggers for a child's asthma attack and where his or her inhaler will be kept; noting what to do if a child has an epileptic fit or that a child with diabetes needs to eat regularly. All adult helpers should have copies of this form. Children's degrees of mobility need to be taken into account when considering distances to be covered, and potential resting places should be identified.

Resources and equipment for learning out of the classroom should be chosen to enable all children to participate: for example, children with poor fine motor skills or who are visually impaired can use a robust thermometer, one metre in length, with a large, clear scale. Children should be able to record their observations in different ways, making full use of technology such as tape recorders and video or digital cameras. Children with sensory impairment need as many sensory clues as possible to make sense of the world. Visual impairment, for example, tends to limit children's spatial skills and ability to find their way around although they respond to auditory and haptic (touch) information (Spencer *et al.*, 1989), and so they should be encouraged to use other senses such as touch, smell or hearing in their enquiries. Sounds in different localities, whether on a farm, by a small stream or in a busy street, can be recorded and used for discussion; objects like smooth pebbles, sand and seaweed can be felt and smelt.

Encouraging children with disabilities to explore the environment

To encourage children, whatever their disability, to explore the environment, all members of the class were blindfolded and, in groups led by adults, followed a sensory trail by holding a rope. There were frequent stops for the children to use their senses in the discovery of the natural and human world:

- touching shapes and textures of bricks, cobbles, bark, fences and railings;
- smelling herbs and flowers; and
- listening to sounds around them when still, and sounds feet and wheelchairs made when crossing different surfaces.

Children were able to describe the trail orally or draw it on a plan of the site and add their own observations; others began to appreciate the need to protect the environment.

Within the classroom or nursery, furniture should be carefully positioned so that all children can move freely, and resources should be clearly labelled and accessible. Some children may find using the computer easier than writing, or may need their work scribed. Where fieldwork is impossible, interactive software enables children to investigate the nature of other places as well as human and physical processes.

Demands on hearing-impaired children can be limited by speaking clearly and naturally when talking or reading, ideally in a quiet atmosphere, facing the child (who is sitting at the front, in the light) and checking that hearing aids are functioning. Teachers should emphasize new vocabulary or instructions and use visual aids such as maps and photographs. For hearing-impaired children (and others who experience difficulties with processing language), it is important to identify geography's 'key language', such as the words for naming features, explaining processes or asking geographical questions. This can be done through, for example, flow diagrams or charts, reinforced by clearly labelled displays (Print, 1999). Visually impaired children may need to use aids such as a desk stand or magnifier and sit near the front in a well-lit area when the teacher is writing on a board or using maps or photographs. Children with colour deficiency will need to use symbols rather than colour when drawing maps.

Helping children with disabilities take part in lessons

Vicki was extremely short-sighted. She was able to participate in geography lessons more fully by:

- touch-typing her work on the computer or using voice recognition software;
- completing worksheets, reading text or graphics which had been scanned and enlarged or enlarged using a photocopier; and
- using a tactile globe and maps.

Learning Difficulties

Learning difficulties range from mild to severe and from specific to complex. In some cases the difficulties may result from other problems, related to a child's physical or emotional development. Other learning difficulties are cognitive and, if not identified and tackled appropriately, can lead to problems with literacy and numeracy, which may hinder progress in other areas of the curriculum. Language acquisition in particular is essential for learning in many areas, and communication problems, like a physical impairment, can mask a child's real potential and intelligence. Furthermore, if children are unable to make themselves understood, they can become frustrated and develop behavioural problems.

Table 9.2 **Key characteristics of some learning difficulties**

Condition	Characteristics
Autistic spectrum disorders (ASD)	Autism is a lifelong disability which affects the way children communicate, relate to others and make sense of the world. Children with Asperger syndrome are at the higher-functioning end of the autistic spectrum. Children with autism find difficulty: <ul><li>with social relationships;</li><li>with verbal and non-verbal communication;</li><li>in the development of play and imagination.</li></ul> They often have repetitive behaviour patterns and resist changes to routine. Some children may also have areas in which they are particularly capable, e.g. drawing, musical ability, memory tasks.
Aphasia	Children with aphasia experience difficulties in understanding the meaning of words or difficulties in expressing themselves whilst knowing what they want to say.
Cerebral palsy	Children with cerebral palsy may have good verbal, reading and comprehension skills but poor visuo-spatial perception and thus difficulties in making relative judgements in time and space and with abstract visual information such as maps and diagrams.
Down syndrome	Down syndrome is a genetic condition caused by the presence of an extra chromosome. Children with Down syndrome may have: <ul><li>poor motor co-ordination skills;</li><li>a short concentration span;</li><li>limited understanding of the world (they do not learn well from incidental learning);</li><li>behaviour more characteristic of younger children.</li></ul> They respond well to structure and routine and benefit from multi-sensory activities and the use of strong visual cues such as photographs.
Dyspraxia	Dyspraxia is a neurological disorder that affects gross and fine motor co-ordination. Children with dyspraxia may have poor perceptual skills, a short attention span and auditory memory, poor articulation, difficulties with balance and underdeveloped social skills.
Dyslexia	Children with dyslexia may have a number of areas of weakness alongside abilities which may be creative, or highly developed verbal skills. Their difficulties might include: <ul><li>poor concentration, easily distracted;</li><li>difficulty following instructions;</li><li>spoken and/or written language slow;</li><li>poor personal organization;</li><li>poor reading progress;</li><li>poor standard of written work compared with oral ability.</li></ul> However, they may have a good understanding of physical processes and the 3D world.
Emotional and behavioural difficulties (EBD)	Children with EBD may exhibit a wide range of behaviour from extreme withdrawal to highly volatile, aggressive and disruptive conduct. Their problems are clearer and greater than sporadic naughtiness or moodiness but not so great as to be classed as mental illness. They may be caused by multiple factors such as frustration as a result of another impairment or learning difficulty; physical, sexual or emotional abuse; lack of security as a result of parental separation; comparisons being made with other siblings; or self-fulfilling prophecies. Dealing with EBD can be particularly frustrating for teachers as the difficulties are caused by factors that are beyond their control. Indicators that may suggest a child has emotional and behavioural difficulties include: <ul><li>seeks friendships with other age groups;</li><li>aggressive towards peers;</li><li>distant or a loner;</li><li>clingy;</li><li>precocious or immature;</li><li>disruptive, attention-seeking;</li><li>poor self-image: 'my map's rubbish';</li><li>anxious;</li></ul>

- restless and easily distracted;
- tearful, irritable or moody, prone to tantrums.

Attention-deficit (hyperactivity) disorder (AD(H)D)

Attention-deficit (hyperactivity) disorder is a clinically recognized condition that affects five times as many boys as girls. Not all children with AD(H)D are necessarily hyperactive. There is uncertainty about what it actually is; diagnosis can be problematic and there is considerable debate as to whether the condition should be treated with drugs (Ritalin).

Indicators of an attention deficit are:
- failure to give close attention, being careless and making regular mistakes;
- forgetful of regular activities such as going to assembly;
- problems in sustaining enthusiasm; avoids tasks requiring extended effort;
- appears not to listen when addressed verbally;
- appears unable to follow instructions, regularly fails to complete tasks;
- difficulties in organizing self, often 'loses' the tools necessary for the task;
- very easily distracted.

Indicators of hyperactivity are:
- constant fidgeting with hands and feet;
- often unable to stay seated;
- moves inappropriately around the room, for example running, climbing over or under tables;
- difficulties in playing without excessive noise;
- interrupts and intrudes upon the activities of peers;
- talks incessantly, blurting out answers to questions without observing classroom conventions;
- difficulty in waiting for a turn.

Indicators that may *suggest a child has learning difficulties*

A child may have learning difficulties if he or she:

- shows little apparent awareness of, or interest in, the world around;
- draws on very limited previous experience;
- struggles with creative approaches to geography;
- has few interests;
- has difficulty in following instructions;
- has difficulty in relating learning in one area to work in another;
- has limited vocabulary, poor speech;
- shows reluctance to contribute to discussion;
- has a limited concentration span, is easily distracted;
- is hyperactive, constantly off-task;
- struggles with literacy and numeracy;
- avoids work through activities such as tidying up;
- prefers practical activities;
- shows lack of interest in books and reading;
- constantly requests adult help; alternatively, never asks for adult help;
- rarely finishes work;
- finishes quickly, carelessly or incompletely, pretending to have finished;
- has a propensity for losing things.

Supporting the geographical learning of children with learning difficulties

Children with learning difficulties usually derive little benefit from teacher-centred ('chalk and talk') or unstructured, high pupil autonomy methods of teaching and learning geography. If teachers are familiar with different ways in which they can provide for differentiation (see Chapter 4), they are more likely to enable these children to make progress. Children with particular difficulties may need more specific support. For example, it is more effective to give autistic children instructions than to give them choices or ask them questions, and they may need extra support in group settings (Siddles, 1999). Geography can also be incorporated into the IEPs of children with statements in mainstream schools (Smith, 1999).

A child with learning difficulties

Beth (Year 4) had moderate learning difficulties. Her IEP concentrated on comprehension, time (with special reference to sequencing), cause and effect, and social skills. Her targets for one term included the following:

- Recognize three signs of spring.
- Use appropriate language to describe the weather.
- Use own records to tally and graph the weather.
- Draw a plan of a journey round school, showing the route and sequencing landmarks.
- Write about 2 events of the journey in order.

Criteria for success such as *use words such as cloud, sun, windy, misty* were identified for each target.

Teachers may have to keep referring to previous work and experience and use visual cues such as photographs to help children make links, and make sense of their learning. Children will also need opportunities for repetition and reinforcement as well as using vocabulary and ideas in different contexts. For example, geographical language such as *up, down, behind, in front of, across, near* and *far* can be used in other areas of the curriculum. Children with learning difficulties need to be encouraged to participate: teachers can foster discussion of what other children have said in order to develop incorrect or partial answers. Where children have been taught group work skills, it helps them to see how they can contribute rather than focusing on what they cannot do (Sebba *et al.,* 1993). Addressing environmental issues and undertaking geographical enquiries lend themselves particularly well to group work.

Investigating places

Investigating their local area can be important for children with SEN: place attachment includes a sense of daily security and stimulation, and so place is seen as basic to personal well-being and development (Spencer and Blades, 1993). Some children will need to develop an awareness of their own body and its position in space through work on left and right and simple orientation before progressing to following a route round school and then investigating features further afield.

Once children are aware of their own locality and have used primary and secondary sources of information, they can begin to make comparisons with contrasting localities. For children who need the concrete experience of a place, it is advisable to choose somewhere, perhaps within the same city, which can be visited. Linking with another school to exchange information and resources and support fieldwork would also be beneficial in providing regular contact for children.

Investigating distant places may not be regarded as suitable for children who find abstract concepts difficult to deal with, but most children are likely to have images of other places through either the media, stories or holidays on which to build. It is useful if the class teacher or a member of the class has visited the place and can share their experience, for instance by using postcards or their holiday photographs as a starting point. Teachers need to use a broad range of resources such as video, music, food, artefacts and visitors to enable children to develop a sense of place.

They will also need to scaffold children's observational skills, when using secondary sources or undertaking fieldwork, through careful questioning, encouraging them to pay attention to detail, ask their own questions and look for similarities and differences. Some children may not be able to handle large amounts of information; a more effective approach might be to focus on finding out about another child's life.

Motivating children with learning difficulties

Children with learning difficulties are often motivated by puppets. Barnaby Bear, for example, can help children learn about different places around the world. They can suggest what he might need to pack to go on holiday and how he might travel there, or locate and describe places he has been to using the postcards he sends (via staff, parents or governors!) (Jackson, 2000).

Children with learning difficulties can find human geography relatively accessible as they can experience human features such as transport, housing and jobs in some form, either directly themselves or through those around them. Investigating physical features also lends itself to fieldwork and practical work: model landscapes with features such as hills, valleys, rivers, roads and buildings can be formed out of sand or earth. Physical processes can be conceptually less accessible, perhaps because they do not relate closely to people. Weather is more easily linked to people through activities such as matching clothes or activities to weather.

Maps and photographs

The concept of plan view needs to be developed through a series of small steps, such as:

- drawing round objects;
- matching objects to outline plans or images projected using an overhead projector;
- identifying plans of objects;
- matching side and plan views to objects;
- drawing plans of objects or models; and
- identifying/locating features on a classroom plan.

Aerial photographs can help children grasp the concept of plan view and thus acquire a better understanding of maps. They need to start using and interpreting ground-level and then oblique (near and further away) photographs which are less abstract and more recognizable as a representation of reality than vertical photographs. A high vantage point either within or near the school is an advantage. Practical activities, such as walking a route before mapping it, will help children reduce three dimensions to two.

Photographs or video clips are also a particularly valuable resource for stimulating enquiry. Children can identify features in the local area and perhaps use a digital camera as a means of recording. Back in the classroom they can use these photographs in activities such as labelling, sorting and sequencing. Again, once children have become used to using photographs in a familiar situation, it should be easier for them to study, compare and contrast those of unfamiliar places. Other geographical skills, such as using positional vocabulary, route-finding and directional skills, can be developed at different times of the day, for example in PE lessons, and help to build up children's level of independence.

Children's literature

The use of stories and poems can make most areas of geography more accessible to children with learning difficulties, as well as helping to develop their geographical vocabulary. *Rosie's Walk* (Hutchins, 1990), for example, can introduce children to mapping a route; poems by Monica Gunning (1994) can help them appreciate some of the characteristics of the Caribbean. There are also numerous poems and stories that make reference to the weather, seasons and natural events which enable a concept to be grasped within a familiar context before it is considered more widely.

Using stories to make geography accessible

During a trip on a local canal with her class, a Year 1 teacher took digital photographs of various features they passed. She then produced an illustrated storybook featuring the adventures of Colin the Carp. The book traced an exciting journey Colin made *under a bridge, over the road, past the church, through the reeds* and so on. He also became trapped in some of the litter they had seen.

Drama and simulations

Using drama and simulations can again increase access to the geography curriculum. This might take the form of a 'geography day' where the class focuses on a particular country; or of a rainforest environment in the classroom, complete with tropical plants and sounds. Addressing environmental issues lends itself particularly well to this approach and can enable children to develop skills such as expressing a point of view and listening and responding to the ideas of others. Playing games which involve discussion, where, for example, children can gain points only by giving an opinion, can help develop their oral skills as well as their ability to concentrate.

ICT

There may be a temptation to overuse the computer with children whose behaviour or learning difficulties appear to subside when working on it. Nevertheless, research consistently demonstrates that ICT has the power to transform the educational experience of children with learning difficulties, facilitating access to the curriculum, encouraging motivation and developing confidence and skills (Peacey, 1999). In geography, ICT has a variety of uses.

Use of ICT with children with learning difficulties

ICT can:
- be used as a technological aid for children with poor or undeveloped motor skills, for example to produce graphs or maps;
- enable children to record and communicate (including emailing) their work by using computer-generated symbol systems, banks of pictures and words, voice processors, tape recorders, video and digital cameras, concept keyboards;
- enable poor readers to access information from software with sound;
- motivate children as well as develop their geographical understanding through, for example, simple simulations and adventure games, mazes, mapping software, or information retrieval where other methods lack appeal;
- help develop geographical concepts such as plan view;
- help develop a sense of direction (through using a programmable floor turtle);
- be used by gifted or talented children for research or more creatively;
- enable children to use teacher-generated material such as worksheets.

Making reading and written tasks accessible

Geography does not rely heavily on text-based teaching and learning, as children can work with maps, photographs, video, tape recorders, graphical information, role-play, fieldwork and model-making. Access to tasks involving reading or writing should not be limited because of reading or writing demands involved.

Strategies to make reading and writing tasks more accessible include:

- adapting or simplifying text such as a newspaper article;
- presenting information in graphical form;
- the teacher reading or children listening to a tape recording as they read;
- marking pages in reference books;
- using short, simple sentences on any worksheets and, where possible, graphics;
- using a concept keyboard;
- teacher/other adult acting as scribe;
- providing a visual stimulus for reference;
- helping to generate appropriate vocabulary or providing keywords;
- providing a writing frame to help children structure their writing; and
- modelling the task first.

Poor writers often have difficulty in organizing their thoughts in order to write. Preliminary planning may help, but, where appropriate, children should be able to record or summarize their geographical learning by other means such as photographs, pictures, maps or diagrams, symbols and ICT. Children with dyslexia, for example, learn more effectively through graphics than through words and can demonstrate their understanding in graphical form rather than describing it (Nichols and Greenwold, 1999).

A child with dyslexia

James has dyslexia. His class (Year 6) was investigating coasts. Following fieldwork, he was able to demonstrate his understanding of coastal processes by drawing a diagram showing how the features he had noticed had been formed. (Alternatively, his teacher could have asked him to explain orally how the features in the photographs she had taken had been created.) He was also able to contribute some imaginative suggestions when the class was engaged in group work, discussing how the environmental quality of the beach area they had seen could be improved.

Children with Emotional and Behavioural Difficulties

Children with challenging and disturbed behaviour are perhaps some of the most difficult to teach. It is worth trying to identify the factors that appear to cause, contribute to or exacerbate undesirable behaviour, and think about ways in which these might be altered. Does it occur:

- during particular kinds of lessons (e.g. tightly structured or more open-ended)?
- at particular times of the day?
- when particular types of classroom organization are used?
- when the child is doing a particular type of activity (e.g. practical)?
- when you act or respond in a certain way?
- when other children act in a certain way?

As well as trying to promote the self-esteem and independence of these children, through praise and positive feedback, teachers need to ensure that they take account of their problems.

Effective teaching of children with EBD

- Plan carefully paced and well-structured lessons which anticipate what might happen.
- Plan short, relevant and rewarding bursts of activity to help with lack of concentration or inability to deal with too much abstract thought.
- Manage a well-organized classroom with no blind spots and which you constantly scan.
- Establish routines and clear expectations of behaviour which are consistently applied and positively reinforced.
- Involve children in group work when their awareness of others has developed.
- Take a calm, non-confrontational approach and use facial expressions or gestures rather than verbal interventions to express disapproval.
- Intervene to divert or defuse a potential outburst by perhaps suggesting a change of location or a task for which they can receive praise.
- Maintain the pace of class discussions and keep them as focused as possible, while encouraging participation.
- Ensure success and involve children in short-term target-setting.

Helping a child with EBD

Mandy (Year 2) found it difficult to work with her peers in a group. She was therefore paired with one of the more tolerant members of the class to work on labelling features on photographs of the local area (one of which included her house). When she appeared to be tiring of this task, her teacher quickly praised her for her efforts so far and suggested that she could either answer some questions about these features on a mapping program on the computer or paint a picture of her house.

Gifted and Talented Pupils

All teachers encounter children who are bright, but those who are gifted or talented have abilities and achieve levels of attainment which significantly exceed those of their peers. Identifying children as gifted is sometimes seen as an elitist approach to education, and as potentially damaging, since it can raise expectations which put undue pressure on a child. Parents' reactions can range from feelings of inadequacy to immense pride, and teachers may need to suggest how they can be supportive, for example by watching and discussing particular television programmes with their children. Nevertheless, all children are entitled to have their educational needs met and teachers need to ensure that gifted and talented children are interested, motivated, appropriately challenged and enabled to achieve their potential. Most gifted and talented pupils:

- have a thirst for knowledge and learn quickly;
- have a very retentive memory;
- can concentrate for long periods on subjects of interest;
- have a wide general knowledge and interest in the world;
- enjoy problem-solving;
- have an unusual imagination;
- show strong feelings and opinions and have an odd sense of humour;
- set high standards and are perfectionists; and
- possess keen powers of observation and reasoning, seeing relationships and generalizing from a few given facts.

In addition, they may be:

- artistic or musical;
- socially or ethically gifted;
- imaginative or creative thinkers.

Gifted and talented children may not achieve highly in all areas. A child could be an outstanding artist or technologist, or creative in using his or her imagination, yet poor at writing. The child might be visual-spatial (better at seeing and doing than at talking and listening). Unless talented children are sufficiently challenged they may become bored or unhappy, may underachieve or even become disruptive. However, it is important that these children have the opportunity to work with their peers as well as independently and for sustained periods as they are likely to be emotionally and socially at their chronological age. Teachers need to handle these children sensitively: they can be intolerant and critical, and they will often know the answer (and want to tell everyone else!), but they may be hypersensitive to criticism or be tempted to underachieve to conform. They need thoughtful, positive teacher intervention which includes challenge and constructive criticism and encouragement to think at a higher level.

Gifted children often make considerable demands on teachers to accommodate the speed and pace at which they may work. Teachers may worry about their lack of particular geographical knowledge but should not be afraid of admitting that they do not know all the answers: 'No, I'm sorry I don't know where . . . why . . . how . . . Where do you think you could find out? . . . Could you come and tell me the answer so I'll learn something as well?'

Supporting the geographical learning of gifted and talented children

Geography can offer gifted and talented children a range of challenging opportunities for pursuing their learning in greater depth or breadth and at a faster pace than their peers. This may mean drawing on material from later Key Stages or higher levels and planning further differentiation and extension by extending the breadth and depth of study, or by planning work which draws on different subjects. This could involve children in:

- being exposed to more challenging vocabulary and language (and if necessary finding out what it means);
- using a range of methods of enquiry;
- identifying and explaining patterns and processes;
- using and applying their geographical understanding in different contexts; and
- sharing their findings and so developing the knowledge and understanding of the whole class.

Children who are imaginative and creative thinkers may be able to envisage sophisticated solutions to environmental management; those who are socially or ethically gifted may be able to demonstrate considerable insight into the opinions of others; those who are artistic may be able to express themselves through well-developed cartographic skills.

Encouraging a gifted child

A Year 5 class was investigating plans to cut down a nearby copse. Caitlin's teacher asked her to put the enquiry in a global context. She used various resources such as newspaper reports and the Internet to find out about deforestation in other parts of the world. She also tried to identify whether there were similar issues involved. She presented her findings to the rest of the class at the end of the unit of work.

Reflective Questions

- Do you set appropriate learning objectives for children with SEN when teaching geography?
- Do you anticipate difficulties which may occur?
- Do you use geographical vocabulary and language at an appropriate level?
- Do you adjust your questions according to ability?
- How do you encourage children to set their own learning goals?
- Do you plan tasks which are challenging but achievable?
- Do you structure lessons in a clear sequence of manageable and achievable steps?
- How do you make full use of ICT to support children with SEN?
- How do you monitor and record children's achievements and use this information to inform your future planning?

FURTHER READING AND INFORMATION

Benton, P. and O'Brien, J. (eds) (2000) *Special Needs and the Beginning Teacher.* London: Continuum.

British Dyslexia Association: www.bda-dyslexia.org.uk/

British Epilepsy Association: www.epilepsy.org.uk

DfEE (SEN): www.dfee.gov.uk/sen

Down's Syndrome Association: www.downs-syndrome.org.uk

National Association for Gifted Children: www.rmplc.co.uk/orgs/nagc

National Autistic Society: www.oneworld.org/autism_uk/

Scope [cerebral palsy]: www.scope.org.uk/

Sebba, J. (1995) *Geography for All.* London: David Fulton.

Stakes, R. and Hornby, G. (1996) *Meeting Special Needs in Mainstream Schools: A Practical Guide for Teachers.* London: David Fulton.

REFERENCES

Blyth, A. and Krause, J. (1995) *Primary Geography: A Developmental Approach.* London: Hodder & Stoughton.

DES (1978) *Special Educational Needs* (The Warnock Report). London: HMSO.

DfEE/QCA (1999) *The National Curriculum Handbook for Primary Teachers in England.* London: DfEE/QCA.

Gunning, M. (1994) *Not a Copper Penny in Me House.* London: Macmillan.

Hutchins, P. (1990) *Rosie's Walk.* London: Penguin.

Jackson, E. (2000) *Barnaby Bear Goes to Dublin.* Sheffield: Geographical Association.

Nichols, S. and Greenwold, L. (1999) 'Geography roles KO!', *Primary Geographer* 36, 8–9.

Peacey, N. (1999) 'Inclusive geography', *Primary Geographer* 36, 4–7.

Print, A. (1999) 'Teaching geography to hearing-impaired children', *Primary Geographer* 36, 18–19.

Sebba, J., Byers, R. and Rose, R. (1993) *Redefining the Whole Curriculum for Pupils with Learning Difficulties.* London: David Fulton.

Siddles, R. (1999) 'Teaching children with autistic spectrum disorders in mainstream primary schools', in *The Autistic Spectrum: A Handbook.* London: National Autistic Society.

Smith, S. (1999) 'What? IEPs for mainstream geography?', *Primary Geographer* 36, 16–17.

Spencer, C. P. and Blades, M. (1993) 'Children's understanding of places: the world at hand', *Geography* 78(4), 367–73.

Spencer, C. P., Blades, M. and Morsley, K. (1989) *The Child in the Physical Environment.* Chichester: Wiley.

Co-ordinating Geography

Before the advent of the National Curriculum, teachers were often awarded curriculum co-ordinator posts in recognition of long service and experience. They may have had little more to do than manage resources. Since 1989, however, nursery and primary teachers have had to develop their expertise across a broad range of subjects or areas of learning. It has been suggested that schools can deliver the curriculum more effectively by capitalizing on their staff's subject strengths and giving co-ordinators responsibility for developing teaching and learning within their subject area (Alexander *et al.*, 1992). Consequently, curriculum co-ordination has become an increasingly complex task.

Most teachers are expected to co-ordinate one or more areas of the curriculum, yet are given little if any non-contact time in which to fulfil their responsibilities. In many cases they have to take on this multifaceted and accountable role at the very start of their careers. The position and title of those responsible for geography vary widely. They may be a class teacher, deputy head or headteacher; team leaders may also find that aspects of the Early Learning Goals related to geography are part of their concern. They may have the title co-ordinator, postholder or subject leader. This chapter uses the term 'co-ordinator', since it implies that this person works with and through colleagues, rather than on or at them, to develop good practice.

Some teachers may be asked to take responsibility for areas of the curriculum in which they have little subject expertise. In addition, for many, the skills and knowledge associated with curriculum co-ordination would appear to have been 'caught', not taught (Webb, 1994). Curriculum co-ordination, particularly of the foundation subjects, also needs to be considered against a background of constant change over the past decade. The introduction of the national literacy and numeracy strategies and an increased emphasis on ICT, accompanied by testing, target-setting and league tables, have all increased curriculum time spent on 'basic skills', as well as the pressures on teachers. This is reflected in the requirements for initial teacher training (ITT) (DfEE,

1998a), which focus on the core curriculum and ICT. Fewer places are allocated for specialists in the foundation subjects and the time spent on these subjects by non-specialists has been reduced. Thus, this chapter is aimed at supporting practising teachers without a background in geography as well as encouraging ITT students with a subject specialism in geography to take a lead in the development of the subject within a school. It outlines the roles and responsibilities of a geography co-ordinator and the knowledge and qualities that person needs in order to fulfil them and carry them out successfully. It also considers the challenges and problems the co-ordinator may face and how these might be addressed.

The Geography Co-ordinator's Role

Geography co-ordinators should have a clearly defined role, recognized in the school development plan and backed up by a job description. Essentially, they are expected to develop the quality of teaching and learning in geography across the school. This will involve them in performing a number of different functions (Table 10.1).

In order to perform these functions successfully, geography co-ordinators require expertise in two main areas: subject knowledge and interpersonal skills. The ability to motivate and lead colleagues is particularly important if geography is not seen as a priority in the school and co-ordinators have to 'sell' the subject.

Table 10.1 **The geography co-ordinator's role**

Nature of role	The geography co-ordinator might:
Initiator	• Produce an outline plan for involving the school in the Geographical Association's Geography Action Week • Suggest ways in which the school grounds could be used for geographical enquiry
Facilitator	• Check that each unit of work is supported by appropriate resources • Pre-OFSTED, be available to discuss colleagues' proposed lessons
Co-ordinator	• Ensure colleagues complete thorough risk assessments before undertaking fieldwork • Liaise with the feeder nursery and local secondary school to promote continuity and progression
Educator	• Teach colleagues how to use new mapping software • Introduce new QCA units of work
Evaluator	• Evaluate the school's scheme of work in the light of the National Curriculum (2000) and Early Learning Goals • Recommend which digital camera the school should purchase
Monitor	• Observe a newly qualified teacher (NQT) colleague who has identified geography as an area for development • Plan a staff meeting when colleagues will assess and level children's work

Subject knowledge

To be effective geography co-ordinators, it is essential that teachers are enthusiastic about the subject, committed to its place in the curriculum and keen to develop good practice. They also need the subject knowledge which has been identified as a precursor to teaching of high quality. This involves rather more than the skills and knowledge that have been acquired through A level and further study. It also includes an understanding of the nature of the subject: knowledge of the factors which promote learning in geography, and the skills needed to teach it successfully at different levels (Knight, 1993). In practice, this could mean possessing the ability to:

- explain 'sustainable development' to a new governor using jargon-free vocabulary;
- refer colleagues to appropriate Web sites for weather data;
- teach a colleague how to use a compass correctly and suggest appropriate activities for children;
- suggest appropriate geographical vocabulary that should be taught in the nursery; and
- explain to a colleague why children may find learning about river processes difficult and how their difficulties could be tackled.

Co-ordinators should also feel confident in their knowledge of the local area.

Geography co-ordinators need to understand how the subject fits into the whole curriculum framework as well as being thoroughly familiar with the National Curriculum Programme of Study, such as the localities to be studied in depth at each Key Stage and the themes to be covered at Key Stage 2. They should know where geography features in the Early Learning Goals and the kind of geographical experiences children are likely to have had before embarking on Key Stage 1. They will also be aware of the form that geography takes at Key Stage 3. More specifically, they should understand how children make progress in each of the four aspects of geography.

Geography specialists will have a degree of expertise upon which to build when they become qualified teachers, but all co-ordinators need to keep abreast of current developments. These include:

- initiatives, whether at local or national level, such as material produced by QCA which would support geography teaching, or opportunities to become involved in a Local Agenda 21 project;
- OFSTED's reviews of inspection findings and whether the strengths and weaknesses identified in geography teaching nationally apply to their school;
- research into primary and early years geography.

This information can be accessed through various means such as

- LEA geography co-ordinator meetings;
- local Geographical Association meetings;
- conferences such as the National Primary Geography Conference;
- INSET courses;
- summaries of research such as those in publications edited by Scoffham (1998) and Bowles (2000), and briefer accounts in, for example, the *Times Educational Supplement*, *Primary Geographer*, *Child Education* and *Junior Education*; and

- Web sites such as the Staffordshire Learning Net for Geography (http://www.sln.org.uk/geography).

Simply meeting others involved in geography can be a positive experience for co-ordinators, renewing their enthusiasm for the subject and helping with the isolation and frustration they may experience in their own schools. However, it is important that relevant information or ideas acquired from these sources are relayed to colleagues, perhaps as an item in a staff meeting. Updating their subject knowledge not only will help co-ordinators in their own teaching and when advising others, but may also inform discussion about the development of the subject.

How a co-ordinator can influence the development of geography teaching

While reviewing the school's scheme of work, some staff say that they think it is inappropriate to investigate distant localities with young children. The geography co-ordinator is able to persuade them otherwise. She explains how young children come into contact with people and places beyond their direct experience on a regular basis. She then confidently summarizes research indicating that there is a strong link between knowledge of other people, places and cultures and attitude formation (Wiegand, 1992; Palmer, 1994), and suggests appropriate activities for the nursery and Key Stage 1 classes.

Continuous professional development (CPD) has been identified as essential to effective curriculum leadership (Krause, 1998). However, it is unlikely that externally provided INSET will cater for updating co-ordinators' knowledge and skills adequately.

One way of enhancing professional development is through undertaking small-scale research, which might focus on, for example, analysing one's own teaching, assessing children's learning or examining children's understanding of a particular aspect of geography. Indeed, research and evidence-based practice is now encouraged by the DfEE (1998b), and teachers may be able to gain funding for research through, for example, the Teacher Training Agency's Teacher Research Grant Scheme. Foskett and Marsden (1998) and Bowles (1997) provide comprehensive sources of information on previous research, while Catling (2000) suggests many areas of primary geography, such as teaching strategies, assessment and the impact of resources, where there is a need for further research in order to create a sound foundation for geography's effective development.

The following titles indicate the type of research that has been undertaken by practising teachers:

- strategies to encourage children to ask geographical questions (Chapman, 1999);
- gender differences in spatial awareness (Till, 1997);
- young children's perceptions of their immediate environment (Poulter, 2000);
- children's perceptions of farmers and farming (Wilson, 2000).

The Geography Co-ordinator's Responsibilities

Documentation

Geography co-ordinators are ultimately responsible for the production of various pieces of documentation. Two points are worth bearing in mind here. First, co-ordinators do not simply generate a sheaf of papers for rubber-stamping by the rest of the staff. Rather, they consult colleagues who contribute to the end product. By feeling that they have some ownership of, say, a geography policy, staff are more likely to feel willing and confident about putting it into operation. Second, documentation needs to be used, monitored and evaluated. Review points should be agreed so that policies and schemes of work are not merely written and put in a cupboard to gather dust.

Consulting colleagues

The school's geography scheme of work had been in place for three years. The co-ordinator asked all class teachers for copies of units of work they had taught, annotated with brief comments. This enabled him to identify, for example, where more resources were required, where the content could be cut in some units and where more variety in activities was needed. He also took this chance to suggest how opportunities to include ICT and citizenship could be developed.

The establishment of OFSTED in 1992 has provided an added impetus to ensuring that documentation is in place. It is therefore unlikely that geography co-ordinators will be required to produce a policy or scheme of work from scratch; they are more likely to be involved in evaluating and fine-tuning documentation.

Geography policy

Most schools produce policies which follow a similar format, and often one that has been suggested by the local education authority (LEA). A geography policy should be a concise and clearly written document that reflects a consensus of staff views on the school's rationale for teaching the subject. It should identify the broad principles that underpin the way in which the subject is approached and thus provide a framework for planning. Geography policies will have a number of common features but they will also reflect the particular situation and needs of a school such as its location or the ethnic make-up of the school community.

Geography policies

A geography policy will usually include brief statements that refer to:

- the nature of geography;
- the school's aims for teaching and learning in geography;
- allocation of time;
- curriculum organization;
- approaches to teaching and learning;
- classroom organization and management;
- continuity and progression;
- equal opportunities;
- differentiation and special educational needs;
- meeting the needs of early years pupils;
- links with other subjects and elements of the curriculum;
- assessment, recording and reporting;
- resources;
- the role of parents;
- health and safety;
- links with the wider community;
- the role of the geography co-ordinator; and
- arrangements for monitoring and evaluation.

Geography scheme of work

A geography scheme of work shows how policy is translated into practice. Based on statutory documentation, it sets out the detail of the geography curriculum. It is not something that can be produced quickly: it might be compiled by combining units of work which teachers have taught successfully with appropriate QCA units, in order to meet statutory and school requirements.

Geography schemes of work

The following elements should be clearly identifiable:

- where the four aspects are taught and assessed;
- balanced, integrated study of places, themes and skills;
- study of a variety of places, near and far;
- progression, for example in the development of mapping skills;
- continuity, for example in use of fieldwork;
- variety in enquiry-based teaching and learning approaches;
- variety in classroom groupings;
- how differentiation can be achieved;
- provision, for example of resoures, for children with special educational needs;
- cross-curricular elements such as citizenship;
- links with other curricular areas;
- opportunities to develop and reinforce skills in literacy, numeracy and ICT;
- how health and safety requirements are met;

- details of resources and their location; and
- arrangements for monitoring and evaluation.

Geography schemes of work can vary in the amount of detail they contain. A scheme which, for example, stipulates particular localities, lists activities and resources and includes the worksheets to be used could be seen as a godsend, enabling teachers to concentrate on differentiation in their short-term planning. Others would argue that this stifles teachers' creativity. Perhaps a compromise is the answer, where learning outcomes or objectives are stated and accompanied by a list of suggested activities and resources.

Assessment, recording and reporting

Geography co-ordinators are responsible for ensuring that the assessment, recording and reporting of geography are carried out to meet statutory requirements. These processes should also be purposeful, manageable and of benefit to teachers, pupils, parents and other interested parties where appropriate. Assessment, recording and reporting of geography should be in line with whole-school policy and practice. However, it is useful if the geography co-ordinator produces guidelines for colleagues, linked to the scheme of work.

Guidelines for the assessment, recording and reporting of geography teaching

Guidelines should include the following information:

- what is of significance in geography and what colleagues should be assessing (that is, the four elements);
- the range of assessment methods that could be used;
- how and when assessments should be recorded;
- suggestions about marking children's work and providing feedback, again reflecting whole-school policy and emphasizing that it is geographical content that is being marked, rather than, for example, a child's ability in English;
- suggestions as to how colleagues might report on children's work to parents; and
- suggestions as to how children can assess their own work.

These points have been explored in more detail in Chapter 7.

Geography portfolio

As geography co-ordinators are responsible for monitoring what pupils are learning as well as what teachers are teaching, it is good practice to collect evidence of children's attainment. This can be achieved by compiling a portfolio of work. This should cover the four aspects of geography, accurately reflect the geography being taught in the school, and demonstrate characteristics of children's performance at different levels. Ideally the contents of this portfolio should have been discussed and moderated, and levels agreed upon by colleagues. It can have many uses, such as

- developing a shared interpretation and understanding of the characteristics and differences between levels;
- demonstrating the standard of consistency between teachers;
- helping the co-ordinator to monitor the quality and standards of geography across the school;
- demonstrating continuity and progression across the school;
- demonstrating how differentiation takes place;
- helping teachers understand progression in learning in geography;
- helping new colleagues to develop appropriate expectations;
- exemplifying how 'best fit' judgements can be made; and
- demonstrating to interested parties such as OFSTED inspectors, the LEA, governors and parents what children are learning in geography and the standards they are attaining.

As well as a range of written and graphical work, the portfolio may include:

- photographs of models and displays;
- photographs of children using fieldwork skills;
- teachers' notes, particularly on younger children's attainment, as evidence of this is likely to be more ephemeral;
- a range of work from one pupil to indicate how 'best fit' judgements are made; and
- work which demonstrates a range of achievement within one particular level.

Whatever is included in the portfolio needs to be annotated, where appropriate, to indicate:

- the context (what instructions were given; how much support was given; what resources were used; whether the child worked individually or in a group; any constraints); and
- evidence the work provides of geographical knowledge, understanding and/or skills.

Resources for teaching and learning geography

Geography co-ordinators are responsible for ensuring that teaching and learning are supported by appropriate resources. This involves:

- auditing resources;
- consulting with colleagues on their needs;
- organizing and maintaining resources; and
- budgeting for, evaluating and selecting resources.

One of the first tasks of a new geography co-ordinator should be to undertake an audit of resources, including the features of the local area such as people, buildings and environments.

- What resources does the school have?
- Are they reasonably up to date and in good condition?
- Is there a range of reference books, maps, photographs, videos and software?
- Do resources cater for children of different abilities?
- Are they educationally sound, for example avoiding stereotyping?
- Do resources support active, enquiry-based learning?
- Where are resources stored? How accessible are they?

Expenditure can then be prioritized to ensure that all units of work focused on geography are adequately resourced. Co-ordinators can also provide colleagues with a list of resources and where they are stored. This should include generic ICT software and hardware as well as children's fiction and non-fiction which could be used to support geography.

A co-ordinator's ongoing task will be to monitor resources, ensuring that they are well maintained, disposing of any of poor quality, and cataloguing and labelling new materials. It is a good idea to photocopy any instruction booklets and keep the original copy. Acquiring new resources will involve decisions, made preferably with colleagues, such as what is essential and whether class sets are preferable to a more limited range of good-quality, more interesting equipment (which would have implications for how the subject might be taught). Co-ordinators should be creative about looking for funding and resources beyond the school budget: the Parent–Teacher Association, local industry and commerce, charities such as Learning through Landscapes, European Union funding for European initiatives, and local or national competitions with geographical themes such as environmental improvement are all worth considering.

New resources should reflect good geographical and educational practice – for example, fostering enquiry-based learning and avoiding stereotyping as well as being cost-effective. However, good resources are of little use unless colleagues are aware of their existence and how they should be used. They could be displayed in the staff room or made the focus of an assembly. Educational catalogues and conference displays can be perused for new resources, and reviews in publications such as *Primary Geographer*, *Nursery Education* and the *Times Educational Supplement* consulted. Representatives from educational suppliers can be asked to display and talk about their products. In this case, it is important to be critical: it is their job to sell!

Communication

Communicating effectively with teaching colleagues is of considerable importance and is considered in more depth in the section on developing good practice across a school. However, there are also other individuals, agencies and groups of people with whom geography co-ordinators may communicate (Table 10.2). They need to consider their audience carefully and tailor their message accordingly in terms of content, style and delivery. Co-ordinators should aim to find a balance between providing too much information and too little, and should ensure that it is relevant, clear and, in most cases, free from educational and technical jargon and unfamiliar acronyms and abbreviations.

Table 10.2 **A geography co-ordinator's responsibilities for communication**

Communication with	Examples of when co-ordinators may communicate
Headteacher	• Engaging the headteacher's interest in geography, if necessary (headteachers can provide time, money, support and authority) • Keeping the headteacher informed of progress in monitoring geography teaching in the school
Governors	• Explaining the geography development plan (governors are responsible for the curriculum, staff and budgetary constraints and opportunities)
Parents/carers	• Informing parents through the school newsletter about a local environmental project in which certain classes are involved • Writing a paragraph on the geography curriculum for inclusion in the school prospectus • Asking the Parent–Teacher Association for funds for fieldwork equipment • Involving parents in field trips and producing resources such as the laminating of photographs
Pupils	• Motivating children and raising the profile of geography by involving the school in Geography Action Week
NQTs/students	• Acting as mentor to an NQT with geography as a main subject • Inducting and supporting non-specialist NQTs
SENCO	• Suggesting appropriate activities for gifted/talented pupils • Ensuring that children with physical disabilities can participate in fieldwork
Staff in feeder/ secondary schools	• Exchanging information on which localities and issues children have studied and where fieldwork has been undertaken
The wider community	• Contacting people such as shopkeepers who work in the local community, and local education and business partnerships, for information and for arranging visits and visitors
Other teachers	• Planning INSET with another geography co-ordinator • Emailing other teachers to develop work on contrasting localities (educational publications often include requests for links) • Arranging an exchange (Central Bureau for Educational Visits and Exchanges)
LEA	• Making and maintaining contact with the geography adviser and finding out what is available in terms of advice, support and training
Professional organizations	• Becoming a member of the Geographical Association
University education departments	• Negotiating placements for geography specialists • Developing joint research projects

Communication and liaison with a university education department

The school receives a letter from the local teacher training institution asking if it will take four final-year geography specialists to focus on curriculum co-ordination. The co-ordinator attends a meeting at the university to discuss the placement with university tutors and other primary colleagues. She then negotiates and helps plan a two-week programme with the students, which will be of benefit to both the school and the students. This includes them:

- contributing to the school's portfolio by assessing and levelling children's work;
- planning and teaching geography-related activities in the nursery;
- observing each other teaching;
- compiling a list of Web sites to support units in the school's scheme of work;
- devising and trialling an orienteering course in the school grounds; and
- discussing the co-ordinator's roles and responsibilities with her.

Geography co-ordinators will also come into contact with OFSTED inspectors. Inspection is invariably a stressful time but it is possible to minimize the anxiety by being well prepared. The responsibilities of the geography co-ordinator in relation to inspection can be summarized as follows (Table 10.3).

It is worth remembering that critical comments in an OFSTED report can be a positive force. They can focus attention on a subject and good practice, attract resources and indicate where staff development is necessary.

Table 10.3   **The geography co-ordinator's responsibilities in relation to OFSTED**

Before inspection	Check that: • Comments made on previous inspections have been addressed. • Documentation is in order, up to date, understood by staff and reflected in practice. • Geography is well integrated into the curriculum. • Resources are adequate to support teaching, well maintained and where they should be. • Colleagues are clear about geography's distinctive contribution to the curriculum as well as to its wider aims and basic skills. • Colleagues are motivating and challenging children in their teaching. • Fieldwork is not postponed or cancelled: it is part of good practice, and well-planned and well-organized fieldwork with appropriate follow-up can impress inspectors. • There is evidence in planning and children's work if geography will not be observed. • High-quality geographical work is on display.
During inspection	• Ensure that colleagues are confident about the geography they are teaching by running through lesson plans with them if necessary. • When interviewed, be truthful; demonstrate knowledge of what is happening in the school, stress the positive and how teachers are supported, but also indicate an awareness of what needs doing. • Use the oral feedback session to pick up advice for the future.
After inspection	• Read relevant parts of the published report, including general comments, for example on assessment, which are applicable; plan to address any weaknesses identified.

205

CO-ORDINATING GEOGRAPHY

Developing Good Practice across a School

The publication of documentation such as the National Curriculum and schemes of work for geography have not automatically led to a dramatic increase in the quality of geography teaching in schools. Improving teaching and learning geography is therefore central to the role of co-ordinators, particularly since research suggests that the major factor in effecting change and development is felt to be the influence of the curriculum leader. Monitoring, in particular, can be a very powerful tool for improving the learning environment and raising standards of pupil achievement, although direct monitoring of teaching can be difficult to arrange (OFSTED, 1999).

A number of factors, both external and internal, may stimulate the development of geography, from new statutory requirements to a general feeling of dissatisfaction amongst staff with the way geography is taught. However, it has been suggested that many co-ordinators feel more comfortable acting as a helper or fellow worker rather than as an adviser or decision-maker. They see their role as providers of documentation, ideas and resources, rather than as monitoring and evaluating teaching and learning and helping colleagues to develop (OFSTED, 1999). Thus the remainder of this chapter explores how geography co-ordinators can develop the subject by successfully initiating and implementing change.

Problems and challenges

Geography co-ordinators have a range of responsibilities, some of which, like managing resources, are relatively straightforward to manage successfully. However, developing the subject can be more problematic for a variety of reasons:

- the history of the school: 'we've never done much geography here';
- the ethos of the school: the school focuses on the core curriculum in spirit as well as in practice;
- lack of communication and lack of a culture of co-operation amongst staff;
- poor leadership: the head has considerable influence on the culture of the school and thus upon its practices and policies;
- familiarity: some co-ordinators may find it difficult to take on a more proactive role with colleagues in order to develop good practice as this may be construed as judgemental;
- hostility: NQTs appointed as geography co-ordinators may face opposition from those who feel that they have been teaching for a long time and there is little anyone can tell them about teaching geography: 'we always go to Whitby in June for our geography trip – the children have a lovely time collecting shells and looking in rock pools . . .'

Teachers' attitudes to change

Underlying many of these problems are teachers' attitudes to change in general. They may have become accustomed to change but this does not mean that they find it any easier to accept, and geography co-ordinators may encounter a range of perspectives, from the 'rational apathetic' to the 'Stone Age obstructionist' (Doyle and Pounder, 1976, cited in Pollard, 1997). Colleagues may feel that their competence is being threatened and lose confidence if they consider that they do not possess the skills or knowledge to implement initiatives. Colleagues may object to having established practices challenged and disrupted. Alternatively, it may be that their own school experience has left them with a dislike of geography.

Helping a colleague who is unwilling to expand her geography teaching

A Key Stage 1 teacher with some 20 years' experience had shown little interest in developing the school's geography scheme of work. On reviewing what had been taught over the first year, the geography co-ordinator found that children in this class had received little teaching that would have developed their geographical skills, particularly in map work. Tactful discussion with the teacher revealed that she was fascinated by other places but had had an unhappy experience of geography at school and had been confused about aspects of mapping such as scale and grid references. The co-ordinator lent her a book which explained progression in developing children's geographical skills clearly with exemplar activities and then helped her plan a forthcoming lesson. She made a note to check with her colleague after this lesson how effective she thought her teaching had been.

Implementing change

It can be a daunting prospect for geography co-ordinators, particularly at the beginning of their careers, to attempt to enthuse colleagues and make a case for the subject to be a priority in the face of a multitude of other pressures. Furthermore, subject expertise alone will not enable them to bring about curriculum change: co-ordinators need to possess (or develop quickly) certain personal and interpersonal skills. Colleagues are more likely to respond positively to initiatives that are led by a co-ordinator who can answer in the affirmative to most of the following questions.

A co-ordinator's attitudes and approach

- Do I appear confident and enthusiastic about geography?
- Am I clear about what change is required and why?
- Am I positive, whilst recognizing that change is a process that takes time?
- Am I well prepared and organized?
- Am I aware of my strengths and weaknesses – for example, am I better at leading staff meetings or supporting staff on a more informal one-to-one basis?
- Am I prepared to be challenged about my proposals and can I accept constructive criticism and acknowledge that I do not know all the answers?
- Do I acknowledge that some staff will not follow my proposals and that I may have to make compromises?
- Do I have high expectations but recognize that it is never easy to bring practice into line with ideals?

Positive educational developments are almost impossible to sustain without teamwork (Pollard, 1997). Ensuring progression and continuity in geography, for example, calls for whole-school co-operation. Teamwork is particularly important in early years settings where large numbers of staff, teaching and non-teaching, may be involved in children's learning. Consequently, the attitudes of those involved are a significant factor in the successful implementation of change. However, a co-ordinator needs to provide leadership and direction, rather than feed colleagues theory, give them some new resources and then leave them to get on with it. In order for co-ordinators to gain colleagues' interest in and commitment to developing geography, they need to possess certain interpersonal skills which are identified in the following questions.

A co-ordinator's interpersonal skills

- Do I respect and value colleagues, seeking their ideas and suggestions?
- Can I convince colleagues of the need for change?
- Am I approachable, willing to listen to colleagues' concerns and prepared to negotiate so that perspectives are shared and collective strategies for action agreed?
- Do I choose my time and place carefully?
- Do I encourage and praise colleagues to motivate them?
- Do I provide appropriate, focused advice and support and in different ways, such as working with colleagues on an individual basis and running workshops?
- Am I realistic in what I ask colleagues to do, acknowledging their priorities as well as their strengths and weaknesses?
- Am I willing to give of my time to talk through a lesson, or look at a half-termly plan?

Geography co-ordinators inevitably have to work within the constraints of the nature of their colleagues, and not everyone may share their vision. Presumably most teachers want the effect of their efforts to be maximized and would like to teach as effectively as possible, but for staff to be committed to curriculum development, they have to recognize that change is desirable. This might mean, for example, that encouraging enquiry-based learning is presented as an opportunity to develop skills that can be applied in other areas of the curriculum; or that reviewing the scheme of work could be a way of highlighting interesting and meaningful contexts in which skills in literacy, numeracy and ICT could be developed and reinforced. If change is to last, it needs to be 'bottom-up' rather than 'top-down'; in other words, staff need to recognize that change is necessary, know where it is going, and be agreed on, and involved in, curriculum development. Finally, any change should be focused, particularly at areas where the co-ordinator, staff or inspectors have identified weaknesses.

208

Where to start

New geography co-ordinators will initially need to take stock of the situation in which they find themselves. One way of doing this is through a SWOT analysis: this involves identifying strengths, weaknesses, opportunities and threats (Table 10.4) in relation to the development of geography, which can then be built on, addressed or maximized. This will arise from the responses to a number of questions.

Some questions to be considered in doing a SWOT analysis

- Is good practice in geography well established or is radical change required?
- Where does geography feature in the school development plan?
- What ideas does the headteacher have and what level of support can be expected?
- Does the co-ordinator need to respond to a critical OFSTED report and what needs to be prioritized?
- What is the level of staff expertise and interest in geography? Where would they welcome support?
- Is it possible to identify where geography is well taught and where there is scope for development?
- Do children have a recurring, balanced experience of geography (from the scheme of work)?
- What does the present policy say and is this reflected in practice?
- What do children's work and displays say about the state of geography?
- What resources are available and where are they stored?

Table 10.4 **An example of a SWOT analysis**

Strengths	• A range of good-quality resources • Staff generally receptive to change
Weaknesses	• A number of new staff with little expertise in geography • Children arrive from feeder infant schools with varying experiences of geography
Opportunities	• Geography prioritized in school development plan • Local ITT institution looking for schools to support geography specialists, with funding
Threats	• School is failing to meet targets, so extra time may be allocated to literacy and numeracy • Cut in the school's subsidy for residential fieldwork has been proposed

Table 10.5 **Example of an easily achieved short-term target**

Target	To develop geography on residential field trips
Criteria for success	Clear enquiry-based learning objectives are identified for each visit
Action	Focused planning
Staff responsible	Geography co-ordinator and class teachers
Action date	End of term
Resources/costs	None

The geography co-ordinator needs to identify priorities and set realistic short-, medium- and longer-term aims with which colleagues agree. These will form a curriculum development plan, probably for the next three years, as part of the whole school development plan. Success is motivating, so it is advisable to set some short-term targets which can be achieved reasonably painlessly and cheaply. Some examples are shown in Table 10.5.

Staff development

Once colleagues' strengths, weaknesses and needs have been identified, geography co-ordinators can plan for staff development. This can take a variety of forms:

- informal: discussing a lesson over coffee at playtime;
- indirect: demonstrating good practice through a display of children's work on an enquiry or through describing fieldwork in an assembly;
- good practitioner: co-ordinators develop their own classroom as an example of good practice and invite colleagues to observe them teaching;
- work alongside staff: planning and managing fieldwork with a colleague;
- structured: inducting new colleagues and NQTs;
- formal training: school-based INSET which could be run by the co-ordinator or a well-briefed visitor and could range from part of a staff meeting to a whole day involving support staff and including fieldwork, demonstrations and workshops. Krause and Garner (1997) suggest a wealth of activities for use in school-based INSET sessions.

The final section of this chapter looks at how a geography co-ordinator might respond to an OFSTED report (Box 10.1), first drawing up an action plan and then planning an INSET session to address some of the identified targets. The geography co-ordinator analysed and summarized these findings, identifying those aspects in which standards were satisfactory and could be built on as well as the areas for improvement. An action plan was then drawn up for inclusion in the whole-school plan. It used the same headings as the development plan and identified the following targets:

- to produce guidelines on assessment, recording and reporting in geography;
- to observe all colleagues teaching geography;
- to plan for coherence and progression in the development of children's mapping skills;
- to identify opportunities for differentiation in planning and devise appropriate activities for the less and more able; and
- to integrate the use of ICT into the teaching and learning of geography.

The following action then took place:

- The headteacher agreed to make time available at a staff meeting to obtain feedback on the action plan.
- The draft proposals were circulated to colleagues.
- The proposals were discussed and agreed at the staff meeting.
- It was decided to start with half a day's INSET focusing on assessment and ICT but which would also take into account the needs identified in the co-ordinator's staff audit.
- The co-ordinator prepared the programme for this training.

Box 10.1   Section from an OFSTED report concerned with geography

---

Geography

119.   Only a small number of lessons were observed during the inspection. However, scrutiny of pupils' work and teachers' planning and discussion with pupils shows that standards in geography are in line with national expectations at Key Stage 1 and exceeding expectations at Key Stage 2. The quality of teaching varies between good and satisfactory. This enables pupils to make satisfactory gains in the acquisition of geographical knowledge, skills and understanding. Often pupils' own backgrounds are used as a basis for teaching.

120.   Good progress is made in Key Stage 1 in raising pupils' awareness of the world. A residential visit and fieldwork in the local area help pupils to observe similarities and differences in the human and physical characteristics of a place. Pupils begin to make and use maps although the work is disjointed and does not build mapping skills sufficiently systematically.

121.   By the end of Key Stage 2 pupils have a good understanding of their local environment and the different countries represented in the school. They can compare and contrast lifestyles in these places with their own. However, little use is made of ICT, for example when looking for information on these countries.

122.   The quality of teaching is satisfactory overall. Teachers are confident and display a good knowledge of the subject matter. In a Year 5 class, for example, where pupils were engaged in a debate focused on the development of tourism on St Lucia, the teacher's enthusiasm and expertise gave them a clear understanding of environmental and development issues. All lessons observed were well planned, with the key ideas and concepts identified. However, planning does not always enable the needs of all pupils to be met. The work for the least able is sometimes too difficult and higher-attaining pupils are not always given sufficiently challenging work.

123.   Pupils' attitudes to learning are satisfactory. Pupils enjoy their work in geography and display interest in the topics they are engaged in. They listen well and pay attention to the teacher. Pupils work together in small groups and evidence from fieldwork indicates that they work well together outside school.

124.   The subject is effectively led and managed by the co-ordinator. However, because it has not recently been a whole-school development priority, she has had little opportunity to monitor the quality of teaching and learning to ensure that the needs of all pupils are met. Assessment and recording have not been developed systematically and teachers have only limited information about what pupils already know to help them in their planning.

- Staff were asked to collect examples of children's work for assessment and levelling purposes, familiarize themselves with the levels in geography, and look at *Expectations in Geography* (SCAA, 1997).

Co-ordinators need to remember that there is usually pressure on the time available at staff meetings and they need to be chaired efficiently in order to be productive. In other words,

- discussion is kept on track and to time;
- colleagues are encouraged to read any documentation to be discussed beforehand;
- the chair seeks to involve everyone and demonstrate that all opinions are valued; and
- the chair summarizes discussions, ensures that there is agreement on decisions and ensures that these are minuted.

Box 10.2   Geography INSET

9.00–9.10   **Introduction** (headteacher, followed by geography co-ordinator)
- purpose and aims of morning
- plan for morning

9.10–10.20   **Assessment**
- what to assess in geography
- how to assess in geography
Staff to work in Key Stage groups:
- assess and level children's work; which pieces are most useful for assessment purposes?
- devise recording format

10.20   **Plenary**
- feedback from groups
- developing self-assessment

10.30–10.40   **Coffee break**

10.50–12.00   **Literacy, numeracy and ICT, and geography**
English, maths and ICT co-ordinators to lead mixed-age groups
- take two different types of units of work and identify opportunities for skills development in these areas
- plan two activities in detail

12.00   **Plenary**
- feedback from groups
- review aims and summarize the morning's achievements
- what next?
- arrangements for monitoring

12.20   **Lunch**

However, staff may not be at their most creative in staff meetings, and curriculum development activities are best planned for half or whole days. Box 10.2 outlines a half-day programme which the geography co-ordinator might have planned.

Planning INSET is similar to lesson planning: it needs to have a clear purpose which is shared with colleagues and to be thought through carefully so that the best use is made of the time available. It also needs to address colleagues' needs. As can be seen, this programme does not try to cover everything at once. It focuses on assessment and ICT, which were identified as weaknesses by OFSTED. However, it also includes activities on literacy and numeracy, which had been identified as concerns by staff. In this case, the headteacher introduced the day (the afternoon would focus on history). The geography co-ordinator then explained the purpose of the morning and how it would address staff and school needs, recapping on the OFSTED report and what was revealed by the staff audit. She then outlined the activities for the morning. Following a brief summary of assessment in geography, she decided to 'float' between groups as they assessed children's work, using a pro forma that she had devised, and then related their assessments to aspects of the level descriptions. Plenary sessions were seen as important so that each group would know what the others had been doing.

The co-ordinator delegated leadership of the next session to the relevant curriculum co-ordinators in order to make use of their subject expertise as well as contributing to their staff development. Colleagues were encouraged to think carefully about, for example, whether children's writing could take the form of a postcard, a poster or a poem, or how they might organize the use of a database.

In the second plenary session, she looked at how far the aims for the morning had been met and indicated what she would do with the material that had been produced. Staff suggested what they saw as the next step. Finally, the co-ordinator put forward her proposals for monitoring teaching for discussion, emphasizing that these were intended to be supportive rather than threatening.

Reflective Questions

- What do your colleagues think geography is or involves?
- Are they confident in teaching geography?
- What geographical work takes place in the nursery?
- How far is the geography policy reflected in practice?
- What do you see as future developments in geography?
- How do you monitor provision and quality in geography?
- How do you influence practice across the school?
- What opportunities do you have to support staff?

FURTHER READING AND INFORMATION

Geographical Association: http://www.geography.org.uk

Geographical Association (1999) *Leading Geography: National Standards for Geography Leaders in Primary Schools*. Sheffield: Geographical Association.

Halocha, J. (1998) *Co-ordinating Geography across the Primary School*. Lewes: Falmer Press.

Teacher Training Agency (1998) *National Standards for Subject Leaders*. London: TTA.

REFERENCES

Alexander, R., Rose, J. and Woodhead, C. (1992) *Curriculum Organisation and Classroom Practice in Primary Schools*. London: DES.

Bowles, R. (1997) *Register of Research in Primary Geography*. London: Register of Research in Primary Geography.

Bowles, R. (ed.) (2000) *Raising Achievement in Geography*. London: Register of Research in Primary Geography.

Catling, S. (2000) 'The importance of classroom research in primary geography', in R. Bowles (ed.) *Raising Achievement in Geography*. London: Register of Research in Primary Geography.

Chapman, J. (1999) 'Stimulating curiosity', *Primary Geographer* 38, 18–19.

DfEE (1998a) *Teaching: High Status, High Standards. Requirements for Courses in Initial Teacher Training*. London: Teacher Training Agency.

DfEE (1998b) *Teachers: Meeting the Challenge of Change*. London: DfEE.

Foskett, N. and Marsden, W. E. (1998) *Bibliography of Geographical Education*. Sheffield: Geographical Association.

Knight, P. (1993) *Primary Geography, Primary History*. London: David Fulton.

Krause, J. (1998) 'The geography co-ordinator', in R. Carter (ed.) *Handbook of Primary Geography*. Sheffield: Geographical Association.

Krause, J. and Garner, W. (1997) *Geography Co-ordinator's Pack*. London: BBC.

Office for Standards in Education (OFSTED) (1999) *Primary Education 1994–98: A Review of Primary Schools in England*. London: OFSTED.

Palmer, J. (1994) *Geography in the Early Years*. London: Routledge.

Pollard, A. (1997) *Reflective Teaching in the Primary School*. London: Cassell.

Poulter, L. (2000) 'Young children's perceptions of their immediate environment', in R. Bowles (ed.) *Raising Achievement in Geography*. London: Register of Research in Primary Geography.

School Curriculum and Assessment Authority (SCAA) (1997) *Expectations in Geography at Key Stages 1 and 2*. London: SCAA.

Scoffham, S. (ed.) (1998) *Primary Sources: Research Findings in Primary Geography*. Sheffield: Geographical Association.

Till, E. (1997) 'What's in a picture', *Primary Geographer* 28, 18–19.

Webb, R. (1994) *After the Deluge: Changing Roles and Responsibilities in the Primary School*. London: Association of Teachers and Lecturers.

Wiegand, P. (1992) *Places in the Primary School*. Lewes: Falmer Press.

Wilson, A. (2000) 'Methods used in researching children's perceptions of farmers and farming', in R. Bowles (ed.) *Raising Achievement in Geography*. London: Register of Research in Primary Geography.

Index